Linguistic Policies and the Survival of
Regional Languages in France and Britain

*Palgrave Studies in Minority Languages and Communities*

*Titles include:*

Anne Judge
LINGUISTIC POLICIES AND THE SURVIVAL OF REGIONAL LANGUAGES IN
FRANCE AND BRITAIN

Máiréad Nic Craith
EUROPE AND THE POLITICS OF LANGUAGE

Glyn Williams
SUSTAINING LANGUAGE DIVERSITY IN EUROPE
Evidence from the Euromosaic project

*Forthcoming titles:*

Maya David, Vanithamani Saravanan and Peter Sercombe
LANGUAGE, IDENTITIES AND EDUCATION IN ASIA

Nancy Hornberger
CAN SCHOOLS SAVE INDIGENOUS LANGUAGES?
Policy and Practice on Four Continents

Yasuko Kanno
LANGUAGE AND EDUCATION IN JAPAN

Máiréad Nic Craith
LANGUAGE, POWER AND IDENTITY POLITICS

Anne Pauwels, Joanne Winter and Joseph Lo Bianco
MAINTAINING MINORITY LANGUAGES IN TRANSNATIONAL CONTEXTS

Vanessa Pupavac
LANGUAGE RIGHTS IN CONFLICT
Serbo-Croatian Language Politics

Graham Turner
SOCIOLINGUISTIC HISTORY OF BRITISH SIGN LANGUAGE

---

**Palgrave Studies in Minority Languages and Communities**
**Series Standing Order ISBN 978-1-4039-3732-2**
*(outside North America only)*

You can receive future titles in this series as they are published by placing a standing order.
Please contact your bookseller or, in case of difficulty, write to us at the address below with
your name and address, the title of the series and the ISBN quoted above.

Customer Services Department, Macmillan Distribution Ltd, Houndmills, Basingstoke,
Hampshire RG21 6XS, England

# Linguistic Policies and the Survival of Regional Languages in France and Britain

Anne Judge
*Professor of French (Emeritus)*
*University of Surrey*

© Anne Judge 2007

Softcover reprint of the hardcover 1st edition 2007 978-1-4039-4983-7

First published in 2007 by
PALGRAVE MACMILLAN
Houndmills, Basingstoke, Hampshire RG21 6XS and
175 Fifth Avenue, New York, N.Y. 10010
Companies and representatives throughout the world.

PALGRAVE MACMILLAN is the global academic imprint of the Palgrave
Macmillan division of St. Martin's Press, LLC and of Palgrave Macmillan Ltd.
Macmillan® is a registered trademark in the United States, United Kingdom
and other countries. Palgrave is a registered trademark in the European
Union and other countries.

ISBN 978-1-349-52598-0       ISBN 978-0-230-28617-7 (eBook)
DOI 10.1057/9780230286177

This book is printed on paper suitable for recycling and made
from fully managed and sustained forest sources. Logging,
pulping and manufacturing processes are expected to conform
to the environmental regulations of the country of origin.

A catalogue record for this book is available from the British Library.

Library of Congress Cataloging-in-Publication Data

Judge, Anne.
    Linguistic policies and the survival of regional languages in France and
Britain / Anne Judge.
        p. cm.—(Palgrave studies in minority languages and communities)
    Includes bibliographical references and index.

        1. Language policy – France – History. 2. French language – Political
aspects – History. 3. Linguistic minorities – France. 4. Language
policy – Great Britain – History. 5. English language – Political
aspects – History. 6. Linguistic minorities – Great Britain. I. Title.

P119.32.F7J83 2007
306.44'944—dc22                                         2006049381

Transferred to Digital Printing in 2012

*To my husband, Steve Judge, whose help and support have, as always, been invaluable*

# Contents

# List of Illustrations

## Tables

## Figures

# List of Maps

# Acknowledgements

I am deeply indebted to many people, both in the academic world and the regional language communities, for much of the information in the book and numerous suggestions as to how best to present it. In particular, I would like to thank Michel Alessio of the *Délégation générale à la langue française et aux langues de France*, for his untiring support, and similarly Jean-Michel Eloy, Professor in Linguistics at the Université d'Amiens, for reading the draft chapters on French and the French Regional Languages and for their suggestions and constructive criticism.

I am also greatly indebted to Peadar Morgan, Language Planning Manager for the Gaelic Language Board, *Bòrd na Gàidhlig*, to Jenefer Lowe, Cornish Language Development Manager and Ian Jones, CAMOC, for his contributions on Welsh. Last but not least I would like to thank John Salters, previously Director of the Centre for Modern Language Teaching, for his contribution on Irish.

Regional Languages is a burning issue, and many of my views have been fed by numerous conversations with academics, such as my colleague Dawn Marley, but also with many people whose own lives are affected by the issue. This book is the result of talking to many such people, both in Britain and France, over many years. My thanks go to them all, and particularly to Jean-Louis Gontard who has been a wonderful 'informant' over the years.

# Series Editor's Preface

Worldwide migration and unprecedented economic, political and social integration in Europe present serious challenges to the nature and position of language minorities. Some communities enjoy protective legislation and active support from states through policies that promote and sustain cultural and linguistic diversity; others succumb to global homogenisation and assimilation. At the same time, discourses on diversity and emancipation have produced greater demands for the management of difference.

This book series has been designed to bring together different strands of work on minority languages in regions with immigrant or traditional minorities or with shifting borders. We give prominence to case studies of particular language groups or varieties, focusing on their vitality, status and prospects within and beyond their communities. Considering this insider picture from a broader perspective, the series explores the effectiveness, desirability and viability of worldwide initiatives at various levels of policy and planning to promote cultural and linguistic pluralism. Thus it touches on cross-theme issues of citizenship, social inclusion and exclusion, empowerment and mutual tolerance.

Work in the above areas is drawn together in this series to provide books that are interdisciplinary and international in scope, considering a wide range of minority contexts. Furthermore, by combining single and comparative case studies that provide in-depth analyses of particular aspects of the socio-political and cultural contexts in which languages are used, we intend to take significant steps towards the fusing of theoretical and practical discourses on linguistic and cultural heterogeneity.

Gabrielle Hogan-Brun
University of Bristol

# Introduction

It has traditionally been assumed in many European countries, including Britain and France, that having a single official language was a necessary condition for the well-being of the state. There are now, however, citizens who are questioning this assumption and attempting to revitalise – or in some cases revive – their regional languages (RLs). This represents a major political headache for governments who must decide how far they can go in encouraging this revival without damaging the fabric of the state, and how much of the national revenue should be diverted to such a cause. This is also a major problem for newly independent states, which are often inherently multilingual, but wish to adopt a single language for practical reasons of communication between their citizens.

It is hoped that the comparative study of such problems in metropolitan France and Britain may help shed some light on the nature of these issues, since they both have a long history in this matter. It is also hoped that it may help people in France and the UK understand the importance of their RLs and their place within the nation. This is important first of all because linguistic policies may affect us all, whether settling elsewhere in France or the UK, or simply visiting: it is both tactful and useful to be aware of the issue. Secondly, because linguistic policies entail matters of principle, some of which may appear at times incompatible with one another. Thus the principle of monolingualism in the name of equality of opportunity dominated the scene until quite recently in both countries. Now it is the principle of freedom of speech and language as a human right which have come to the fore, helped in the UK by the impact of devolution. Hence efforts to save the RLs from extinction.

The story of the suppression of the RLs is, in fact, similar in both countries, which is not totally surprising if one considers the underlying historical continuity of both France and Britain: although French history

1

appears, on the surface, marked by revolution and sudden change, whereas the trade mark of Britain is evolution, this apparent difference masks the similarities in many areas. Thus, as far as language is concerned, both saw a steady move towards the establishment of a single official language at the expense of the RLs.

And yet, many of the RLs have survived. One reason is that for some people, language is not only a tool for communication, but is fundamental to their sense of identity. This is particularly true where a language symbolises resistance to a regime (e.g. Basque in Franco's Spain) or an overpowering culture (e.g. Welsh in relation to Anglo-Saxon culture). The RLs then take on an iconic value. Their presence today is the result of a variety of social, religious and political situations which developed over the centuries. Their relevance and importance extend, therefore, well beyond the linguistic policy issue.

There are a number of conceptual and terminological problems associated with the RLs. One is the use of 'language' versus 'dialect'. The term 'dialect' is problematic because it is seen to refer to a sub-category of a language, rather than a language in its own right. Whereas this is not problematic in a historical context, it may cause offence in a contemporary situation since it denies a particular form of speech the autonomy and importance of a full language. A typical example is Scots, seen by its defendants as a 'language' and by others as a 'mere dialect' of English. An even more patronising term is 'patois' with its insinuation of lowly, peasant status. And yet this term, now much frowned upon in France where it is only used between inverted commas, is useful when referring to a speech form functioning purely at a very local level, and only in a familiar spoken context.

A different but related problem concerns languages which are so close as to be seen by some as variants of the same language, whereas others maintain their separateness. The concept of 'collateral language' has been recently developed in France (Eloy 2004) to deal with the problem: collateral languages, such as Picard versus French, or Scots versus English, have a common origin, but have developed differently. There may be differences between them at all levels – phonological, morphological, syntactical and lexical – but they remain close in so far as they are considered to be mutually intelligible.

This in itself may depend on a hidden political agenda: claiming that a dialect is a language, or variants of a language are separate languages, is not only determined by linguistic factors, but is a matter of politics, and fits into a broader context. This is because nothing is static where language is concerned. A language may break up into different 'dialects' or 'varieties', each evolving in its own particular way, depending on historical, geographical, economic and cultural factors. Thus Latin broke up into numerous romance 'dialects' which eventually became our modern romance 'languages'. More recently, Swedish, Norwegian and Danish, originally classified as dialects of the same language, have acceded to the title of separate languages. This kind of phenomenon has led to a massive expansion in the number of minority languages recognised in Europe. This expansion has been encouraged by the European Bureau for Lesser Used Languages (EBLUL), by the Council of Europe's Charter for Regional or Minority Languages and also by non-linguistically related political decisions. Ulster Scots, for example, only appeared on the European linguistic map as a result of the Good Friday Agreement in 1998; hence G. Falconer referring to a 'moderate relax-ation in the criteria of languageness, particularly for those idioms which formerly enjoyed language status' (Falconer 2005: 48). This, he points out, may create its own problems with language communities becoming ever smaller.

The opposite is also true since one of several 'dialects' or 'varieties' of a language may be chosen as the basis for a codified language to be used for education and in official contexts. This may cause problems with speakers wishing to maintain their local variant. There is a paradox here: codification is a necessary evil if a language is to become used in all public domains and decline hence reversed, but codification also leads to a reduction in local varieties, which presents sociolinguists and policy-makers with another dilemma.

This book recognises as British RLs those recognised under the European Charter for Regional or Minority Languages: Welsh, Gaelic and Irish for the Celtic languages, and Scots and Ulster Scots for the languages collat-eral with English. Cornish is also included since it was added in 2002. As far as France is concerned, this book restricts itself to the traditional RLs of metropolitan France: Alsatian, Basque, Breton, Catalan, Flemish, Occitan, Provençal, and the *langues d'oïl*.

The book is in three parts. The first part deals with the emergence of French and English as official national languages, and the consequent decline of the RLs. The second and third parts deal respectively with RLs in metropolitan France and in Britain. The aim is to give an overview of the situation: each language is described in terms of its history, its current status and the efforts made to promote it. The focus is on linguistic policies (and not on linguistic descriptions), with the aim of establishing their degree of success. It is important to remember, in this context, that intervention in their favour may not appear to produce immediate results since it takes a long time for new speakers to emerge. Thus negative figures, although the subject of alarm, are not always indicative of later outcomes. Or at least it is to be hoped so, since all of the RLs in France and Britain are classified, at present, as 'endangered' languages.[1]

# Part I

# The Rise of French and English and the Destruction of the Regional Languages

# Introduction

A common feature of most accounts of the emergence of English and French as official national languages, is their failure to refer to the regional languages (RLs) displaced in the process. On the other hand, any account of the surviving RLs has to be made within the context of this struggle for dominance. It is also important to compare the different ways in which French and English became official national languages since this explains the different situations in which the RLs of France and Britain find themselves today.

One has to look to politics to understand why France traditionally adopted the same negative policies towards all the RLs whereas Britain had different policies towards different languages according to circumstances. History also highlights the importance of linguistic differences between the two languages in terms of their respective glottopolitical development. Thus whereas French was the language of the kings of France, English was the language of the people. In addition, whereas French only had to displace Latin to become the official language of France, English had to displace both Latin and French. A further factor is that whereas the Romans were successful in imposing Latin in France, they did not do so in Britain, whereas the Germanic tribes imposed their language(s) in Britain but were unable to do so in France, although they strongly influenced the development of French.

Another interesting difference between the two countries is that whereas France is famous for its long and explicit history of linguistic intervention, the same degree of awareness does not exist in Britain. As a result, accounts of the emergence and domination of English and French tend to adopt different points of view, those for French insisting on the legalistic and institutional aspects of the process, while those for English tend to dwell on its social and cultural implications.

There are also differences in the way in which French and English have been codified and standardised. In France there has been a tradition of codification and standardisation achieved mainly through official bodies, with the agreement of the elite. In England the process was more haphazard, although both countries ended up being intensely prescriptive, institutionally in France, socially in Britain. This is important for the RLs for two reasons. Firstly it was the codification and standardisation of French and English which brought the RLs to their knees, the fact that both countries were very prescriptive only accentuating the process. Secondly because it demonstrates that some form of agreement in terms of codification and standardisation, however they are achieved, seem necessary to the survival of the RLs. This, however, goes against the principle of language preservation, since codification and standardisation imply by definition loss of local characteristics and identity (see Parts II and III).

Where the RLs were local varieties or dialects of French or English, this process usually led to their disappearance from normal speech, although some of their traits may have passed into the official language. Nowadays various forms of 'regional French' or 'regional English' bear witness to this past. The RLs traditionally seen to have survived are those seen as 'clearly' different from the official languages, and in particular those furthest from the centre of power. But a survey carried out in France by INSEE in 1999 (see Part II) showed, to everybody's surprise, that some of the languages collateral with French, seem to have survived, mainly in a spoken form. Their survival is largely due to their having remained until then unrecognised as 'languages', which meant they survived as 'dialects' or 'patois', in the shadow of French. They are now demanding recognition. In some cases there is a cline which goes from the official language containing traits from the RL, to a completely separate language (e.g. Scottish English and Scots). And in some cases the status and present relationship of the RL with a collateral official language may be far from clear (e.g. Alsatian and German).

The following chapters deal with the origins of French and English, their emergence as official national languages, their codification and standardisation and the impact this had on the RLs.

# 1
# The Rise of French as an Official National Language

French emerged from Latin to become first of all the language of the king and his court, then an international language during medieval times, and finally the only official language of France. Later it also became a world language through the process of colonialism. This did not happen in a haphazard way, but through a careful process of legislative and educational policies spread over five centuries. These have been strengthened in recent years because of the perceived threat of English. These policies excluded the RLs from public life in the name of equality. As a result, they are now classified as 'endangered languages'. In recent years, however, a new climate of thought has brought forth the desire to save them, although this desire is far from shared by all. The following chapter examines the policies which destroyed them, particularly those still in force, in order to assess the nature of the problem facing the RLs today. As will be seen, reversing the trend constitutes a formidable task.

## The origins of the French language

French is a romance language, and as such derived from Latin. The Romans first came to Gaul in 125 BC, when their help was requested by the Greeks (established since around 600 BC in Marseilles, Nice, and Antibes) to put an end to the raids constantly being carried out by the Gauls. Having achieved this in 124 BC, the Romans stayed on and created the first Roman province, or *Provincia Narbonensis* (Provence). The locals quickly became so Romanised that they even took to wearing togas instead of the traditional Gaulish breeches. Their speech, derived from Latin, became Occitan.

In 58 BC, the Gauls (who had originally been invaders who had displaced the Ligurians in Provence, the Iberians in the south west and the Aquitani in Aquitaine) themselves called upon the Romans for help,[1] which gave Caesar an excuse to invade not yet Romanised northern Gaul. Having thus moved beyond the limits of the *Provincia Narbonensis*, the Romans again stayed on and spread further afield. They conquered the Armoricans (Gauls), who inhabited the area roughly corresponding to present-day Brittany, and the Aquitanians. Finally the Celtic centre of Gaul was taken in 52 BC after the fall of the first 'French' hero, the Gallic chieftain Vercingetorix. The whole of Gaul was declared a Roman province in 51 BC.

After the conquest, the Gauls, who spoke according to Strabon hundreds of Celtic languages, quickly became Latinised partly because Roman policy was to make their way of life look as attractive as possible and partly because of the ease with which people could integrate into the Roman professional classes. Thus the Gaulish aristocracy became Gallo-Roman, which explains the general willingness to learn Latin, and particularly to write it, since Gaulish was not basically a written language. But, whereas written Latin remained for a long time reason-ably close to Classical Latin, spoken Latin became a 'vernacularised' form, 'Gallo-Romance', with Gaulish functioning as a 'sub-stratum'. In other words the Gauls imported some of their speech habits into Latin.

It was the flexibility of the administrative system and the mobility of the society thus created, which made Latin the language of integration and social progress (just as French has aimed to be since the 1789 Revolution, and as English is today). Tacitus tells how, in AD 21, the sons of the most illustrious Gaulish families attended Roman schools (the only schools which existed) whenever possible. Sidonius Apollinarius wrote in the 5th century AD that the Arvene nobility – a Celtic people in the Auvergne – had at last 'got rid of the "dross" of the Celtic language'. This means that, in the intervening period, the nobility was bilingual in a diglossic situation. Gaulish continued to be spoken in the country probably for another century by the peasants and is regarded as having died out finally by the end of the sixth century, except in a few isolated areas. It may also have acted as a substratum for the form of Breton spoken in the Vannetais area (see Chapter 4).

The next influence was Germanic. The Germanic migrations started well before the 'invasions' proper. As early as the third century AD, the Franks started moving in with their families and animals, fleeing the insecurity which reigned east of the Rhine. They were able to do so having been given permission by the Romans to occupy deserted land. They soon began to occupy the northern part of France, except for Brittany. They naturally learned the Gallo-Romance spoken in the area, giving it their own Frankish flavour.

The Germanic invasions proper started around the time when Romanisation was more or less complete. They were made possible because of the weakness of the Roman Empire, which finally collapsed in AD 476. From AD 406 and through the course of the century there was a whole wave of invasions and settlements (mainly Franks, Visigoths and Burgundians, many of them fleeing problems themselves – particularly in the shape of the Huns). This led to major ethnic migrations, and Gaul was torn apart by violent conflicts between the parties involved. In the final event, the Franks were the most important from a linguistic point of view, being established in great numbers in the north. Their influence was much diluted south of the Loire, where the Visigoths held sway, but since the latter were outnumbered by Gallo-Romans their linguistic influence was slight.

The most important historical event of the period was the conversion to Christianity of Clovis, king of the Franks, in 496. This ensured an alliance between the Franks and the Gallo-Roman Church, which in turn meant the survival of Latin through the development of monasteries and cultural centres. The Church acted as a unifying factor for all the populations, irrespective of their language or culture, as they gradually converted to Christianity. In addition, in those Frankish areas where the Franks were outnumbered by the Gallo-Romans, intermarriage and alliances of interest meant the distinctions between the two peoples gradually disappeared. A new 'nation' was gradually emerging.

The Franks did not impose their language, many having already moved over to Gallo-Romance, except on the left bank of the Rhine, where Alsatian and Franconian are still spoken. But although they failed to impose Frankish, a Frankish super-stratum was gradually superimposed on to the Gallo-Romance they learned to speak. In the north this contributed to the development of the *langue d'oïl*, from which standard French gradually emerged (the word *français* derives from the Latin *franciscus*, originally meaning Frankish). In the south (corresponding to Provence, Languedoc, Dauphiné and Savoie), Romanisation and Latinisation were much stronger, having been much less affected either by the Gauls or the Germanic invasions: Aquitaine and Provence did not come under Frankish rule until 732 when Charles Martel repelled a Saracen invasion. This explains the survival to this day of the *langue d'oc* or Occitan and its closeness to Latin.

By the late eighth century the Gallo-Romance language spoken in the northern part of France had changed so much that it could hardly be called Latin. As a result, Charlemagne (742–814) decided that Classical Latin should be properly taught and established schools for young clerics in every monastery and in every bishop's house. This resulted in the great cathedral schools, which were to have a lasting influence. These were to train not only priests but also administrators and civil servants to give the new regime a more stable basis, which implied the need for written documents. Classical Latin became the language of law, administration, and the Church for theological matters, and the written language in general, while the people continued to speak their versions of Gallo-Romance. But the fact that the two languages had become mutually unintelligible created a problem for the Church, which decided in 813 at the Council of Tours that, in order to be understood, priests should preach in the *rustica romana lingua*. From that point on Latin would become the language of the elite. The diglossic situation typical of the Roman period was therefore equally typical of the period which followed. Bilingualism in Latin/Gallo-Romance was the necessary passport to success. It was also fundamental to the class system.

Although the Gauls turned to a scholastic form of Latin for administrative, judicial, academic and religious purposes in the later period, it was the vernacular Gallo-Romance (or 'Romance') which became French. The *Strasbourg Oaths* are generally considered to be the first text in French, albeit Old French. The Oaths arose from the fact that Lothair, the grandson of Charlemagne, wished to inherit the whole of his grandfather's Empire. His brother, Louis the German, and his half brother, Charles the Bald, wanted the Empire to be split between the three of them, which was more in keeping with Frankish tradition. The two brothers formed an alliance and defeated Lothair at the battle of Fontenoy in 841. They then cemented this alliance in 842 by oaths of support for each other while they tackled the difficult task of dividing up between the three of them a very heterogeneous empire.

The actual text of the Oaths is cited by Nithardus, a grandson of Charlemagne and cousin of the princes, in his *Histoire des fils de Louis le Pieux*, written in Latin. He reproduced the text of the Oaths in the vernaculars in which they were pronounced. As it was important that each army should hear and understand the oaths pronounced by their leaders, Louis took the oath in Gallo-Romance, while Charles[2] took it in the Germanic version. After the leaders had each taken the oath, their followers took a different oath, each in their own language. The very act of transcribing the Oaths into Gallo-Romance transformed the vernacular in which it was spoken into a legitimate language. Hence 842 is frequently given as the date of the birth of the French language.

The translation of the Oaths highlights the importance of language in politics, and vice versa, so fundamental to the construction of the future

European nation-states. Indeed an important aspect of the *Strasbourg Oaths* is that they illustrate a very early use of language as a marker of national identity. They also mark the passage from Gallo-Romance to Old French. Thus Renée Balibar wrote in fairly lyrical style in her *Histoire de la littérature française* (1996: 3):

> French literature was born one winter morning at Strasbourg on 14th February 842. That day an oath of allegiance between two kings, proclaimed in two languages, representing Germanic and Romance speech, contained the seed of European vernacular literature.[3] Once officially written down, the vernacular languages bore witness to the divisions between populations but also to their common destiny: thanks to writing, the vernacular languages were born into the world and developed through translation from one into another.

Another important text is a religious poem, which dates from 881, the *Cantilène de sainte Eulalie* (author unknown). It is the oldest known example of a literature which was to flourish soon after, giving such social prestige to the language that little by little it replaced Latin in all contexts.

The variety of Romance which became French, was the one spoken in the Ile-de-France, which became a meeting point of Norman, Picard, Champenois and others. This did not constitute a dialect in its own right (it is now widely recognised that *Francien* was a nineteenth-century invention), but rather a supra-dialectal form, from which dialectal trait forms were excluded. It acquired, as such, considerable prestige, particularly after the election by his peers of Hugues Capet, Duc de l'Isle-de-France, to the position of king, and his consecration by the Church, in 987. This gave him both political and religious prestige. The fact that this marked the beginning of a dynasty which lasted until 1848 (in contrast to Britain with its frequent changes of dynasty) symbolises the importance of the event. From then on, although the kingdom of France proper, i.e. the Ile-de-France, was initially small, its prestige was disproportionately large, and the language spoken at the Court rapidly became the model to follow.

The result was the emergence of the concept of 'good' and 'bad' written French, the latter containing features belonging to other varieties of Northern Romance speech, such as Champenois or Picard. This is known from various comments such as one poet writing 'Mi langages est buens, car en France sui nez', i.e. 'my language is good because I was born in France' (i.e. the Ile-de-France), whereas others, such as Conon de

Béthune, from Picardy, deplored in 1180 the fact that his French was laughed at when at Court: 'The Queen, along with her son the King, acted discourteously when she criticised me: although my speech is not that of the Ile-de-France, one can still understand me in French. And those who criticised me for using words from Artois, are not courteous or polite, for I was not born in Pointoise' (Lodge 1993: 99). In other words, despite a high level of mutual intelligibility between the various Romance dialects of northern France, there was early on a hierarchy in terms of the degree of acceptability of their most characteristic traits.

By the early Middle Ages, there were, in fact, many varieties of Romance spoken in France, for the imposition of a feudal system meant ordinary people's lives were lived in the shadow of their overlord, and had few exchanges with often quite close neighbouring communities. This played an important part in splitting up Gallo-Romance into ever smaller components, traditionally regrouped under the *langue d'oïl* label for those in the north, and the *langue d'oc* label for those in the south, the latter having been least influenced by the Germanic invasions which helped shape Gallo-Romance in the north.[4]

The smallest speech units were at the parish level, and became known derogatorily as *patois*. Thus Guiraud quotes Marouzeau stating that *patois* refers to local forms of speech used by a population 'whose civilisation is inferior to the one of the common language' (Guiraud 1978: 6). Denying to these forms of speech the status of 'language' had the advantage, after the 1789 Revolution, of removing the concept of local identity, seen as detrimental to the concept of the nation-state. Thus Guiraud quotes Gaston Paris as stating that 'there is nothing that separates the Northern French from the Southern French since from one end of the country to the other all the local vernaculars gradually meld into one unique tapestry' (Guiraud, *Patois et dialectes français*, 1978: 21).

The desire to establish a nice clear lineage for the national language was common, until recently, among many linguists. As recently as 1995, Rossillon explained in his *Atlas de la langue française* (1995: 17) that the French of the *Strasbourg Oaths* was already a 'national' language. He bases this assertion on the fact that no dialectal origin has been found for them. He concludes that the language was therefore drawn up by intellectuals trying to elaborate a national language. Codification, in other words, long before the French Academy was founded.

There is, however, a more likely explanation for this lack of a known dialectal origin: the Oaths are in 'a Latin consciously vulgarised by adaptation to the most common features in the vernacular of the day, features which were widespread over northern France' (Elcock 1960: 336).

Elcock (basing himself on Professor Ewert's work) gives as an argument for this theory the impressive ease with which the French version slips back into notarial Latin (1960: 339).

It is important, therefore, to remember that any past 'scientific' work on the RLs is likely to be tainted with prejudice in France since denying languages their very existence goes back to times nearly immemorial. But this has always been the result of an enduring hidden political and ideological agenda: it stresses the perfection of French (*langue universelle* according to Rivarol, 1784)[5] and led to complete contempt for the local languages, hence the sad fate of the RLs. Matters have only changed recently in this respect (see Chapters 3 and 4).

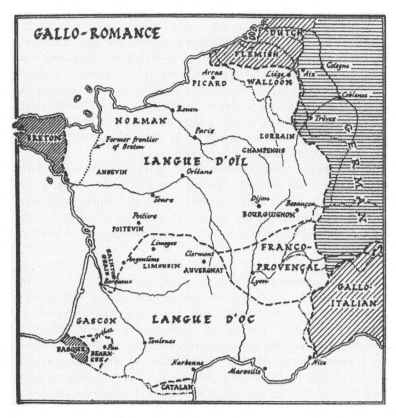

*Map 1*  Map of Gallo-Romance

## The rise of French as an official language

The rise of French as an official language is linked with the rise of France as a centralised state, which started with the Romans. Later Charlemagne encouraged the development of a powerful and unifying Church and finally the Capetian kings and their successors built a country around their base in the Ile-de-France base. As different areas were integrated into the royal domain, the regional languages suffered competition from French. But the process of annexation was often slow and complicated, the region or province ceasing first to be independent before finally becoming fully part of the realm, through war, marriage or inheritance. Thus Normandy ceased being under the rule of the kings of England in 1204 but only became part of France in 1468; Anjou was annexed in 1205 and became part of the realm in 1481; Brittany was united to the kingdom of France through marriage in 1491 and voted for union with France in 1532; the Languedoc area came under the rule of the French kings during the thirteenth century, but kept its customs and privileges after the crushing of the Cathars; Burgundy was conquered and became a French province in 1477; while Provence became French in 1481, Corsica as late as 1768, Nice in 1860 and the valley of Tende in 1947; and Alsace and Lorraine changed hands several times. It was the disparate nature of these annexations and the fact that prior to 1789 only the elite was affected by these changes which helped some of the regional languages to survive.

The first major administrative blow to the RLs was the 1539 *Ordonnance de Villers-Cotterêts* (named after the castle where it was signed), in 1539, when Francis I made French (the langue maternelle française) the official language for all legal and administrative matters[6] instead of Latin. It was an extremely successful law since it took less than twenty years for French to establish itself as sole official language. This success was due to a number of factors. One was that natural linguistic evolution in this direction had taken place, and was already encapsulated in previous laws. Thus the *Ordonnance de Moulins* of 1490 decreed that witness statements in court cases in the Languedoc area could be written either in French or in any other mother tongue (instead of Latin). Although Charles VIII passed this decree for legal reasons rather than to promote linguistic unity, it was, however, a first move in this direction. Then, in 1510, Louis XII decreed that all criminal trials would be carried out in the language of the area where the crime was committed. Finally in 1535 Francis I, in the *Ordonnance d'Is-sur-Tille* aimed at reforming justice in Provence, decreed that all criminal trials would be in French, or at least in the vernacular. The *Ordonnance de Villers-Cotterêts* just went one step further in requiring that all administrative and legal matters were to be in French *et non autrement,* i.e. 'and not otherwise'. (One reason for this law is supposed to have been the king's poor knowledge of Latin.) It is still in place today and constitutes the foundation of French as the official language of the state. As such it is a thorn in the side of the RLs.

There are numerous reasons for its success. One was that the other most widely spoken language was the *langue d'oc* (now often called Occitan). Being a Romance language like French, it was relatively easy to move from one to the other. There is the famous and apocryphal[7] story of representatives of the Languedoc area going to see Francis I after the passing of the decree, complaining that they did not know French and could only function in Latin for official purposes. Having been left waiting for an audience for three weeks, when they were finally received by the king he spoke to them in French, which by then, they could understand. Francis I then pointed out triumphantly that it was not difficult to learn French, and that now they could go back home speaking the king's tongue, thus showing their superior status not only in dress,[8] but also in speech.

Another reason for its success was that by 1539 numerous documents were already written in French rather than Latin. This was partly due to the way in which the French legal system developed. Originally, or at least after the Frankish conquest, each ethnic group had its own law: this was called a *système personnel* under which it was possible to have different people in the same village subject to different laws. Then, with the development of the feudal system, law became territorially based and customary law developed. The judge's task was to establish whether the law invoked by a party existed or not. Uncertainty as to the existence of certain customs led to their being written down in what were termed *coutumiers,* i.e. books recording the legal customs of an area. These were often in French for the convenience of those litigants who had no knowledge of Latin. Thus *Le grand coutumier de Normandie,* written in the thirteenth century, existed in three versions, one in Latin, one in French prose and one in French verse (for mnemonic reasons). The most famous of all the *coutumiers* was *Les coutumes de Beauvaisis* by Philippe de Beaumanoir written directly in French *c.* 1280.

The importance of the *coutumiers* increased through time, particularly when in 1454 Charles VII proclaimed in the *Edit de Montil-les-Tours* that from then on they would have the force of law. In 1498 Charles VIII additionally required all the customs and usages in the north of France to be written down in an official form. Furthermore, the documents issued from the Chancellerie Royale were often in French, particularly charters granting privileges and rights to towns. This was usually because many of the kings – not just Francis I – did not master Latin particularly well. The tendency was for the Comtés (the regional administrative areas) to follow suit. At first these documents were written in the vernacular of the area, but this changed in the second half of the thirteenth century, when Acts appeared in French rather than in the local languages. The move was accentuated during the next two centuries as the monarchy became increasingly centralised, leading to a considerable increase in the number of legal and administrative documents.

Famines and epidemics played an important part in the process which led to a disastrous shortage of clerics with sufficient knowledge of Latin to draw up official documents. As a result, individuals ended up writing documents such as wills in their vernacular, which increasingly became French. This practice had already started at the time of the Crusades, but it took on a much greater momentum when whole swathes of the population were struck by famine and disease. Thus during the famine of 1315–17, the accounts of Ypres giving the cost of burying the victims are in French. The Hundred Years War had a similar effect. Finally the papal Schism of 1378 weakened the position of the Church, and therefore of Latin. Also the Church itself had already contributed to the spread of the vernaculars: the Council of Tours had decreed in 813 that sermons, aimed at a local audience, should be in the vernacular whereas mass was to remain in Latin, because of its universal appeal.

The distinction between local and general audiences was carried through into other fields. Thus a tendency developed according to which 'national law' was in Latin (Charles V's Ordinance of 1376 proclaiming the majority of kings at fourteen) whereas local customs and regulations were in French, or more rarely, in the local vernacular. Decisions affecting the individual were increasingly in French (e.g. the *lettres de naturalité* granted by Louis XI in 1476 to three printers), as were deeds, wills, receipts and official letters (see Judge and Lamothe 1995). On the international level, however, Latin continued to be the norm although some treaties appeared in French very early on, such as the Treaty of Paris of 1250 between Henri III and Saint Louis, the letter of provocation from Edward III to Philippe VI in 1340 and the Treaty of Arras between Louis XI and Maximilian, archduke of Austria in 1482.

In some cases French and Latin appeared side by side, particularly in court cases. The three main law suits of Louis XII (1462–1515) are interesting in this respect: his divorce from Jeanne de France was in Latin, since divorce came under canon law; but when Anne de France tried to establish the validity of her marriage, the case starts in Latin, continues in French and reverts to Latin, often mixing the two; and in his trial for *lèse-majesté* against Pierre de Rohan the case was pleaded in French in front of the Grand Conseil, then referred to the Parlement de Toulouse where most of the case was in French, but the first two pages of the *reprise de l'instruction* (resumption of the indictment) were in Latin. The *arrêt* or decision starts with two short paragraphs in French and continues in Latin. The final speech of the *procureur* (prosecutor) was in French as were six out of sixty-eight pieces of documentary evidence; finally the judgement of the Parlement condemning Pierre de Rohan was in Latin, while the sentence was in French.

Finally the success of *Villers-Cotterêts* was also due to the literary prestige of French, acquired much earlier on: the first historical work written directly in French prose was Villehardouin's *La conquête de Constantinople*, an account of the Fourth Crusade (1198–1207); letters were frequently in French, from the thirteenth century, although often conforming to Latin style; and literature proper became extremely rich and varied from the twelfth century onwards. Hence Brunetto Latini, author of the first French encyclopaedia, wrote in the late thirteenth century: 'And if anyone were to ask me why this book is written in Romance after the French manner, given that we are Italian, I would say that it is for two reasons, firstly because we are in France, secondly because [French] speech is the most pleasant and the most widely spoken among all languages' (Lodge's translation 1993: 131). Its role as an international language was also important in this respect.

Although the king's French was the main vernacular to be written, it was not the only one. Occitan in particular had a rich written tradition while still spoken by the upper echelons of society (Alienor of Aquitaine and her son, Richard Lion Heart spoke *langue d'oc* or Occitan which gave it considerable prestige). On a different level, 'French literature' included Picard, Norman and Champenois varieties (they are studied under the label 'Old French' in French universities). But by 1549 there were few traces of the local vernaculars in texts. Even in southern France, French had become the normal language of writing. Thus Montaigne (1533–92) who was purposefully brought up by his father speaking Latin as his mother tongue (all the servants in the household also had to speak Latin), chose to write not in Latin, nor in *langue d'oc*, the language spoken all around him, but in French.

Other factors which encouraged the spreading of written French were the development of Protestantism (the Reformation movement broke away from the Church of Rome when Luther was excommunicated in 1520), the influence of printing (the first printing press was set up in Paris in 1470) and the Humanists who linked the new emphasis on individualism with the growth of the vernaculars. From then on Latin, and also Greek, were studied more and more and used less and less. This was both a result of an increasing sense of national identity, and a factor which encouraged its development.

Education also played a major part. In 1530 Francis I created the Collège des Lecteurs royaux, which became the Collège de France, and similar schools were created in other towns where the teaching was supposed to be in Latin but was in fact in French. This was very much in keeping with the spirit of the time: in 1549 Du Bellay's *Défense et illustration de la langue française* was an enthusiastic manifesto in favour of French over Latin. The group of poets called the Pléiade, to which Du Bellay belonged, worked hard for this end and in 1550 Meigret published the first French grammar.[9] In 1570 Charles IX created an Académie du Palais specifically for the advancement of French in all fields, particularly those which had been the prerogative of Latin. The Académie du Palais closed down in 1581, but was recreated in 1625. It eventually became the Académie française in 1636 and was registered by parliament in 1637, which made it into a governmental agency with an official brief. Its task was to develop the language so that it could replace Latin in all areas of communication. This was the beginning of French prescriptivism, which is still with us today.

The general replacement of Latin by French constituted an important blow for the RLs but it only affected the elite, whereas the linguistic policies of the 1789 Revolution affected the whole population. Indeed language was one of the first preoccupations of the Revolutionaries for how could Republican ideals be popularised if most of the nation did not understand the language in which they were proclaimed? In 1790, they commissioned the first ever linguistic survey of France, the *Rapport Grégoire*. It established that French was the exclusive language of only 15 *départements*[10] out of a total of 83 and that more than 6 million mainly rural citizens did not understand French, that another 6 million could speak some French but insufficiently to carry on a conversation, that only 3 million could speak the language properly, and still fewer actually wrote it.[11] This caused consternation.

The initial reaction was to adopt a policy of multilingualism. The argument in favour of this approach was based on the practical recognition that it takes a long time to learn a language and that the French population needed to be made aware immediately of the principles of the Revolution. It was therefore felt necessary to translate all important texts into the local languages, which meant, in some cases, establishing an official spelling. This was the position adopted by the 'federalists', or 'Girondins' (many delegates were from the Gironde). Thus in January 1790 a decree was promulgated encouraging the translation of official texts into the local languages, and in May 1790 another decree instituted an increase in salary for bilingual teachers. The term 'Girondin' is still used today to refer to a policy favourable to decentralisation, and, indirectly therefore, to the RLs. It was, however, the Jacobins, who favoured extreme centralisation and the imposition of French, who won the day[12] and, from then on, national linguistic unification became one of the main ideals and aims of the new Republic: democratisation through a common language. The term 'Jacobin'[13] is still used in France today to refer to a centralist approach to government which opposes the RLs.

Although the Jacobins knew it to be utopian to believe in a world in which all could understand each other, they felt it to be an ideal they should at least aim for: 'This undertaking, which has never yet been achieved by any nation is a worthy goal for the French people, who are centralising all branches of social organisation; they must insure with unswerving zeal and as soon as possible the unique and invariable use of the language of liberty (i.e. French) in a Republic which is one and indivisible.'[14] As a result the *Convention*[15] decided to appoint a French language teacher in every *commune*,[16] to commission a French grammar suitable for schools, and establish a list of acceptable vocabulary (*Projet de loi Le Peletier* of 1793). French was to be the language of all municipal councils and of the army (the idea of a Breton, or even worse, a Corsican battalion as the equivalent of the Welsh Guards is unthinkable in France even today). Grégoire even suggested making knowledge of French a necessary condition for marriage!

A lack of financial resources, civil war, the rise to power of Napoleon and the first Restoration postponed the implementation of most of these decisions until much later. But French became – and remains – one of the most important symbols of the new nation-state defined as an indivisible community within a defined territory, sharing a common cultural heritage, common economic interests, a common attitude towards religion – it ignored all of them – and a common language. Indeed French has often, since then, been described as the 'cement' of the nation: 'Since the ordinance of Villers-Cotterets in 1539 – which established that justice was to be dispensed in French – and the creation of the French Academy in 1635 – which gave our language a guardian – the French language, *the cement of our national unity* and a fundamental aspect of our heritage, has been the object of public policies'[17] (Ministère de la culture et de la francophonie, 1994, in the context of discussion on the Toubon law, see below).

French has also been described as a passport to Frenchness, i.e. as a means of assimilating foreigners. Thus in 1994, referring to people who had recently acquired French nationality, J. Toubon stated: 'the French language is their first possession, the sign of their dignity, the means towards integration and to tuning into a universal culture; it enables them to have share in a common heritage and *the French dream*.'[18] Hence an element of continuity in French education policy, whatever the government, is the preoccupation with the teaching of French, seen as essential to a successful education programme leading to integration.[19] In 2005, this was again clearly restated by D. de Villepin in his introduction to the *Rapport au Parlement sur l'emploi de la langue française*.

The move towards a common language after the 1789 Revolution, was also fuelled by political factors as is clear from the frequently quoted Barère report drawn up in the name of the Comité de Salut Public in 1794:

> The voice of federalism and of superstition speaks Breton; the émigrés and those who hate the Republic speak German. The counter-revolution speaks Italian; fanaticism speaks Basque. Let us smash these instruments of damage and error . . . For our part we owe it to our citizens, we owe it to our republic, in order to strengthen it, that everyone on its territory is made to speak the language of the Declaration of the Rights of Man. (De Certeau, Julia and Revel 1975: 295 and 298)

This became law on 20 July 1794: 'No public document may be written in any part of the territory of the Republic in any language other than French' (Wardhaugh 1987: 102). Similar arguments are still used today by opponents of the RLs who consider that speaking a second language is socially divisive, and that these languages could be hijacked by separatist movements.

From then on French was imposed on the nation through the schools, army and civil service, and the compulsory nature of French as the official language of the nation was reiterated on numerous occasions. Thus the 1851 memorandum on the application of the 1850 Falloux law on education stated categorically that all education had to be in French. This law still holds to this day, and is frequently referred to.

The result of this onslaught was that by the 1930s only one person in four still spoke a RL, by the 1950s this figure had dropped to one in ten, by the 1970s to one in twenty and by the 1980s to one in over thirty. This steady decline in the number of RL speakers was due to the same unifying linguistic policies still being pursued (see below). These culminated, accidentally, with the change made to the Constitution in 1992 which made French the official language of the Republic. This had, of course, long been the case in practice, but it had not been previously felt necessary to include such a statement in the various constitutions. Its inclusion was no longer symbolic of the fight against the RLs, but against the domination of English in Europe, since at the time of the signature of the Maastricht Treaty, some people in France feared the imposition of English as a working language within the EU. Although this change was not originally designed to harm the RLs, it has certainly been used since then in this way (see Part II).

Similarly, in 1994 the *loi Toubon*[20] was passed, officially to protect the French consumers and indirectly the French language, by making its use compulsory in a number of contexts such as retail, business transactions and science and technology (see below). But whereas a rather similar law, the Loi Bas-Lauriol, had been passed unanimously in 1975, the Toubon law gave rise to much controversy in Parliament and much ridicule in the press, the mood of the country having changed partly because English had become an inescapable aspect of French life. Doubts were also growing as to the justification of the destruction of the RLs since the modern concept of human rights, as championed by the European Parliament and the Council of Europe, proclaims the right to linguistic freedom. Hence the RLs attempting to stage a comeback just when French was feeling under threat.

## The codification of French: a very formal affair

The codification of French, enthusiastically espoused from very early on, constituted another blow for the RLs. The aim was to make French as good and dependable as Latin had been, since it was replacing it in all domains. Codification implies making choices in terms of vocabulary and structures, and even pronunciation; the chosen forms then become the 'standard' form of the language. In the case of French the guiding principles in making such choices were clarity (the famous *clarté française*) and precision, hence the removal of all vocabulary and structures felt to be redundant. This explains why the French language has a much smaller vocabulary than English, which did not follow the same route. (Most large French dictionaries include around 150 000 words, against the Oxford English Dictionary, which accounts for more than 600 000.)

This process started in 1498 when Charles VIII ordered that the customs and usages of northern France be written down in an official form. It was then that the need to adapt French to the legal context by coining new terms and defining others precisely first became apparent. This desire for clarity was not limited to the law and scientists and philosophers followed suit. The greatness of French was proclaimed in the sixteenth century by Du Bellay and the Pléiade poets. But it was Malherbe (1555–1628), however, who was the first to set out rules of style and grammar which were to have a lasting impact. They included the rejection of foreign words, archaisms, Latinisms, and dialectal expressions. Polite language was to be simple and avoid all scientific, technical and legal terms, thus creating a sense of *bienséance du vocabulaire* (i.e. rules governing the polite use of vocabulary).

The role of the French Academy created in 1636 was to enforce such rules. It did not, in fact, immediately accept the idea of becoming an official body because to acquire this power it had to give up its intellectual freedom. Pressure was brought to bear, however, and with its official status it acquired the brief to give French proper rules, to pass judgement on the language used by authors, and to write a dictionary, a grammar, a rhetoric and a treatise on poetics. The dictionary was to become the 'law' both in matters of meanings and spellings since Louis XIV gave it legal recognition in 1674, before it was completed, by forbidding all printers to publish any other dictionary. The need to adopt a standardised spelling had already been established the previous year. To quote Henriette Walter (1988) in a section entitled 'martyrs to spelling':

> All the children who nowadays struggle to learn French spelling may curse Monday 8 May 1673, the fateful day when the academicians decided to adopt a single spelling, compulsory for themselves and that they would try to ensure was adopted by the general public. Despite the permanent anxiety caused by the fear of a zero in dictation, spelling, which is both loathed and venerated, continues in the XXth century to have its martyrs and its worshippers.[21] (Walter 1988: 101)

Whereas codification of the law in the Middle Ages had led accidentally to linguistic codification and linguistic legislation, codification of French under the aegis of the Academy was an end in itself. Vaugelas'

*Remarques sur la langue française,* published in 1647, soon became its Bible, the very foundation of *le bon usage,* which was to become a rallying cry for centuries to come. Vaugelas produced many sayings of the *dites peu, dites bien* ('say little but say it well') type and recommended the removal of all vulgarity from language. Since such views were widely held in the literary salons, they encountered little resistance (even Corneille and Racine meekly corrected their 'mistakes' when these were pointed out to them).

The rules of *bon usage,* although not enforceable by the courts, were enforced indirectly through access to posts of influence. This constituted a kind of delegated legislation, but proved to be just as powerful since the Academy's decisions were generally followed for at least two centuries by all those in positions of power and by most important writers. This general consensus was perhaps due to the Academy's conservative and often *ad hoc* approach to linguistic matters.[22] Indeed the Academy was so much the subject of general approval, despite internal dissensions, that it survived the Revolution, despite its association with the elite. Although dissolved in 1793, it was reconstituted in a diminished form in 1795 and re-established in its original form in 1816, mainly because the Revolutionaries too wanted a codified form of French.

In the present day, although the Academy has seen its power decline, it still retains some of its influence. It awards some 150 annual prizes each year for literary works which contribute to 'le rayonnement de la langue et de la culture française',[23] one of which is explicitly called le prix du *Rayonnement du français,* an unthinkable concept in Britain. It also subsidises literary associations and literary reviews and it collaborates with various governmental bodies which are required to consult it in linguistic matters. Its position was strengthened in 1986 when its permanent secretary was given a seat on the Commissariat général de la langue française (see below). It is also consulted by the Minister of Education on matters of linguistic reform, usually functioning as a force for conservation.

1832 is supposed to be when the government decided that the orthography of the *Dictionnaire de l'Académie* (made official by the king in 1674) would be compulsory for all examinations and official documents, making access to civil service posts subject to this rule. Whether such a governmental decision was taken or not[24] matters little for the result was the same: the Académie and printing presses (i.e. newspapers, administrative documents, school textbooks, and everything which needed printing) 'ruled supreme over the writing system' (Catach 1993: 140). Their norm was adopted during the Revolution in schools, and primary school teachers, throughout the nineteenth century, came to see 'correct' spelling as the gospel.

This made 'correct' or 'official' spelling, for the first time, synonymous with 'correct French'. There were objections to this because of the often irrational nature of the orthography imposed, which led to many calls for reforms. These fell on deaf ears until an *arrêté* in 1901 drew up a small list of acceptable alternatives for examination purposes; they were again proposed in February 1975 and published by the *Journal Officiel* in 1977 as *tolérances*. But the enforcement of what was only tolerated was doomed to failure. Another mild reform followed in 1990, which was published in the *Journal Officiel*, but given the virulence of the debate which followed its proclamation, the Academy declared that the proposed modifications were merely recommended rather than compulsory. Prescriptiveness has therefore reigned supreme until very recently, when cracks started to appear in the edifice, partly due to the importance assumed by the spoken word in the information and communication revolution.

## The standardisation of French

The French language inherited by the Revolutionaries was codified, but only used by an elite. Their task was to spread its use throughout the country. This turned out to be either fatal or near fatal to the local languages. Their destruction was made possible because, as was stated in the Grégoire Report, they themselves wished to be 'délivrés de leur patois' ('freed from their vernaculars'). In 1791 this led to Talleyrand presenting a report to the *Assemblée Constituante* asking for the establishment of primary schools in each commune where teaching would be in French and in which French would be taught as a subject. This was in the name of equality through education. Thus Danton declared that 'après le pain, l'éducation est le premier besoin du peuple' ('immediately after the need for bread comes the need to educate the people') and Condorcet declared to the *Assembée Nationale* in 1792: 'He who needs to have recourse to another to write or even to read a letter, to calculate his expenses or his taxes, to calculate the size of his field or to share it, to know what the law allows him or forbids him; [. . .] that person is necessarily in a state of personal dependency, in a state of dependency which makes exercising his rights as a citizen impossible or dangeous'[25] (*Rapport et projet de décret sur l'organisation générale de l'instuction publique*, read out to the Assemblée Nationale on 20 and 21 April 1792).

A lack of financial resources and serious political upheavals meant that it was not until 1833 that a general primary system of education was established by Guizot (the 'loi Guizot', see Léon and Roche 2003). Then came the memorandum on the application of the 1850 Falloux law which made French the sole language of education, which became free in 1881 and compulsory in 1882 (*lois Jules Ferry*). Progress in enforcing French had been slow previous to this, to the extent that the Ministry of Education deplored in 1861 that there were still 24 *départements* out of 89 where more than half the population still spoke no French. In these the RLs had survived more or less intact. But after 1881, French was to make devastating progress.

Other factors also had a major impact on the spread of French to the detriment of the RLs: an improved transport system, the imposition of compulsory military service for all in 1875, and World War One. The latter has traditionally been considered to be the most important factor since it brought together people from all over France. Another factor, now considered by some to be equally or even more important, was the strong growth in urbanisation characteristic of the period from the middle of the nineteenth century until World War One. The ultimate result was that by the 1930s only one person in four spoke a RL, and from the 1940s there were no new monolingual speakers of the RLs. There were still some monolingual speakers left among the elderly in the 1950s, but from then on, all newborn children had French as their first language. There is a famous passage by Duneton (1973) in *Parler Croquant*, in which the author describes his first day at school in the south west in 1941, when he discovered he was the only monolingual speaker of French in his class, while another, whom he describes as 'the last of the Mohicans', was the only monolingual speaker of Occitan. The rest of the class was bilingual.

## French on the defensive and the resurgence of the RLs

It is paradoxical that scarcely had French become the unifying element of the nation, indeed one of its main pillars, than it was forced on the defensive. This was partly because its traditional position as an international language was threatened by English, and partly because the multiplication of multinationals in metropolitan France had led to a certain Anglicisation of the workplace. This only happened very gradually, without the French realising it, until a book, *Parlez-vous franglais?* (Etiemble 1964), alerted the nation to this danger.

As always the French sought institutional answers to the problem, with the creation over the years of a number of governmental institutions to defend the integrity of French. These changed as the mood in the European Community, then the European Union evolved. The first governmental institution to be founded was the *Haut Comité de défense et d'expansion de la langue française,* created by decree in March 1966 under the influence of Charles de Gaulle and placed directly under the prime minister's control. Its main role was to protect French from English borrowings, with terminology the main focus of interest, hence the 1970 decree establishing the need for ministerial commissions on terminology. The results of their deliberations are published in the *Journal Officiel,* which makes them 'law', at least for the army of workers which makes up the French Civil Service.

In 1973 this body was replaced by the *Haut Comité de la langue française,* the change of name reflecting a change in orientation, the term 'expansion' being seen as too 'colonial' and the term 'defence' too negative. In 1984 it was replaced by two bodies, the *Comité consultatif de la langue française* and the *Commissariat général de la langue française.* Finally, in June 1989, they were replaced respectively by the *Conseil supérieur de la langue française* and the *Délégation générale à la langue française,* known as the DGLF. The two new bodies resemble those they replace except that their goals are more specific and their brief broader. The *Conseil supérieur* deals with linguistic problems, while the DGLF promotes governmental linguistic policies.

It is also worth noting that many laws passed during this period include linguistic sections aimed at protecting the French language. Thus a decree on the code of ethics for doctors (decree 79–506, 28 June 1979) was passed in 1979 which includes an article (article 41) which states that all medical certificates, prescriptions or other medical documents delivered by a doctor must be in French, although a translation into the language of the patient is authorised.

On a more general level, the *loi Bas-Lauriol,* first presented to the *Assemblée Nationale* in May 1973, was passed in a less rigid form in December 1975. It made French compulsory in three domains in which French was to become compulsory: (i) in commercial and advertising contexts, to protect the consumer; (ii) in work contracts, to protect the employee; and (iii) in the context of information given to consumers either by private firms or public bodies, usually in the form of leaflets. It also established that new terminology decided by the terminological commissions would be compulsory in all governmental documentation, in all contracts, in education and in all other state institutions. It was completed by the *circulaire* (memorandum) of March 1976, again modified by the *circulaire* of October 1982 because, reasonable as the law may have seemed at the time, its scope had to be subsequently limited because of the laws governing the Common Market.

It was, in fact, around this time that it became obvious that France was no longer free to legislate on internal linguistic matters if the insistence on the use of French contravened the anti-discrimination policies under the Treaty of Rome. Thus any linguistic legislation which contravened the basic principle of the freedom of movement of workers or goods between member states would be illegal at the supra-national level. This was why the *loi Bas-Lauriol* had to be watered down. France also ran into problems in insisting on French alone on the labelling and marketing of foodstuffs since this contravened Directive 79/112. The French government also ran into problems when it tried to discriminate against non-French speaking workers where French was irrelevant to their work, as in the case of foreign tourist guides looking after foreign tourists.[26] Another law, similar to the Bas-Lauriol law was passed in 1994, the Toubon law, which ran into similar problems and it too had to be watered down.

The European problem led French governments to adopt a new approach to the defence of French. If French could not be defended through protectionist policies, it would fight against the growing monopoly of English within the EU in the name of all the other official languages. This gave birth to the French policy of plurilingualism: all children in schools should be taught at least two foreign languages to stop English ousting all the others. Thus article 11 of the Toubon law states that 'mastery of the French language and knowledge of two other languages are part of the fundamental aims of education'. This offered an interesting opening for the RLs.

It was, moreover, around the same time that the RLs were gaining ground, within the general European climate which favours regionalism (the European Charter for Regional or Minority Languages was drawn up in 1992). From the 1980s onwards a number of politicians (including Mitterrand) made many promises to RL militants and when the Toubon law was drawn up some time later, it contained articles referring to them. Thus article 11 states that although the language of education and exams is French, there were justifiable exceptions such as the teaching of RLs and their culture or foreign languages. And article 21 states that the Toubon law is not to be seen in any way as prejudicial to the RLs and in no way opposes their use. These important articles seem to have passed unnoticed by the general public, most debates having been on the wisdom of linguistic legislation, which itself marked a fundamental change of attitude on the part of a section of the population.

A leaflet was produced by the *Délégation générale à la langue française*, dated 1999, with the title 'La valorisation des langues régionales', i.e. 'the promotion of the RLs', although the word 'promotion' leaves out the connotation of 'worth' and 'worthiness' implied by the French term. It lists a number of measures taken in favour of the RLs in recent years, starting with the 1951 *loi Deixonne* which allowed, for the first time, the RLs into the classroom and the guarantees given to the RLs by the Toubon law. The leaflet also refers to the speech given by the French Prime Minister, Lionel Jospin, to the Council of Europe in 1997 in which he stated that the identity of Europe was based in part on an important linguistic heritage, to which special attention should be given. The leaflet also lists the appointment of Nicole Péry and then Bernard Poignant, who were asked to draw up a report on the RLs spoken in France, for educational purposes, and make suggestions for their preservation. This was handed in to the government in 1998 and it was suggested France should sign the Charter for the Protection of Regional and Minority Languages. Finally a major symbolic step was taken in 2001 when the *Délégation générale à la langue française* (DGLF) became the 'Délégation générale à la langue française *et aux langues de France'* (DGLFLF). Its annual report for parliament now always contains a section on the RLs and two very capable members of staff are committed to working on their behalf.

This progress was achieved under the Socialists, but the present government remains deeply committed to the protection of French as a pillar of the nation. Thus, in 2002, the Prime Minister, Jean-Pierre Raffarin, in a leaflet published and distributed by the DGLFLF stated: 'Although a policy in favour of the French language remains a constant of governmental action, it must also be the object of constant vigilance, of unfailing determination. It must also constantly evolve, be renewed, be modernised to remain efficient.'[27] There are now four priorities: (1) establishing the primacy of French with the state setting the example; (2) the fight against illiteracy in the name of social cohesion; (3) the fight to maintain the position of French internationally, mainly through the Organisation Internationale de la Francophonie; and (4) *the encouragement of plurilingualism at all levels*. This was meant to refer to the policy of teaching at least two languages, so that English should not displace all others. On the other hand it is clearly difficult to back a plurilingual policy from which the RLs would be excluded. Some accept this fully (mostly the Socialists, but with some notable exceptions), while others drag their feet as much as they can, particularly the *Conseil Constitutionnel* and the *Conseil d'Etat*, who have outlawed numerous efforts to give the RLs an official legal existence.

## Present impact of past policies

Past legislation starting with the 1539 Edict of Villers-Cotterêts, and unifying linguistic policies, in particular the Falloux law amendment making French the sole language of education, have led to the total elimination of the RLs from all public domains. These laws and policies constitute a formidable obstacle to any revival of the RLs. From a legal point of view they still have no status. They are merely tolerated.

The edict of 1539 is still used to exclude them from all legal and administrative contexts. The edict itself does not provide for sanctions where a language other than French is used, nor does it state whether the documents are invalid. The *Cour de Cassation* (the highest court in the land) decided, however, in the Corsican case of *Giorgi vs Masaspino* (4 August 1859), that the 1539 edict should be broadly interpreted, namely that the legal document drawn up by the lawyer in Corsican should be declared null and void. But in the case of *Orféi vs Orféi* (22 January 1879), the *Cour de Cassation* took a different view. The case concerned the validity of a marriage certificate written in Corsican. The judgement specifies that neither the 1539 edict, nor the decree of 2 Thermidor of Year II, nor the *arrêté* (ruling) of 24 Prairial of Year XI state that such acts were null and void. This was, according to the judgement, because the imposition of harsh penalties would be counterproductive to the gradual imposition of the law. It was pointed out that since the couple to be married only spoke Corsican, the failure to use French could hardly be seen as an act of bad faith. Other court cases reached the same conclusion, namely that the law was to facilitate the development of national unity, but could not be imposed directly on annexed regions.

More recent judgements have, however, not been so tolerant, and have established that any document addressed to a court or tribunal in a language other than French would not be considered (*Cour de Cassation*, 22 July 1986, *M. Cucca vs M. Del Pozo*). In another case where the defendants wished to present their case in Alsatian, the court decreed this to be unacceptable. Their request for an interpreter was also refused since they were both French nationals and known to be French speakers.

1539 also still holds strong in administrative matters. Thus in 1985, a petition filed in Breton was rejected as inadmissible (*Cour d'Etat*,

22 November 1985, *Quillevère*). This decision was specifically based on *Villers-Cotterêts*. Matters were slightly different in *Société Max-Planck-Gesellschaft* (number 206341, 18 October 2000). In this case the judge specified that a petition should not be turned down if in a foreign language, including the RLs, but only if accompanied by an officially recognised translation.

The language of the courts is therefore still French. An interpreter may be assigned to a person who does not know French, but this does not apply to the RLs, if the judge decides that the parties are bilingual. The same applies in the public domain (*la sphère publique*). This is why the imposition of an official terminology in all state organisations, such as education and the Civil Service, is seen as so important. The text most often invoked in this respect is article 2 of the Constitution which states that the language of the Republic is French. Thus it was held that correspondence addressed in Breton to a tax office was not acceptable (CAA, Nantes, 14 November 1990, Le Duigou). And the Post Office, which often goes to considerable efforts for letters clearly written by foreigners, refuses to deliver letters addressed in Breton (see CE, 15 April 92, Le Duigou). Similarly, although Memorandum 1619 (10 August 1979) allowed bilingual road signs, these were resisted by some representatives of the state, on the basis of their being contrary to both *Villers Cotterêts* and article 2 of the Constitution. Thus the *Préfet* for the Pyrénées Orientales tried to stop bilingual signs appearing in Perpignan. He also sent a letter to all Catalophone *communes* forbidding the use of Catalan, if they were not to lose their subsidies. Similarly in 1998, the *Sous Préfet* of Apt, in the *département* of the Vaucluse, demanded the reprinting of tickets giving entry to a Provençal castle, because they were partly written in Provençal.

France adopts a similarly cautious approach when signing and ratifying international agreements. Generally, whenever France has signed an international treaty in which one or more articles has the effect of recognising the existence of ethnic, religious or linguistic minorities, it has always been subject to the following reservation: 'the government of the Republic declares, taking account of article 1[28] of the Constitution of the French Republic, that article [. . .] does not apply in respect of the Republic'. This was the solution adopted for article 30 of the national Convention on the Rights of Children, which contained an article in respect of minority groups, when it was adopted in January 1990. This is not always possible, which is why the European Charter for Regional or Minority Languages has not been ratified by France (see Chapter 5).

## Concluding comments

Revival of the RLs demands first of all their legal recognition. This means, in practice, either changing the Constitution so as to include the RLs, or being willing to interpret the wording of article 2 differently. This could easily be done since stating that 'French is the language of the Republic' need not necessarily mean that it is the only one. It is simply that the members of both the Conseil Constitutionnel and the Conseil d'Etat have chosen to interpret the article in a narrow sense, in accordance with their Jacobin beliefs.

Either changing the wording of article 2 or interpreting it more generously is, in fact, all that is required to be able to treat the RLs as legally legitimate, since Villers-Cotterêts, used in the past against the RLs, does not in fact imply sanctions if they are used. The Toubon law is also often invoked, but with no good reason since it contains statements to the effect that none of its articles are to be interpreted to the detriment of the RLs.

At present it is therefore article 2 of the Constitution which remains the main stumbling block. An increasing minority is vocal in its demand for a revision of the Constitution, but it is still a minority, hence efforts being made to ensure their survival through other means, namely education and, to a much lesser extent, the media.

# 2
# The Rise of English as an Official Language

English emerged as an official national language by using the same devices as French, namely imposing English in all spheres of life, either by force or through the law, and by spreading English through the medium of education. But unlike in France, where the same policies applied throughout the country, they differed from region to region, with levels of coercion varying according to the levels of resistance encountered *in situ*. Religion also played a part, with voluntary conversion to the Church of England helping the survival of the RLs. This was the case in Wales, whereas the opposite applied in Cornwall.

The fact that different approaches were adopted towards different RLs was due to Britain's linguistic policies merely reflecting the pragmatic needs of a conqueror, and not a national ideal as in France. As regards codification, on the other hand, there was much discussion as to whether or not to follow the French path. In spite of finally deciding not to follow the example of France, a concept of *bon usage* emerged in England much as it did in France, although through different social forces. Standardisation was conducted in both countries in a similar fashion, with compulsory education being introduced in England slightly earlier than in France.

Bearing in mind that, unlike in France, the official national language is a Germanic as opposed to a Romance language, there is a puzzle as to the origin of English and why the Celtic languages and cultures have had such little impact, and indeed still attract so little recognition. The term 'Celtic fringe' is still used in a pejorative sense. This chapter starts with what Crystal calls the 'Celtic puzzle' since it is fundamental to the problems faced by the Celtic languages to this day.

## The origins of the English language

English is a direct descendant from the languages brought to Britain by the Germanic tribes in the course of the fifth century. They had a very different impact in Britain and in France: whereas French goes back to a Gallicised form of Latin, with a mainly Celtic sub-stratum and a Germanic super-stratum, in Britain it was the language(s) of the invaders which won the day, the others becoming peripheral RLs. The Germanic languages imported into Britain were, moreover, surprisingly unaffected by the Celtic languages widely spoken at the time. This is again in contrast with France where, in the same period, Gaulish was becoming extinct. The reason for this was that the Romans had had little impact in Britain linguistically, except for producing a very small Romanised Celtic elite. The Celtic languages were therefore spoken for much longer in Britain than in France (Breton not being a descendant from Gaulish, but an import from Britain in the sixth century).

Despite the cultural importance of the Celtic languages and cultures, and their having held sway over the Isles for the best part of a thousand years, most books on British history do not even include them, a fact deplored by the historian Norman Davies:

> Even though the Ancient Celts were the earliest group of ethnically and culturally identifiable inhabitants of the Isles, few general histories pay them much attention. Most histories of 'England', 'Britain', or 'the British Isles' begin with the coming of the Romans, starting either with Caesar's expedition in 55 and 54 BC or with the Claudian conquest. The preceding period of the Celtic supremacy, which lasted for the same length of time as that dividing Claudius from Bede or Tony Blair from the Black Prince, is usually glossed over or simply cut. (Davies 1999: 73)

(To which one could add that most school history books traditionally started with 1066 and the Norman conquest.)

Starting with the Roman conquest (the Romans were in Britain from 43 BC to AD 410) has a certain logic about it, because of the British traditional and ingrained admiration for the Classical world, rather than their Celtic heritage. But although Classical culture has certainly had a major influence on English culture, the same cannot be said of Latin, which was not implanted in Britain as it was in France in any permanent form, except in terms of Latin loan words. This is assumed to be because the Romans in Britain were so heavily outnumbered by the Britons (the early Celtic inhabitants of the land). They were, however, also outnumbered in Gaul, so other complex factors must have come into play.

Whatever the reasons, in Norman Davies' words, 'Latin civilization proved to be a veneer, an implantation that did not take root.' To back this point he quotes Barry Cuncliffe, Professor of Archaeology in Oxford as having 'dared to write': 'For nearly four hundred years, Britain was occupied and governed by an alien power. Yet, remarkably, the impact of that long period of rigid control was comparatively slight' (1999: 119). The influence of Latin came later through the Church and via the Normans, through French.

The origins of French and English are therefore complete opposites: a gradual and on the whole peaceful move to Latin in France, Roman civilisation being seen as superior and the route to social success, contrasted in England with the move from the Celtic to the Germanic languages, by-passing Latin nearly completely, a move which has been associated with brute force. It is interesting to speculate on why this should have happened.

According to the Venerable Bede (*c.* 672–735),[1] early in the fifth century, the Picts, who had arrived in the north of Britain from Scythia via northern Ireland, and the Scots, who had also come from Ireland, were attacking the Britons. The Britons therefore appealed to Rome for help. Bede states that the letter to the Roman consul spoke of 'the groans of the Britons' and that the invaders were referred to as 'the Barbarians who drive us to the sea. The sea drives us back towards the barbarians – we are either slain or drowned' (Crystal 1995: 6). But Rome was too busy fighting off the attack of the Barbarians to send help. So, still according to Bede, the Britons 'consulted on what was to be done and where they should seek assistance to repel the cruel and frequent incursions of the northern nations; and they all agreed with their King Vortigern, to call over to their aid, from the parts beyond the sea, the Saxon nation' (quoted in Crystal 2004: 16). This was clearly a mistake, since the Saxons took over nearly the whole land, either displacing or massacring many Britons in the process.

Bragg states colourfully:

> That is one powerful image – English arriving on the scene like a fury from hell, brought to the soft shore of an abandoned imperial outpost by fearless pagan fighting men, riding along the whale's way on their wave-steed. It is an image of the spread of English which has been matched by reality many times, often savagely, across one and a half millennia.

But then he adds:

> But there is another story. There were many who came as peaceful immigrants, farmers seeking profitable toil and finding a relatively peaceful home as they transported their way of life from bleak flatlands to rich pastures. Through their occupation English was earthed. This ability to plant itself deep in foreign territory became another powerful characteristic of the language. (Bragg 2003: 1–2)

This last point, of course, is not strictly true since the Germanic languages were unable to 'earth' themselves in France, except in very small areas where the Germanic tribes outnumbered all others, as in Alsace. It seems that in England they either pushed the local populations west, until they could take refuge behind the Welsh mountain ranges, or else they absorbed the local population.

The theory that there was a shift in the population from east to west seems to be backed by genetic evidence. Thus Crystal reports on a 2002 study which 'showed a major difference in Y-chromosome markers between men from a selection of seven towns along an east–west transect from East Anglia to north Wales, suggesting a mass migration of Celts from England, with at least half the male indigenous Celtic population of England being displaced' (Crystal 2004: 31). Crystal also ponders about what he calls the 'Celtic language puzzle'. By this he means the fact that the Germanic tribes did not end up speaking the Celtic languages of the local occupants, albeit in a Germanicised form, and that, apart from place-names, the influence of the Celtic languages was so small as not even to constitute a sub-stratum, as they had in France. He puts forward two opposing theories to explain this.

The first is that 'there was so little in common between the Celtic way of life as it had developed in Roman Britain, and the Anglo-Saxon way of life as it had developed on the Continent that there was no motivation to borrow Celtic words' (Crystal 2004: 30). He points out that, since the Germanic tribes were victorious in their conquest, either the Celts were seen as inferior, or they were seen as superior because of their highly Romanised culture. Whatever the explanation, the Germanic tribes would have tended to avoid all Celtic influence.

The opposite theory is that their two ways of life were so similar that the Anglo-Saxons 'had all the words they needed . . . Celtic words which the Anglo-Saxons might most usefully have adopted might already have come into their language from Latin because of the Roman presence in Europe. At the very least they would have been familiar with many Latin words, from encounters with Romans on the Continent' (Crystal 2004: 30). Moreover, Latin, the language of political power, would have been the more attractive source of borrowing. To which must be added the fact that many of the Celts spoke Latin themselves. The arrival of St Augustine and other Roman Catholic missionaries in 597 also played an important role in strengthening Latin since they introduced the Roman alphabet. But by the middle of the seventh century, the numerous scribes in monasteries were starting to incorporate Old English forms into their work, adapting the alphabet in the process (Crystal 2004: 27).

But again Crystal proposes a counter-argument to the 'distaste for all things Celtic' previously advanced: the use of Celtic personal names does not support this scenario, since although infrequent, when they were adopted it was by members of the Anglo-Saxon nobility. Crystal therefore concludes that if Anglo-Saxon noblemen were giving their children Celtic names, they must have had respect for the Celts, at least in some parts of the country, and intermarried (Crystal 2004: 32–3). In which case more Celtic loan words could be expected. Crystal's conclusion is that this remains one of the great puzzles in the history of the English language.

Other specialists have claimed that although the Germanic languages were largely unaffected by the Celtic languages, Celtic culture has had a deep impact on English culture. Thus the bard Eluned Philipps, winner of the Eisteddfod Crown,[2] commenting on the distinctive Welsh contribution to English literature, stated that 'You can always tell when a Welshman is writing in English because of the flamboyance of their descriptions. I think that comes down from the old Celtic warriors who used to go into battle [against the Anglo-Saxons] not only with terror in their veins, but with red hot waves of ecstasy' (quoted in McCrum et al. 1986: 56). The historian Norman Davies makes much the same claim, although in less flamboyant terms (he is not after all a bard), attributing to the Celtic sub-stratum (although he does not use the term) much of the English sense of poetry, romanticism and mysticism, without the English ever acknowledging their debt.

Davies complains in particular that 'all too often the English casually subsume the insular Celts, or callously ignore them, as the mood dictates' (1999: 81). He gives several explanations for this historical neglect. One is that the pre-Roman era is judged to be prehistory, while another relates to classical prejudices: traditionally educated Englishmen received a 'Classical' education, which did not include anything to do with Ancient Britain. Instead, generations of British schoolboys learned from Tacitus that the Celts were barbarians, since the Romans were seen as the sole bearers of civilisation (Davies 1999: 124). Which indirectly made English civilisation also superior.

Another factor is the English approach to archaeology which is 'reluctant to enter those realms of research and speculation in which their well-tried scientific methodology is not relevant' (Davies 1999: 74), i.e. to take into account Ancient Celtic literature, an oral tradition which was written down in the early Middle Ages. According to Davies, some have even asserted that the Ancient Celts never really existed and were no more than a modern invention: 'There are archaeologists working with the Celtophiles, and others working against them, often suspected of dire English nationalism. The idea that archaeology is a neutral science is a mirage' (Davies 1999: 74). Yet another complaint is the manner in which Celtic studies have nearly always developed inside their own 'watertight compartment'. And finally, although the Welsh followed the Reformation movement, Ireland did not and its association with the papacy was damaging for the prestige of Celtic studies.

Whatever the answer to Crystal's 'Celtic puzzle' and however great Davies' dismay at the lack of recognition of our Celtic past, the fact remains that it was the languages spoken by the Germanic tribes which gave rise to 'Anglo-Saxon', i.e. Old English, while Welsh, Cornish, Manx, Gaelic and Irish became peripheral RLs. How did this take place? According to Bede's account, later incorporated in the *The Anglo-Saxon Chronicle*,[3] the first invaders were the Angles, the Saxons and the Jutes, who sailed across the sea from Denmark and the coastal part of Germany known as Lower Saxony, in AD 449, at which point, according to these chronicles (written, it must be remembered, two centuries after the events, since their author was born *c.* 672) the native Britons (i.e. the Celts) were driven towards the west, fleeing the invaders 'as if from fire' (quoted in McCrum et al. 1986: 60), thus creating the 'Celtic fringe'. The dispossessed Britons were called *wealas*, meaning not only 'foreigner' but also slave, which gave the word 'Welsh'.

This did not happen overnight for the Britons did resist, the most famous of their heroes being probably the legendary King Arthur, who appears to have maintained an element of peace for a while. But by the seventh century the Anglo-Saxons were established in most of England, where they eventually set up seven kingdoms: Northumbria, Mercia, East Anglia, Kent, Essex, Sussex and Wessex. McCrum et al. comment on how deep the divide which existed then between the English and the Celts has remained to this day, the Welsh having retained their language, the Scots their separate legal and educational systems, and the Irish having been in a state of rebellion for centuries. Indeed they comment on the irony of the expression 'the Brits' as it is now used, since the Ancient Britons were in fact the Celts (1986: 61).

In the beginning, according to Bede, the Saxons[4] settled in Essex, Sussex and Wessex, the Angles settled in East Anglia, Mercia and Northumbria and the Jutes took over Kent and the Isle of Wight. Appalling massacres of native Britons took place in the process during the sixth, seventh and eighth centuries leading to the death of the local languages, where they were originally spoken. There emerged, as a result, according to traditional philology, four Old English dialects after the kingdoms where they were spoken: West Saxon, Kentish, Mercian and Northumbrian (the last two are sometimes classified together as 'Anglian').

Four dialects may not seem much, and there were probably many more, their number depending on the level of linguistic 'delicacy' adopted. Crystal explains (2004: Chapter 2) that this small number arises from the nature of the evidence available: Old English material from 600 to 1150 only accounts for 3 million words, i.e. less than the total of a single prolific modern writer. This clearly is not much data to go on, and Crystal marvels that evidence for even four could be found, particularly since this material is extremely varied, including as it does prose works, poetry, charters, laws, local records, medical texts, inscriptions, in fact all manner of records.

Crystal concludes from his examination of the documentation that evidence for the Kentish dialect is thin, but reveals interesting characteristics, spread country-wide later by Chaucer, and which are now part of Modern English. Most of the Northumbrian texts appeared very early since there were many major centres of learning in the north, with Bede and later Alcuin producing important works. The absence of texts between the eighth and tenth century reflects the destructive influence of the Vikings at that time. The importance of Mercia as a political power and centre for learning is reflected in the survival of texts dating back to the eighth century (there are few earlier texts presumably because of the violent impact of the Vikings). But many Mercian features penetrated other dialects, and in particular West Saxon, because King Alfred made his kingdom into a leading political and cultural centre to which others gravitated.

The bulk of the corpus is in West Saxon, which reflects its steadily increasing power, until the arrival of the Normans. It is the dialect of most poetic works of the period, and indeed it becomes over time a 'standard' literary dialect, and the one usually associated with Anglo-Saxon studies. It certainly acted as a unifying force in English politics.

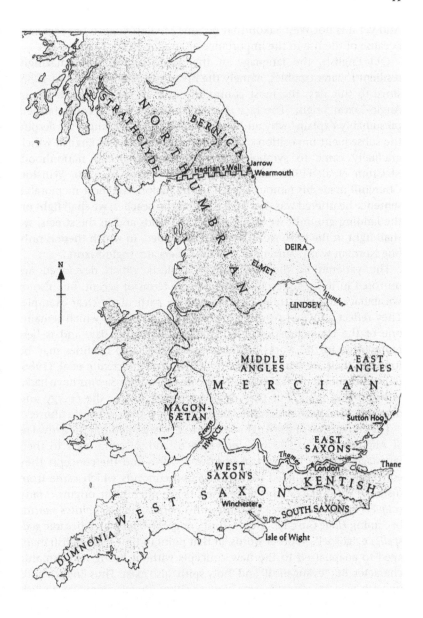

*Map 2* The chief dialect areas of Old English (some of the more important Anglo-Saxon kingdoms are also indicated)

And yet it is not West Saxon that became Modern English but Mercian, because of the rise in the importance of London in the Middle Ages.

Old English, the language of the Anglo-Saxons, was amazingly resilient to later troubles, namely the invasion of the Normans in 1066, since to this day, the most commonly used words in English are of Anglo-Saxon origin. The fact that the invaders had become farmers presumably explains why and how they kept to their language, despite the subsequent imposition of French. It is therefore Old English which gradually came to symbolise English continuity and nationhood. McCrum et al. (1986: 62) point out that when, in 1940, Winston Churchill made his famous speech to the nation, the most memorable sentence he uttered was 'We shall fight on the beaches; we shall fight on the landing grounds, we shall fight in the fields and in the streets, we shall fight in the hills; we shall never surrender', in which there is only one Norman word, 'surrender'. All the others are Anglo-Saxon.

The varieties of the Anglo-Saxon dialects which developed are mirrored in today's speech, particularly in terms of accent, but also of vocabulary and structures, Geordie being a particularly clear example. They reflect a love of word-play, innuendo and riddles which remains one of the characteristics of British English to this day, and is best represented in the works of Shakespeare. The same qualities may be found in their art, which was extremely intricate. McCrum et al. (1986: 64) comment on the fact that 'Historically, the Anglo-Saxons have had a rather mixed press; but they deserve great credit for the energy and determination with which they developed their own sense of culture.'

The conversion of the Anglo-Saxons to Christianity from the arrival of St Augustine in AD 597 was, however, to add an extra layer to their language(s), both in terms of borrowed words and the concepts they conveyed. This included both things and concepts which came from distant exotic places (the Bible itself being oriental in origin). Many *calques*[5] from Latin appeared during this period, such as *spiritus sanctus* becoming *Halig Gast*, i.e. 'Holy Ghost', or *evangelium* which became *god-spell*, i.e. 'gospel'. In other words, at that point in time Old English managed to adapt itself to the new concepts without losing its Germanic character. But 'evangelical' and 'holy spirit' also exist. Thus English ends up with two sets of words, one coming either directly from Old English or via an elaborated form of Old English, and the other coming directly from Latin where religious matters were concerned, and from Norman French after the Conquest, for all others. This also illustrates what Bragg refers to as 'English's most subtle and ruthless characteristic of all: its capacity to absorb others' (2003: 3).

Between AD 750 and 1050 a new migration began in the shape of the Vikings, who came from what is now Sweden and colonised parts of the British Isles. The 'Danes' or 'Norsemen' (who also come under the label 'Viking') also conquered northern France, where they became the Normans who eventually conquered Britain, but by then they had changed their language to French. They, too, were very destructive. Thus they sacked the monasteries of Jarrow and Lindisfarne in AD 793. By the middle of the ninth century half the country was under their power. At this point they turned their attention to the most important of the kingdoms, the kingdom of Wessex, which comprised Dorset, Wiltshire, Somerset and Hampshire. It looked as if there would soon be no English-speaking kingdom left. But Alfred 'the Great', king of Wessex, eventually managed to defeat them and a treaty was signed in 878 which gave the Danes the part of the country east of the 'Danelaw Boundary', which runs roughly from Cheshire, slightly west of Rugby and slightly north of London. (A great white horse carved into the hillside in Wiltshire commemorates his victory.)

No sooner was peace reached with the Vikings than King Alfred had to face a new problem, namely that his forces were too weak to defend the peace. For this he needed allies, if the 'English' culture was to be saved. To this end he appealed to a sense of Englishness shared by all those with the same Germanic origins and who spoke variants of the same language, Old English. It seems that he quite consciously used English as a way of creating a sense of national identity (McCrum et al. 1986: 69). To enhance this concept he built or rebuilt monasteries and schools, where English and not Latin was to be used as a basis for education. This was in part because he found that very few priests were left who were able to read and write Latin. Therefore Alfred (848–900) did the opposite of Charlemagne (742–814): instead of resuscitating a classical form of Latin he went over to the vernacular. He even went to the trouble of learning Latin so that he could translate important works – in particular Bede's *Ecclesiastical History of the English Nation* – into English. He explains in his preface: 'Therefore it seems better to me . . . that we should also translate certain books which are most necessary for all men to know, into the language that we can all understand' (quoted in McCrum et al. 1986: 69).

Within the Danelaw boundaries, where the Vikings settled, Old Norse and Saxon (or Old English) came into close contact. Both being Germanic languages, some communication could take place, but English probably rapidly became pidginised, i.e. simplified. What emerged was a language which was no longer inflected, as it had been, but one in which

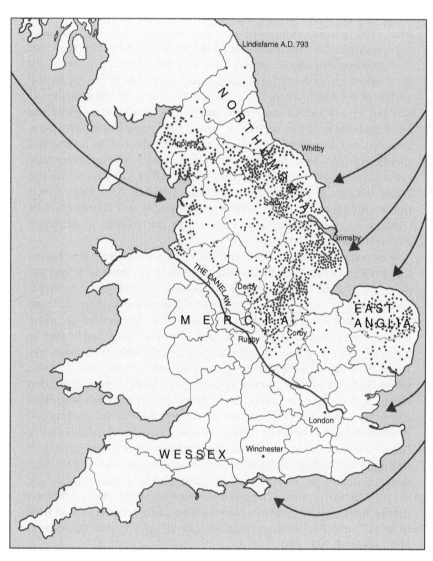

*Map 3* The Danelaw boundary

word endings used to convey functional meaning (i.e. the case system) were dropped and replaced by word order and prepositions. In other words the language became simplified and much closer to Modern English. Old Norse seems to have disappeared as a separate entity in just about a century, having contributed some 900 new words to the language, although borrowings are often difficult to determine given the Germanic nature of both languages (McCrum et al. 1986: 70–1). There are certainly a number of doublets or word pairs which result from the Norse influence: words such as *dike* in Old Norse, and *ditch* in Old English, or *sick* in Old Norse, and *ill* in Old English. Some of these may also have come to symbolise regional variation, such as *kirk* versus *church*..

The 1066 Norman Conquest threatened English with extinction. Yet in the beginning the estimated number of French speakers represented no more than 3–5 per cent of the population, and some specialists say even less. As a result, Old English continued to be spoken by the masses. But although Old English/Middle English (it is difficult to draw a precise line between the two) continued to be spoken, it acquired 'dialectal' not to say *patois* overtones. To quote Bragg: 'it lived in the margins, much as the English dialects did after the triumph of eighteenth century Enlightenment drove them outside the pale of "literature" to the lower reaches of society' (2003: 48). (Which is, of course, what happened to most of the RLs.) This means that there was considerable variation in the forms spoken up and down the country. (Which again is what happened to the RLs.)

Although English survived, it underwent profound changes, to the extent that whereas Old English seems to the modern reader an incomprehensible foreign language, by the time of Chaucer (1340–1400) it had become recognisably English. This was because during the intervening three centuries two major phenomena had taken place. The first was the dropping of cases in favour of word order and prepositions, which had started happening within the Danelaw area and had spread to other areas. The second was the influence of French, bringing new concepts for which there were no Old English terms. Thousands of new Latin-based words had to be absorbed, to the extent that Modern English vocabulary is reckoned to be 60 per cent French-based, making it, according to some linguists, a remarkably successful creole.

The result was the well-documented phenomenon of lexical specialisation, of the *pig/pork* and *house/mansion* type, with the Anglo-Saxon-based word referring either to the basic reality (the live animal) or a less grand reality (the house). As Bragg puts it so colourfully: 'The English laboured, the French feasted' (2003: 51). Such a tradition has endured into the present: a 'casserole' is seen as a much higher class of dish than a 'stew'. It is this hugely lexically enriched and grammatically simplified language which gradually emerged as the national language of Britain. But whereas French was the object of centralised legislation and institutionalisation from the time of the emergence of France as a state, English developed into the official national language in a gradual and piecemeal fashion.

## The rise of English as an official language and the accidental emergence of linguistic policies

The progress of English, like that of French, has to be seen within the gradual absorption of lands and kingdoms under the Crown. But whereas France ended up *une et indivisible* ('one and indivisible'), Britain, or rather the 'United Kingdom' remains made up of four parts: England, Wales and Scotland, which may be defined as separate 'nations', and Northern Ireland, which is difficult to classify since some of the members of its population considers themselves as British while others see themselves as Irish. Many in Cornwall also add the 'Cornish nation', although it now comes under a 'South West England' label.

Linguistically, too, French and English are different, in that French developed directly from Latin, whereas English is much more of a hybrid:

> The making of English is the story of three invasions and a cultural revolution. In its simplest terms, the language was brought to Britain by Germanic tribes, the Angles, Saxons and Jutes, influenced by Latin and Greek when St Augustine and his followers converted England to Christianity, subtly enriched by the Danes, and finally transformed by the French-speaking Normans . . . From the beginning English was a crafty hybrid, made in war and peace. It was, in the words of Daniel Defoe 'your Roman-Saxon-Danish-Norman English' . . . The English have always accepted the mixed blood of their language. (McCrum et al. 1986: 51)

This is in contrast with the *pureté de la langue française*, i.e. the purity of French, the latter coming directly from Latin, which gave it considerable prestige.

English suffered, moreover, considerable loss of prestige after the Norman Conquest in 1066 since it then became associated purely with the lower classes, and its remarkable written tradition disintegrated.

English therefore had to fight back in order to achieve the status it had enjoyed previously. The first factor to help English in this struggle was the defeat of John Lackland, after which the nobility had to declare their allegiance either to the king of France or to the king of England. Thus little by little the French came to be seen as foreigners in England which helped develop the idea of 'our language' as against 'theirs'. This was a first step towards English regaining its former prestige. Then in 1295 Edward I tried to rally the population against the possibility of a French invasion, under Philippe IV of France, and to do so he addressed the people in their mother tongue, English. This was the first time English was used for nationalistic purposes. Similarly, Richard II quelling the Peasants' Revolt in 1381 addressed the rebels and duped them using English, which was not his mother tongue.

It is also said that English spread from the cradle: the Normans often married English women, and they often had English-speaking nannies for their children. Although specialists in the development of the English language do not all agree on this point, one fact is indisputable, namely that by the thirteenth century, although not an official language, English was spoken or at least understood by nearly the whole population.

As in France, legal literature played an important part in the linguistic development of the country. This originated during the reign of Henry I (1100–35) when a little group of treatises attempted to formulate Anglo-Saxon law in a way suited to the Norman age. The most important was Leges Henrici Primi (Laws of Henry I) which appeared around 1118 and whose purpose was to explain the customary law of the local courts to the Norman sheriffs and lords in a language – Latin – that they could understand. But already, according to Plucknett (1956: 256), 'the author suffered under the disability of writing a very bad Latin style and his meaning is often far from clear'. As in France, disease also helped to displace Latin. The plague broke out in 1348, with, again, the clerics and monks the most affected because of living in communities, with the result that legal literature started to appear in French, the language of the Conquest. The most important treatise in French, the *Britton* (c. 1290–2), was based on Bracton, the first great treatise on English law (in Latin of course), during the reign of Henry III (1216–72) (Plucknett 1956: 265–6). This was because lawyers became less and less at ease with Latin and preferred to turn to the familiar French of *Britton*.[6] At roughly the same time the writs, which were always in Latin, were translated into French, the language in which counts[7] in the regal courts were actually spoken, since it was the ordinary language of the upper classes.

This was for the benefit of professional, literate men, who were not automatically familiar with Latin.

The Year Books, the earliest of which originated in the reign of Edward I (1272–1307), present another example of the use of French – the language of pleadings – in a legal context which is particularly interesting since they are accounts of oral debates. They were subsidiary to the various manuals of procedure which consisted of the French oral forms which were used by the 'serjeant' when addressing the court. According to Plucknett, they 'resemble not so much a modern law report as a professional newspaper, combining matters of technical interest with the lighter side of professional life' (Plucknett 1956: 270). (This is because they often included long rambling conversations and irrelevant material.)

It would seem that the Year Books dried up around the thirtieth year of the reign of Henry VIII (i.e. 1538–9), French being gradually replaced by English. Already in 1362 the Statute of Pleading established that all pleas would be in English, *la lange du paiis* rather than in French *qest trop desconue* (i.e. which had become too unknown) in all courts of justice, but that the final written version would be in Latin. It was also in 1362 or 1363 that the opening of parliament took place for the first time in English. The oldest known parliamentary document dates from 1386. Even in the grammar schools, education was gradually ceasing to be in French.

The progress of English may be illustrated by the change in the language used by England's kings. Thus Richard II (1377–99) was the last English king to speak French as his mother tongue. Henry IV (1399–1413), who deposed him, made his first speech to his subjects in English, instead of the customary French, and Richard II also pronounced his abdication speech in English. It is from then on that English became the national language, but without the passing of any decrees to that effect. Although Henry IV spoke in English, royal documents remained in French. It was his successor, Henry V (1413–22) who was the first to use English as his written language. Even his will was in English. (The first known will in English dates from 1387.) As in France, the people followed the example given by the king and in 1422 the Brewers Guild decreed in 1422 that English would be adopted in the written context.

English also started to play a role in the work of the Chancery. Although Latin was used when dealing with the king's interests as universal feudal superior, it was English which was used when dealing with petitions, pleadings or bills of complaint by individuals. Thus, as in

France, Latin tended to be used for universal matters, and the vernacular at the level of the individual.

Finally, English started to compete with Latin in the religious sphere. The principle had traditionally been that the priest was supposed to act as an intermediary between God and His people. But once it was felt that there was no need for such an intermediary, English took over from Latin. Thus John Wyclif (1329–84) inspired the first English translation of the Bible from a Latin version. This was done in secret by a group of scholars who were then sent out to preach the word of God in English. They were the Lollards who were condemned by the Church in 1382 and the Bibles were burnt (and also some of the Lollards). But they continued to operate in secret. In the sixteenth century, there were more translations, all still illegal. Thus around 1530 Tyndale translated the Bible, starting from Latin and Greek, which led to numerous borrowings from those two languages. Although Tyndale was condemned to death for this deed, his translation became the basis for the official translation of 1539, after the Reformation in 1534. The Bible quickly became the most read book in the land and played a major role in the spread of English. Tyndale's version also influenced James I's Authorised Version of the Bible which was used to spread English in Wales, Scotland and Ireland.

Thus English came to compete with Latin and French in all domains. This led to the Courts of Justice Act 1731, which required the use of English in all courts of justice in England and Wales, and in the Court of the Exchequer in Scotland. A similar Act was passed in 1737 for Ireland. The aim was to make the law accessible to all English-speaking lay persons. Another law, the Local Government Act 1889, made English the sole language of the newly founded local authorities in England and Wales. By then, its supremacy was complete.

The gradual rise in status of English was not only to the detriment of Latin and French, but also of the RLs. Generally speaking, the more the Celtic languages were associated with a spirit of rebellion the more they were repressed. The closer to the spirit of the Reformation, the better they survived.

The first area to be affected was Cornwall, annexed *de facto* in 1337 when it became the Duchy of Cornwall. This is such a long time ago that most people are hardly aware of Cornwall having ever been anything else but part of England, which infuriates many Cornish people today. The result of this early annexation is that Cornish fared worst of all the RLs in the UK. This is because there were numerous Cornish rebellions against the English, which were mercilessly put down. One, in particular, in 1549, was caused by the imposition of the Common Prayer Book in English. This caused an outcry in Cornwall, where Latin was the language of religion and Cornish the language of the home. In England, however, this was seen as a stand against the Reformation, and something to be crushed at all costs. As a result, all the monasteries and places of learning were destroyed and Cornish soon started a slow decline. Until quite recently, it was considered to have died out by the end of the eighteenth century but it has re-emerged in recent years.

The first piece of linguistic legislation ever passed in these isles concerned Ireland: in 1366, the Statutes of Kilkenny obliged all English settlers to use English or else lose their land. It seems they were turning 'native' at a worrying rate. Then, from the sixteenth century on, the English Crown fought the Irish in the name of Protestantism, which implied the use of English. Finally in 1801 the Act of Union with Great Britain brought new efforts to anglicise the island, including, in 1832, the foundation of 'national schools' which functioned entirely in English. A few years later, a series of famines killed or drove abroad a large proportion of the Irish poor, who formed the main body of Irish speakers. From then on, Irish was an endangered language. The next important date was of course 1922 when Partition created Northern Ireland, and Irish continued to be spoken in Northern Ireland, but only in a limited number of homes. English was very much the only official language.

Wales was annexed by England by the Act of Union of 1536, which provided that only English was to be used for legal and administrative purposes. But this rule proved impossible to implement fully for practical reasons, namely a lack of competent bilinguals, the country being mainly monoglot at the time. Welsh therefore continued to be used for some time in all contexts. Religion was also a factor in the survival of the language, Wales having readily accepted the Reformation. This meant that the New Testament was translated into Welsh in 1567 and the whole Bible in 1588. As early as 1698 the Society for Promoting Christian Knowledge established schools which functioned entirely in Welsh. This ensured it a certain prestige, not enjoyed by the other Celtic languages in the British Isles. It was no longer, however, the language of social progress and the Education Act of 1870, which allowed for education only in English, dealt a final institutional blow to Welsh.

The 1609 Statutes of Iona include the first piece of linguistic legislation passed in Scotland. It obliged the heads of wealthy families to educate at least their eldest child in English (a 'wealthy' person was defined as one who owned at least 60 cows). Then, in 1616, the Scottish Privy Council set up schools to destroy what they called 'the Irish language'. The 1707 Act of Union accentuated the move towards English but the movement of extreme Anglicisation only began after Bonnie Prince Charles' defeat at Culloden in 1746. The later desire to convert the Gaelic-speaking Catholic Highlanders to Protestantism led to the translation of the New Testament into Gaelic in 1767, which helped save Gaelic from extinction. This was only meant to be a means towards an end, i.e. conversion, and the Education Act of 1872, stipulating that education could only be in English, was the final blow to Gaelic.

The other language spoken in Scotland was Scots, or Lallans, spoken mainly in the Lowlands (Lallans = low lands). It was a literary language and the language of the Scottish Court, and was codified early on, but a number of events led to its early loss of prestige. The first blow came in 1560, when, after the Reformation (1534), English, rather than Scots, became the language of the Church in Scotland. The second blow was when James VI of Scotland became James I of England and settled with his Court in London in 1603. He changed his manner of speech, abandoning Old Scots for English, and the whole Court followed suit. From then on Scots became the language of the people, despite the efforts of numerous poets, the most famous being Robert Burns (1759–96).

Since Scots did not represent any danger for the Crown, it was never subjected to repressive policies, but simply ignored. It even came to be viewed as 'bad English', which was even more destructive than any legislation could have been. The Education Act of 1872, however, again delivered it a final blow.

From a comparative point of view, the most interesting piece of legislation was the 1536 Act of Union between England and Wales, since it made English the language of law and administration, three years before the edict of *Villers-Cotterêts* did the same for French (in France it is usually considered the first ever law of this type, but clearly this was not the case). The big difference is that the 1536 Act only applied to Wales, whereas in France *Villers-Cotterêts* applied to the whole country.

The importance of compulsory education in establishing an official language is similar in both countries. Again France and Britain differ in that educational laws applied to France uniformly, whereas in Britain different acts were passed for different parts of the kingdom. In both cases force, legislation and the institutional framework – particularly state education – were the main factors in ensuring the success of French and English as official national languages.

## The codification of English: an unstructured affair

By the time English started to be used again in official contexts, some form of codification became necessary since by then there were many competing forms (or 'dialects') spoken up and down the country. Thus, when Caxton translated Virgil's *Aeneid* from French into English he ran into the problem of how to translate the word for *oeuf* (egg). He hesitated between *egges*, which came from Old Norse and was used in the north and the east of the country, and *eyren*, the word used in the south and which came from Old English. In this case he chose the Old Norse *eggs*, but in many others he chose words commonly used in London and Kent, and also understood in the Midlands. In other words, traits from many different dialects made their way into English, although it predominantly comes from the forms of speech spoken in the Midlands and London. This led in the long term to a cline between English dialects (now of historical interest only), regionally marked forms of English (the original dialect functioning as a sub-stratum) and standard English.

The first move towards codification is usually ascribed to the first great English writer since the Norman invasion, Chaucer (1340–1400). It was his work that contributed first to the fixing of English grammar and vocabulary. He and his contemporaries worried that their work would not survive or fail to gain recognition because of linguistic variation within the country and they were the first to feel the need for codification. The same problem arises for protagonists of the RLs which have broken up into smaller linguistic units that are no longer mutually intelligible.

The scribes working in the Chancery in Westminster were the first to play a major role in fixing orthography, since it was essential that a document written in London should be intelligible throughout the country. Their form of writing has been referred to as 'Chancery English' but the spelling that they adopted was not always the most logical, sometimes because of a desire to make English look more like Latin, hence aberrations of the *dette/debt*, or *doute/doubt* variety.

When in 1476 Caxton established the first printing press in England (Gutenberg's press was established in 1453), he fixed English spelling for centuries to come. This was unfortunate since his spelling predated the great English vowel shift,[8] which took place between the end of the fourteenth and the sixteenth centuries. This meant that the spelling rapidly diverged with pronunciation, at least where long vowels were concerned. But however illogical 'correct' spelling may have been, it soon became a way of distinguishing the educated from the less well educated, much as it is today.

The importance of printing may be judged by the fact that between 1500 and 1640, over 20 000 works were published, and that half the population could read at least a little. Such a large readership represented a source of enormous profit. It was therefore commercially sensible to publish books that could be read and understood by the greatest number. This meant excluding from the vocabulary words which were unlikely to be widely understood. This also meant eliminating most regional variants which led to the gradual imposition of the form of English spoken in London – the most prestigious city in the country, thanks to its theatres, its social scene and the presence of the Court – to the detriment of other varieties.

A major difference between England and France as regards codification and standardisation was that in France it was largely the result of politics and legislation whereas in England it was the result of competing social forces. Thus the towering figure of Shakespeare (1564–1616) fixed certain aspects of the English language for centuries to come. This was due to the universal appeal of his works which borrowed from all registers and regions. In this respect he was similar to Rabelais for French with the difference that Rabelais' rich style had to give way to the purified version of French promoted by the Academy. Shakespeare's language was allowed to enrich the national language, giving it its flexibility of expression. It may be this very flexibility which has contributed to English becoming an international language.

Other authors, however, introduced prescriptivism into English, making it hard for regional variations to survive due to the recognition of the concept of 'good' as against 'unacceptable' English. The first writer to ask for the establishment of an academy or society at which such matters could be debated was Daniel Defoe in an essay, 'Of Academies' written in 1697: 'The Work of this Society shou'd be to encourage *Polite* Learning, to polish and refine the English Tongue, and advance the so much neglected Faculty of Correct language, to establish *Purity* and *Propriety* of Stile, and to purge it from all the Irregular Additions that Ignorance and Affectation have introduc'd' (quoted in Crystal 2004: 377; my emphasis). This seemed a reasonable request, particularly since a Royal Society for Sciences had been created in 1664. Swift (1667–1745) asked Queen Anne for the creation of such an academy for the glory of her Majesty, but the Queen died in 1714, and the succeeding king, George I, spoke only German, so the plan was abandoned. This did not stop Swift writing a *Proposal for Correcting*,

*Improving and Ascertaining the English Tongue* in 1712. He and Addison (1672–1719), who wrote in the *Spectator*, stood against change in general, their goal being the stabilisation of the language.

There were opponents to the idea, the most important being Dr Johnson, author of the first large-scale English dictionary, *A Dictionarie of the English Language* (1755). He came to the conclusion that the search for stability was similar to the search for an anti-ageing elixir and that a language cannot simply be embalmed. All that could be done was to register usage. His spelling, however, despite not being given force of law, became nonetheless the accepted norm, until the arrival of the *Oxford English Dictionary*, completed in 1928.

Grammar also came under a prescriptive influence. Bishop Robert Lowth's *Short Introduction to English Grammar* (1762) was not only prescriptive but conservative and reflected his own likes and dislikes and was extremely popular, whereas Joseph Priestley's *The Rudiments of English Grammar* (1761) which was based on usage was not a success. Over 200 grammars were published between 1750 and 1800 which illustrates the importance attached to grammatical correctness.

Pronunciation was also seen as in need of codification. The problem was the variation in pronunciation throughout the country and the gap which had developed between spelling and pronunciation. Good pronunciation was supposed to correspond to spelling, hence expressions such as *'Don't drop your 'h's'*. But it was then important to identify the pronunciation that was implied by the spelling. As early as 1589 George Puttenham, the author of a manual on rhetoric, rejected the pronunciation of the north of England in favour of London in the name of mutual intelligibility. Sheridan (1751–1816) became a keen campaigner on such matters. In 1756 he published *The British Education*, and in 1757 gave a series of lectures on the subject. His role is important because, until then, although London and the Court provided a linguistic model in terms of vocabulary and grammar, having a regional or foreign accent was not seen as a problem. After Sheridan, the accent of the middle classes became the model to imitate. In 1762 Sheridan went as far as to proclaim that 'correct' pronunciation was a sign that a person had kept good company in the past and was worth knowing.

Thus, whereas previously codification and standardisation aimed purely at improving communication, Sheridan introduced a new social dimension in that people were divided into those who spoke 'proper' English and those who did not. In particular, he mocked approximate uses of language by creating the character of Mrs Malaprop (from the French *mal à propos*, meaning inapposite) which led to the concept of 'malapropisms'. Later Thomas Bowdler (1754–1825) edited a number of great literary works, including those of Shakespeare, and removed all 'offensive' language. While Jane Austen (1775–1817) became the symbol of *bon usage*.

Bragg has an amusing way of summarising this evolution: 'Wherever you land after Swift's failed academy, Johnson's cornerstone dictionary and Sheridan's class distinguishing elocution, the English are having a high old time tormenting the language into shapes and sounds which reflect strait-laced manners, class prejudice and competing moralities' (2003: 234). In other words, English became the mirror of the prejudices of the period and an indispensable tool for social ascension. Bernard Shaw illustrated this point in *Pygmalion* (which became the musical *My Fair Lady*). It is also a well-known fact that in England (but not to the same extent in France) being well spoken is the first tool of the swindler.

To this day there are innumerable guidebooks to writing 'good' or 'correct' English. Fowler's *Modern English Usage*, first edited in 1926, was updated with the subtitle *the acknowledged authority on English usage*. A recent addition to the canon deals with punctuation and has sold in millions (*Eats, Shoots and Leaves* by Lynn Truss, 2003). Its subtitle, *The Zero Tolerance Approach to Punctuation!*, illustrates both the desire to be correct and the amused contempt in which correctness is held. The ironical element is typical of current British attitudes, which are more liberal than those in France, at least among the 'politically correct' and the linguistically sophisticated.

In conclusion the position can be summarised by stating that 'Proper English' came into existence as a tool for social progress and that it was mirrored by a parallel decline in the local dialects which were unable to compete.

## The standardisation of English

The propagation of a codified, normalised form of English was the result of social pressures, mainly from London, the centre of political power and a focal point for the arts and publishing. But this only affected a small proportion of the population. English was mainly spread throughout the British Isles without the benefit of legislation through education. The public schools[9] started spreading these norms from the sixteenth century on, and by the nineteenth century a large proportion of the sons of the upper middle classes also attended such schools. They then went on to Oxford or Cambridge, and from there to one of the numerous posts created in the wake of the British Empire. The lower classes were not affected and continued to speak their local dialects or RLs, but their lack of use in prestigious and official contexts led to their becoming rapidly debased.

As in France, the biggest blow to the RLs was the establishment of a free state system of education functioning in English which happened a little earlier than in France (the Jules Ferry laws came into effect in the 1880s) and in a more piecemeal fashion. There was an Education Act in 1870 for England and Wales, and another in 1872 for Scotland. Education became compulsory in 1880 and from 1918 it was obligatory until fourteen. This was seen by most people as desirable progress with no thought given to the impact on the RLs.

Dictionaries provide another way of propagating norms, and the *Oxford English Dictionary* played a very important role in this respect (the first volume was published in 1884 and the last in 1927),[10] while works such as Henry Watson Fowler's *Modern English Usage*, meant for those uncertain as to what is 'correct', also helped to spread a codified form of English.

Prior to the advent of radio, English was written in a highly standardised fashion, but the same did not apply to the spoken language since only a small circle of people spoke 'Oxford English' or the 'King's English'. Radio spread what became known as 'Received Pronunciation' or RP, i.e. the accent of the educated classes as spoken in the Home Counties, in the south of England. It was also the accent to be taught to foreigners.[11] The founder of the BBC, John Reith (1889–1971) established RP as the norm, and an Advisory Committee on Spoken English was founded in 1926. In the 1960s and 1970s, BBC English changed in keeping with the changes happening in society. Thus the election of a Prime Minister, Harold Wilson, with a slight northern accent and the success of the Beatles, also from the north, explain a shift in what was considered RP. At about the same time public school accents became a subject of ridicule.

The Advisory Committee on Spoken English was also meant to discuss terminological problems (e.g. whether to use *gyratory circuses* vs. *roundabouts* or *stop-and-goes* vs. *traffic lights*). It included such famous writers as Bernard Shaw and Rudyard Kipling, and its secretary was the phonetician A. Lloyd James. There are, however, no British equivalents to the numerous institutions created in France since the 1960s to develop the language and in particular its terminology. On the other hand no body has such an impact on language as the media.

The propagation of standard English has not only been the prerogative of Britain and its role in the British Empire. The expansion of the

United States of America has played an ever increasing role over the years in spreading a slightly different form of English, codification and standardisation having taken place differently in the States. Rejected for a long time in Britain by purists such as Fowler, it is now more commonly used than British English. Other forms of English have also developed worldwide, such as Indian English, or Caribbean English. Whether or not they should be treated as different 'Standard Englishes' is a matter of political and linguistic disagreement.

## English and its symbolic role in the state

There are three ways of interpreting the codification and standardisation of English in Britain. The first and traditional one stresses the idea of social consensus in order to facilitate effective communication. The second sees codification and standardisation as a tool of social oppression, the intimidation by the speakers of the prestige form of English of those who do not. The third stresses the financial and economic importance of codification and standardisation since it enables communication with the greatest number. This approach has also been linked with the traditional attitude adopted by the BBC. The same argument could be made for French, but there the discourse is overwhelmingly idealistic with language seen as a pillar of the nation and an instrument of integration. The same pragmatic approach was adopted by a recent Home Secretary (Charles Clarke): the white paper, *Making Migration Work for Britain*, published on 7 March 2006, establishes an Australian-style points-based immigration system, which contains a requirement for healthcare staff from overseas to demonstrate their knowledge of English. Only the healthcare workers appear to be mentioned in this respect (*The Guardian*, 8 March 2006).

On the other hand, the French ideal of language as a tool for integration is present in both the British Nationality Act 1981 and the Nationality, Immigration and Asylum Act 2002 which both demand a knowledge of English in order to obtain British citizenship. This seems to have arisen from a need to provide a unifying factor to the multicultural, present-day British Isles. As in France, English is now seen as an essential tool for social cohesion and advancement. Candidates for British citizenship now have to pass two tests, a linguistic one and a cultural one (called the 'Life in the UK' test) which is one step further than France. While in France the hope is that immigrants will integrate into the community and wish to learn French, in Britain it is reckoned that immigrants tend to live amongst themselves and the acquisition of

English is not automatic. The new test aims to prove that the candidate has 'sufficient knowledge' of English, as represented by the ESOL Entry 3 test (English for Speakers of Other Languages).

A very interesting aspect of both nationality acts from the point of view of the RLs is that they both accept Welsh and Scottish Gaelic (but not Irish) as alternatives to English. The documentation provided by the Home Office to applicants for British citizenship is quite clear on this issue: 'For many years, people applying to be naturalised as British citizens have needed to possess "sufficient knowledge" (without it however being put to an official test) of either *English, Scottish Gaelic,* or *Welsh*. There are not many cases in which people claim British nationality by virtue of a knowledge of Welsh or Scottish Gaelic, but anyone who wishes to do so should consult the Immigration and Nationality Directorate for advice' (see press release of 15 June 2005, www.ind.homeoffice.gov.uk, my emphasis).

## Concluding comments

Although English gradually became as codified and standardised as French, it did so in a piecemeal fashion. The result, linguistically, was much the same as far as the RLs are concerned. But nowadays Britain has a much more relaxed attitude towards them than France. This is undoubtedly due to the fact that English, unlike French, is not on the defensive. It is also due to a different approach to nationhood and state, seen as a *fait accompli* rather than intellectualised into a Jacobin ideal. Moreover devolution has changed the situation and has led to frequent questions as to what constitutes being British on the one hand and English on the other. This effort to redefine ourselves – and also within the EU development of the concept of linguistic freedom as a human right with accompanying institutions – led the United Kingdom to sign the European Charter for Regional or Minority Languages in 2000 and to ratify it in 2001 (see introduction to Part III). By doing so, it guaranteed giving protection to a number of British RLs. This protection is maximal in the case of Welsh, Scottish Gaelic and Irish, and minimal in the case of Scots (or Lallans), Ulster Scots (or Ullans) and Cornish (see Part III).

Britain, in so doing, has come a long way from the generally accepted nitons as expressed by John Stuart Mill in *Considerations on Representative Government* published in 1861:

> Nobody can suppose that it is not beneficial to a Breton, or a Basque of French Navarre to be brought into the current of ideas and feelings of a highly civilised and cultivated people – to be a member of the

French nationality, admitted on equal terms to all the privileges of French citizenship . . . than to sulk on his own rocks, the half-savage relic of times past, revolving in his own mental orbit, without participation or interest in the general movement of the world. The same remark applies to the Welshman or the Scottish Highlander as members of the British nation. (Quoted by Dunbar 2003b: 140)

# Part II[1]

# The Regional Languages Spoken in Metropolitan France

# General Presentation

The first question which may be asked is how many RLs are there in metropolitan France? The answer to such a question is not obvious, given the difficulty in drawing the line between *patois*,[2] dialect and language, but the RLs traditionally listed as having survived in some form or other into the present include: Alsatian, Basque, Breton, Catalan, Corsican, (Western) Flemish, Franco-Provençal, *langues d'oïl*, and Occitan (see Map 4).

Of these, three are Germanic: Flemish, which is spoken in a small area around Dunkirk, Alsatian (which comes from Alemanic), which is a rather loose term applied to the Germanic varieties spoken in the *départements* of the Haut Rhin, the Bas Rhin, and Mosellan (or Franconian) which is spoken in the Moselle region also known as known as *la Lorraine thioise*. There is one Celtic language, Breton, spoken in the Basse Bretagne. Catalan, Occitan, Corsican and Franco-Provençal are Romance languages, as are the *langues d'oïl* spoken in the northern half of France. Basque is a non-Indo-European language of unknown or at least disputed origin.

Not all specialists agree with the above list. For example, most specialists have classified Occitan as a single language made up of a number of dialects since the 1970s, whereas others consider Occitan as comprising several different 'languages' (*les langues d'oc*) that have a number of traits in common. Some speakers of Provençal, in particular, prefer to claim separate linguistic status for their variety. There is similar disagreement as to the nature of Alsatian, seen by some as a variety of German and by others as a language in its own right. Similarly there is disagreement as to the classification of Western Flemish either as a language in its own right or a variety of Dutch. As for Corsican, it may have been seen as a variety of Italian in the past, but brave would be the person who adopted such a stance now.

*Map 4*  The regional languages of France

The *langues d'oïl* are even more problematic, having been until very recently considered to be either mere dialects of French, or poor French, or (even worse) extinct, although an association – *Défense et promotion des langues d'oïl* – was founded in 1981. But they only became officially 'languages' with the Cerquiglini Report of 1999, drawn up when the French government thought it would be signing and ratifying the European Charter for Regional or Minority Languages.

It is clear from Map 4 that the linguistic borders of France do not correspond with its political frontiers. Thus Flemish, Alsatian and

Mosellan (the last two if seen as a linguistic forms related to German) are national languages beyond France's borders and Basque and Catalan have official status in Spain, whereas Breton, Franco-Provençal and Occitan do not enjoy any real official recognition, which puts them in an even more endangered position in terms of their survival than the others.

The seriousness of the plight of all the RLs is clearly expressed in the approach adopted by the *Atlas de la langue française* (Rossillon 1995) which states that the RLs are gradually but inexorably disappearing because of the diffusion of French through the education system, rural exodus, television, movements of population for professional reason and intermarriage. As a result the *Atlas* only gives maps for Breton, Basque, Alsace and Lorraine, pointing out that these maps are mainly of historic interest. The other languages quoted as surviving, although endangered, are Occitan with, according to the *Atlas*, only 9000 speakers, Corsican with only 5000, Breton with 4000 and Catalan with 1500. The authors of the *Atlas* justify their position by pointing out that the percentage of parents using their mother tongue with their children is only around 0–5 per cent. The *Atlas* does mention efforts made in recent years to save the RLs from complete extinction, but they state that the measures taken so far have not been very effective in stopping their slow decay.

This gives an unduly gloomy picture of the situation since the figures given are debatable. Those given by the DGLFLF (*Délégation générale à la langue française et aux langues de France*), and based on the (partial) 1999 census, are very different (as published in *Des langues plein les poches, Les langues de France*, 2003) (Table 1). These are far more reliable figures, having a scientific base. As for the fact that in the past many very different figures were given (some of them appear to have been pulled out of thin air), could it be that the results given are affected by the researchers' personal agenda? Clearly those involved in the *Atlas de la langue française* had no interest in the RLs.

Even officially obtained figures, like the ones above, should be treated with care, for interpreting statistics is problematic for a number of reasons. Firstly nearly all figures are based on surveys which are usually self-evaluative, which by definition makes them suspect. Then there is the problem of defining what 'knowing' a language means: speaking it, understanding it, reading it or writing it, or all four elements combined. Other aspects such as age group, professional categories and rate of intergenerational transmission within the family also have to be considered.

Defining the geographical areas to be taken into account is also problematic. One reason is terminological: languages are sometimes

*Table 1*   List of regional languages spoken in France

| List of RLs | Who speaks them? | How is it transmitted? |
| --- | --- | --- |
| Alsatian | Half the Alsatians say they speak it quite naturally in everyday life. | Mainly within the family.* It is mainly German which is taught at school. |
| Basque | 60 000 speakers in France, i.e. 1 Basque out of 4. 750 000 for the whole of the Basque country, i.e. including Spain. | Within the family, in school, particularly in the *ikastolas*.** In all 30 000 pupils learn Basque at school. |
| Breton | 240 000 Bretons maintain they speak it 'rather well'. Only half speak it regularly. | Within the family, at school, particularly in the *Diwan*.** In all 25 000 pupils learn Breton at school. |
| Catalan | 126 000 speakers in France but 5 500 000 if one includes Spain. | Within the family, at school, particularly in France in the *bressolas*.** In all, 11 000 students learn Catalan at school. |
| Corsican | 180 000 speakers, i.e. around 70% of the island's population. | Within the family, at school and in a *scola aperta*.** In all 33 000 pupils learn Corsican in school. |
| (Western) Flemish | There could be in France between 30 000 and 10 0000 speakers, most of them using Flemish but very rarely. | Within the family, mainly. In schools it is more Dutch which is learned. |
| Franco-Provençal | 60 000 speakers in France, i.e. 1% of the Franco-Provençal population + 60 000 in Italy. | Mainly within the family. |
| Langues d'oïl | The number of speakers is unknown. | Mainly within the family. |
| Occitan | 2 million speakers out of the 15 million living in the Occitan area. | Within the family, at school and in the *calandretas*.** In all more than 10 000 pupils learn Occitan at school. |

*: 'transmission within the family' means natural transmission
**: refers to private schools functioning in the RLs

known by the name of the pre-revolutionary province they used to be associated with, but since these were broken up into smaller *départements* after 1789, they also sometimes bear the name of the *département*, while they may also refer to a linguistic entity only. Thus 'Mosellan' and 'Franconian' (*Francique*) refer to the same language.

Another problem in defining languages geographically is the movements of population which tend to take place in a centralised state such as France (civil servants – which includes teachers – may be sent to posts anywhere in the country, irrespective of their personal desires). This means that not only may the figures given for numbers of speakers be disputed, but also the delimitation of the areas where they are spoken in. Figures and maps must therefore be interpreted bearing these possible weaknesses in mind. These problems, general to all linguistic descriptions, are particularly acute in France, where the Constitution does not allow for the census to contain questions on either language use, religion or race, because of France being *une et indivisible*.

It was partly to avoid the constitutional problem forbidding linguistic questions in census surveys that the *Enquête famille* (the Family Survey) was conceived by INED (*Institut national des études démographiques*) and carried out by INSEE (*Institut national de la statistique et des études économiques*) in 1999. It consists of a questionnaire distributed at the same time as the 1999 official census questionnaire to 380 000 people. Instead of trying to work out who speaks a particular language, the questionnaire looked into the problem of language transmission. The questions asked were whether a language, dialect or *patois* other than French was spoken to the respondents in their childhood, i.e. around the age of five years old, either habitually or occasionally, and by mother, or father or both. If the answer was 'Yes', the next question was whether the respondents had transmitted this language to their own descendants.

The *Enquête famille* therefore gives a more subtle picture of the situation. According to the results, some 610 000 adults were spoken to habitually in Occitan, and over one million occasionally; 660 000 were spoken to habitually in Alsatian and 240 000 occasionally; 280 000 habitually in Breton and 400 000 occasionally. All other RLs appear to have been spoken to fewer than 10 000 adults both on a habitual and an occasional basis. The *Enquête famille* also gives figures, and this for the first time, for the *langues d'oïl*: 570 000 had heard it spoken habitually and 850 000 occasionally. Such high figures were a surprise to most linguists. And yet, on reflection, it is not as surprising as it may seem given most Francophones can understand a fair amount of Picard or Norman, particularly in its written form, hence the success of comic strip books in these languages (a Picard version of *Tintin* is said to have sold over 80 000 copies).

On the other hand, matters are grim where transmission within the family is concerned. Thus the survey reveals that 90 per cent of adult males to whom Breton was spoken in their childhood, have not transmitted the language to their children, and the figures are over 80 per cent for Occitan, over 75 per cent for Catalan and Corsican, nearly 60 per cent for Basque and 45 per cent for Alsatian.

But even these figures, although they mark a significant improvement, have to be treated with care. One problem is that only 380 000 persons were questioned: this is a large number by survey standards, but, although the sampling of interviewees was weighted towards RL areas, sampling can never be completely trusted. Another problem is that only analysing transmission may be misleading. Thus, according to such figures, Breton is moribund, which disguises the enormous efforts made at present to reverse this tendency. Similarly, although the figure for the number of Basques having been brought up in a Bascophone environment seems very low (around 60 000), the influence of the Basque militants in the movement to revive all the RLs has been disproportionately large. Numbers may therefore be misleading if seen outside of their specific context.

An important factor in their revival may be whether the RL considered has official status elsewhere or not. Chapter 3 deals with those languages which are officially recognised beyond the French borders and Chapter 4 deals with those which are not. Each chapter attempts to retrace briefly the origin and development of each language, its importance as a written language and the development of its writing system. Another objective is to give some idea of its importance in terms of the number of its speakers and its vitality in terms of intergenerational transmission. Its importance in terms of the identity of its speakers and its potential for artistic innovation, as well as its possible role in local nationalism are also examined. Chapter 5 examines efforts made in recent years to help their revival. Use will be made of the reports published by the DGLFLF which give up-to-date figures in terms of progress achieved so far in terms of education, the media and culture.

# 3
# Regional Languages Official Elsewhere: Basque, Catalan, Flemish and Alsatian

The RLs which are official in other countries tend, by definition, to straddle borders. There are three clear cases in France. Basque and Catalan are both national languages in Spain, and co-official with the state language, Castilian, in the regions where they are spoken. Flemish is both an official and national language in Belgium and Holland.

Alsatian, and Mosellan (or 'Franconian'), which have been included under the same heading, are special cases since it depends on whether they are classified as varieties of German or as separate languages. The *Rapport Cerquiglini* classified Alsatian and Mosellan as German 'dialects' and German is now taught as the standard form of the 'RLs' in those areas. Mosellan, on the other hand, is similar to Luxemburgish, one of the official languages of Luxemburg. Both Alsatian and Mosellan have been classified as 'RLs official elsewhere', but they appear in fourth position, i.e. the alphabetical order adopted in this chapter has been interrupted to highlight their being a special case.

## Basque or 'Euskara', the oldest language in Europe

Of the very early languages such as Aquitanian, Ligurian and Iberian, only the first is thought – very tentatively – to have a distant surviving descendant, Basque. However, evidence of all three of them can be found in the toponymy of France; thus the names of all the important rivers such as the Seine, the Rhône, the Loire, and the Garonne are pre-Celtic. But when Julius Caesar described France in his *Gallic Wars, Book 1*, he referred only to the Aquitani, the Belgae, and the Gauls who formed a loose confederation:

> The whole of Gaul is divided into three parts, one of which the Belgae inhabit, the Aquitani another, and the third a people who in their own language are called 'Celts'; but in ours 'Gauls': They all differ among themselves in respect of the language, way of life, and laws. The River Garonne divides the Gauls from the Aquitani, and the Marne and Seine rivers separate them from the Belgae.

According to toponymical data, the Aquitanian language was spoken through out Aquitaine prior to the arrival of the Romans. Then, from the fifth century BC, a number of Celtic tribes penetrated the area, leaving traces of their migrations in place-names (for example, Calezun and Gaudun include the Celtic suffix -*dunum* meaning 'fortified place'; while others such as Eauze and Lectoure bear the names of Celtic tribes, the Elusates and the Lectorates). The first contacts with Rome date from the second century BC, and in 56 BC a number of the local *peuplades* (or tribes) tried in vain to resist military conquest. After the conquest, most Aquitani must have adopted Latin, seen as the language of progress and social success, while others – gradually or suddenly – moved south to escape its impact. The term *Gascons*, which is etymologically the same word as *Basques*, refers, at least in part, to Latinised Aquitani, mixed with some Latinised Celts, and possibly others. The non-Romanised Aquitani, the Basques, retained their language and culture more or less intact, in the isolation and remoteness of the Pyrenees.

The origins of the Basque language are the subject of an incredible number of unconvincing theories. What is certain is that it predates the Indo-European languages, hence it being considered 'the oldest language in Europe'. The first inscriptions, which are very short, date from about the tenth century. The first list of words appears in a pilgrim's guide book which dates from the twelfth century. The first known book in Basque, a book of poems written by a priest, seems to date from 1545. It was followed in 1571 by a translation of the New Testament, and a book of proverbs and sayings in 1596. The Basque written tradition therefore goes back to the sixteenth century. It exists in four dialects: Labourdin, Souletin, Guipúzcoan and Biscayen. In France, particularly Labourdin was made famous in the seventeenth century, when P. Axular published in 1643 a book on Christian ethics, which remained a linguistic model for centuries. Guipúzcoan literature only started to develop in the eighteenth century and Biscayen in the nineteenth.

The first Castilian–Basque dictionary was written by an Italian, N. Landucchio, in 1562. The first Basque–French dictionary was written only a century later by S. Pouvreau, but remains unpublished to this day. The first grammar was written by a Guipúzcoan Jesuit, M. Larramendi, in 1729. But since Basque was not allowed to play a part in any official domain, it remained mainly a spoken language, used in the home, between friends, and in church. All this changed during the second half of the twentieth century which saw an explosion of Basque literature. To give an idea, between the first book published in 1545 and 1974, 4000 books were published in Basque (*Euskara*), whereas between 1974 and 1994 12 500 were published. At present about 1000 titles are published in Euskara per year, including novels, poetry, academic books and translations of works from other languages (Kurlansky 2000: 326–7). A daily newspaper is published, along with several weeklies and magazines, and radio and television broadcasts on both sides of the border.

It is important to point out, however, that the main engine for the Basque language revival comes from the Spanish side of the border. There are four provinces in Spain, Viscaya, Guipúzcoa and Alava, which form the Autonomous Euskadi Community (or 'Euskadi') and Navarra, which stands on its own. On the French side there are three provinces, Labourd, Basse Navarre and Soule, which make up Iparralde (Pays Basque Nord).

Not surprisingly given the mountainous nature of the area, there are many forms of Basque, although the concept of an overall language, 'Basque', goes back centuries. Its variety was seen as an obstacle by the nationalists, who set up a Basque Academy of Language in 1918. Its brief was to give the language a single written system (previously there had been two systems, derived respectively from Spanish and French). It was not until the 1960s, however, that the Academy was able to establish a common written language, which was called Euskara Batua. This was achieved through the members of the Academy, who each represented a different linguistic variety, working out which forms were most commonly used and, from these, creating a supra-dialectal variety including distinctive elements from all dialects. The aim was not to create a 'pure' language, but a usable one, hence accepting numerous borrowings from Spanish but also from other languages such as English (where computer terms are concerned, for example). This was not, however, a new departure for the Basque language which borrowed generously from Latin from the earliest times. Indeed it is not its vocabulary that makes it a difficult language to learn but its complex grammatical structures which have remained more or less intact through the ages (the language has many cases and a verbal system which may include up to three personal markers – subject, direct object and addressee object – and number).

In Spain, the 1978 Constitution made Basque into an official language. It is now used in all spheres of life. This is a triumph given that under Franco a whole generation of speakers was lost on the Spanish side. But since the 1970s, when Franco started loosening his grip, the percentage of speakers has steadily increased. This is mainly due to bilingual schooling. It is reckoned that if these trends continue, Vizcaya and Guipúzcoa could soon have a Basque-speaking majority.

The same does not apply to the French provinces, where decline is still the order of the day (see figures below). As is the case for all the RLs in France, decline started with the 1789 Revolution. Before that the Basques had enjoyed a certain amount of self-determination, a kind of semi-independence, symbolised by the right to be governed by their own laws and customs (the *Fueros* or 'Foral administration') which dated back – although regularly updated – to medieval times. Customs controls also started at the Ebro, and not at the Pyrenean border, which is still what Basque nationalists on both side of the borders would like to see. But after 1789, one of the first moves of the Revolutionaries was to remove all names of places corresponding to a regional identity or ethnicity, replacing them by neutral geographical names of mountains or rivers. Thus the Basque provinces are now part of the *département des Pyrénées-Atlantiques* (it used to be called the *Basses Pyrénées*) of which the old Basque provinces only constitute a minority. The Basques have repeatedly asked for the creation of a *département du Pays Basque*. The first time was in 1836, when the Bayonne Chamber of Commerce petitioned the king. Then in the 1960s the nationalists again made such a plea. President Mitterrand appeared, in 1981, to agree, as did the Jospin government (1997–2002), but both failed to fulfil their promises, possibly for fear of unrest on the Spanish side spreading to France. Whatever the reason, this left the area without an official name reflecting its specific identity.

The language itself has been gradually eroded by all those factors which have traditionally spelt death for the RLs, such as compulsory French education, the need to speak French in all walks of life, the influence of the media, economic factors etc. Indeed these seem to have been more destructive than the gross abuses and violent repression which characterised Spain's policy towards the Basque provinces from the time of the Carlist Wars in the nineteenth century.[1] But the fact that religious services continued to be held in Basque, and the culture, in terms of music, song and sport continued to be upheld, helped the language survive.

So what is the situation today? According to Walter (1994: 230–1) a survey in 1991 in the French Basque country of 1200 people over the age of 15 showed that, out of a population of 237 000, 32 per cent claimed a good knowledge of the language, 23 per cent claimed some knowledge, and 45 per cent claimed no knowledge. Some degree of knowledge was thus claimed by 55 per cent. If those with a 'good knowledge' are equated with 'speakers' of the language, this is consistent with the information contained in the *Mini-guide* published by the EBLUL (1993): 80 000 out of a population of 240 000. Another survey in 1996 (Nelde et al. in Euromosaïc) gives the figure of 86 000, while the DGLFLF table above gives 60 000 active speakers. Héran et al. (2002), on the other hand, give the much lower figure of 44 000 derived from the *Enquête famille* survey. According to this last figure, matters are not looking good for the future of Basque in France. But it is important to remember that the French Basques represent only 10 per cent of Bascophones as a whole, and a little over 25 per cent of the inhabitants of the French Basque country. On the other hand, if Basque continues receding on the French side, this would mean the first significant loss of territory since the late Roman Empire.

The important factor is not, however, the actual number of speakers but the rate of transmission, which defines the vitality of the language. In the case of Basque, a number of sociolinguistic surveys have been carried out at regular intervals to assess this point. The first, *La continuité de la langue basque I* (i.e. 'the continuity of Basque I'), was carried out in 1991, the second, *La continuité de la langue basque II* in 1996 and the third, *La continuité de la langue basque III* in 2001.

These surveys were aimed at both Bascophones and non-Bascophones over 15 years old and in both the French and Spanish Basque country. For the second and third surveys it was the French INSEE which prepared the sampling for the survey in terms of age, sex and professional categories. It was the Basque institute for statistics (EUSTAT) which worked out the results. The task as a whole was the responsibility of the Basque autonomous government's sub-ministry for linguistic affairs.

The 1996 survey led to the conclusion that on the French side of the border there were around 60 000 active speakers and 15 000 passive ones, which distinction shows marked progress on previous estimations (the numbers on the Spanish side were respectively 450 000 in the Autonomous Euskadi Community, and 50 000 in Navarra). But this survey makes for quite depressing reading as far as transmission of the language is concerned, with the lowest figures of transmission applying to the young which implies natural transmission is not taking place. The figures are 37 per cent for those over 65, 14 per cent for those between 25 and 34, and only 11 per cent for those between 16 and 24. (No figures are given for the 35- to 49-year-olds.) The percentage varies not only according to age but to area, with the lowest percentage in the tourist coastal area, which explains why the Basque militant organisation ETA has traditionally been opposed to tourism.

This contrasts with the figures given for the Autonomous Euskadi Community in Spain which shows an increase since only 29 per cent of those aged over 65 per cent spoke the language as against 33 per cent of those aged between 16 and 24. Which goes to show that the linguistic policies pursued in favour of Basque by the government of the autonomous Basque area of Spain are working, and that linguistic reversal may be possible in certain cases.

J.-B. Coyos (2004) has analysed all three surveys, from which he draws some general conclusions. The first is that during the period 1991–2001, the language has lost 14 500 speakers on the French side. On the other hand, the loss in terms of numbers of speakers on the French side has diminished in intensity, since although between 1991 and 1996, 13 000 speakers were lost, the loss between 1996 and 2001 was of 'only' 1000.

But the figures do not take into account the steady increase in the number of people with a passive knowledge of the language, who listen to the media in Basque, sing in Basque, and who may even attempt to speak the language if they feel that the context is sympathetic to their lack of spoken competence. The increase in their number was of 5000 between 1991 and 1996, and 6000 between 1996 and 2001. Passive knowledge does not help transmission directly, but can help it indirectly since such people are probably more likely to send their children to Basque immersion schools, the *ikastolak* ('school' in Basque), or at least to schools where Basque is taught. The *ikastolak*, i.e. the Basque immersion schools, were originally founded in the Spanish Basque country in 1903. The first French one dates from 1969. It started with eight pupils but by 1998, there were 1630 pupils attending some 33 schools, which are regrouped in a federation, *Seaska*, meaning 'cradle'. Of these, 19 were kindergartens, 12 were primary schools, one was a *collège* and one a *lycée*. Bilingual education is also offered, particularly in the Catholic private sector (there were some 25 Catholic bilingual schools by the 1990s). The first private bilingual kindergarten dates from 1967. The first bilingual state schools, called *Ikas-bi* started in 1983 (see Chapter 5 for further details). This is important since the survival of the language on the French side is now dependent on learning it at school: among the very young Bascophones, only half have learned the language through natural transmission in the context of the family.

A survey was carried out in 2001 by the *Institut culturel basque* which tried to assess the demand for the teaching of Basque in schools on the part of parents of children aged between 0 and 2 years. It shows that the demand is high, even if transmission is low, or perhaps precisely because it is low: 56 per cent of those interviewed expressed the wish that their children be taught Basque at school, 42 per cent from kindergarten. This figure seems remarkably high given that the survey was conducted in the Bayonne–Anglet–Biarritz area, which has the lowest percentage of Bascophones.

Finally, Coyos points out that whereas in 2001, 24.7 per cent of the population had a knowledge of Basque, only 5.8 per cent of those observed speaking in the street were using Basque: to speak Basque it is necessary to have a Bascophone to speak to, and it is not always easy to know who does. It was recently suggested (for Esperanto) that people speaking the language should wear a badge. This idea could usefully be extended to all the RLs.

The strength of Basque is that it spans two countries, in one of which it is recognised as an official language. It also occupies an identifiable territory, although it has shrunk considerably. There is a strong nationalist movement, particularly on the Spanish side, for historical reasons (between 1937 and the early 1960s the teaching of the language was forbidden, books were publicly burned, and inscriptions on public buildings and tombs erased). Hence some Basques wish for a unified state of their own, which is symbolised by the symbol '4 + 3 = 1', the 4 and the 3 standing for the four Spanish provinces and the three French ones.

The Basque language has long been a potent symbol and weapon in the fight for independence led, on the Spanish side, by the revolutionary terrorist movement ETA (*Euskadi ta Azkatasuna*, i.e. Basque Fatherland and Freedom) formed in 1959. (It declared, however, a permanent ceasefire on 24 March 2006 in favour of democratic means.) Its political arm is the Basque People Party (*Euskal Herritarrok*). Its French equivalent is the *Iparretarak* (meaning 'those from the North'), but it represents a much smaller percentage of the Basque population than ETA in Spain and has no political arm. But the existence of ETA and its terrorist activities has created tensions for the French Basques, their area having been often used as a safe haven for Spanish Basques fleeing the police. There is in fact a long history of the French Basque country providing safe houses for those in flight, particularly during World War Two. And, of course, smuggling is a way of life. This makes providing safe houses part of the Basque culture. It also creates problems for the French Basques: are they to be loyal to the Basque nation or to the French state of which they are citizens? It will be interesting to see how the overall picture will be changed by ETA's abandonment of violence.

This may have been because violence is unpopular on both sides of the frontier and the killing of over 800 innocent people since the founding of ETA has not had an endearing effect. On the other hand, since a whole generation, on the Spanish side, has now been educated in Basque, including at university level, there is now an increased sense of nationalism among the educated young in Euskadi. This could filter through to the French side, particularly in a more peaceful context.

So far, judging by the polls and despite the lack of any institutional recognition (unconstitutional in France), the huge majority of French Basques operate within the normal institutional framework, maintain they are French, and are attached to French institutions (particularly the benefits of the health service and the social security system). Many hold the view that the French Basque country is too small to survive independently and recent population shifts mean that the area is less homogeneous. A unification of the Spanish and French Basque country would make for a slightly more viable entity, but this seems unlikely for a variety of reasons beyond the scope of this chapter. On the other hand, the autonomy gained by the Spanish Basques helps preserve the language in the French region, by strengthening its sense of identity. Moreover, its becoming for the first time in history an official language has acted as a huge psychological boost. The French Basques also benefit from the Spanish Basque media, which helps to reinforce the feeling of trans-Pyrenean unity, which is further strengthened by the breaking down of frontiers within the EU. As a result, violent movements such as ETA no longer enjoy the kind of tacit support they enjoyed at various points in the past.

An interesting aspect of Basque identity in relation to nationhood is the slightly changing role attributed to language over the last 150 years. Previously the definition of a Basque had always been linguistic: a *Euskaldun* which meant a 'Basque speaker'. But when Sabino Arana Goiri (1865–1903), founder of the Spanish Basque Nationalist Party, formulated the first programme aimed at the rebirth of the Basque nation (creating in particular the Basque flag and writing the Basque anthem), he considered that 'race'[2] or 'blood' was the most important constituent in defining the Basque nation. This meant having a Basque patronym and four Basque grandparents. Language only came in second position. All other defining aspects of a nation, such as customs, literature, laws, shared moments of glory, were seen as deriving from the first two.

This 'racist' approach has to be seen as normal in the nineteenth century, when so much interest was taken in the origins of man, languages and customs.[3] It is therefore hardly surprising that the 'race' element should have been fundamental to Arana's approach to Basque nationhood. But this view is more than a century old and no longer adhered to. On the contrary, nowadays it is the language which is considered a deciding factor, and no longer the number of grandparents. ETA recognised that the racial definition of a Basque was neither acceptable, justifiable nor practically applicable, if only because so many ETA followers failed to pass the four-grandparent test. Indeed some had none, since the movement with its socialist leanings attracted many descendants of immigrants to the Basque country. This meant a return to the old definition of a Basque, i.e. a *Euskaldun*, 'Basque speaker'.

Customs and laws (the Basque *fueros*) – including such matters as home architecture, which is very distinctive in the Basque country – are also very important. Not having an impressive ancient literary tradition is compensated for by the importance of folk literature, singing and other aspects of culture such as architecture, food and sport (cf. the *pelote basque*). This culture has survived more or less intact to the present day. Indeed the fact that the borders of these cultural zones remain much the same as at the end of the Roman period, shows the strength of the Basque language and culture and illustrates, at least on the Spanish side, a potential for survival. But the same cannot be stated with the same authority for the French side, since only 42 per cent of those having heard Basque spoken during childhood have transmitted it to their descendants. Hence the efforts made nowadays to transmit it through education (see Chapter 5).

## Catalan

Catalan is spoken in the old French province of the Roussillon, which became part of the French Crown in 1659. Its territory corresponds nowadays to most of the *département des Pyrénées-Orientales* and its capital is Perpignan. Although at first a vassal state of France, the area was associated from times immemorial with Catalonia and the House of Barcelona, hence the need to know some aspects of the development of Catalan in Spain to understand its position in France and the help it may expect from Catalonia.

Catalonia's demands for autonomy, from the late nineteenth century onwards, are not surprising given her distant past as an independent nation-state: in 985 Count Borrell of Barcelona asked the king of France for help against the Moors. Having received no help and having defeated them himself he declared his lands to be independent and created the new state of Catalonia. In 1137 Count Ramon-Berenguer IV married the heir to the crown of Aragon, and the two together formed the Catalano-Aragonese Confederation. Although Roussillon only became fully part of Catalonia in 1172, its linguistic and cultural developments had been, nonetheless, very similar well before that date.

Catalan was recognised very early on as a separate language spoken in a large area including Aragon, Valencia and the Balearic Islands, as well as enclaves in Italy, North Africa and Greece (Mar-Molinero 2000: 90–2). It developed between the eleventh and fourteenth centuries, on a par with French and Italian on the one hand, and Castilian and Portuguese on the other. It too competed with Latin in administrative and legal contexts. It was a language of high culture and literary production. It was also the closest to the Latin-derived varieties spoken in other parts of Europe, with the Catalans having their sights firmly on the Mediterranean in terms of trade and influence. But it was closest to Occitan to the extent that Sibille (2000) refers to them as 'twin sisters'. Catalans on both sides of the border participated in the Occitan Troubadour culture, but whereas Occitan started to decline in the fourteenth century, Catalan's literary golden age, on the Spanish side, was in the fourteenth and fifteenth centuries. On the French side, it was between 1276 and 1344, when the kings of Mallorca made Perpignan their capital.

Things changed dramatically, however, when the Castilians organised their resistance to the Moors, the *Reconquista*, at which point Castilian or 'Spanish' emerged as a symbol of solidarity in the face of a common enemy. Moreover, a standardised version of Castilian had emerged as early as in the mid-thirteenth century under Alfonso X, and the first grammar of Castilian was produced in 1492 (also the year of the expulsion of both Arabs and Jews, which makes it a significant date from many points of view). Everything was therefore in place to make Castilian into a national language.

Before that the Compromise of Casp, in 1412, had already brought the *Pays Catalans* under the rule of the king of Castilia. As a result, from the sixteenth century onwards the rise of Castilian power brought the decline of Catalan. This decline was precipitated in 1516 when the last king of the Catalano-Aragonese Confederation died and Catalan lost its status as a national language. Gradually only the lower classes spoke exclusively Catalan, the upper classes being diglossic.

Later, loss of influence was further accelerated by the Spanish War of Succession, which started after the death of Charles II in 1700. The successful claimant was Philip V, a Bourbon, who set about trying to impose a French-style centralised system on Spain. Whereas the Basques supported the Bourbon claim and as a result were allowed to keep their *fueros*, Catalonia along with Valencia and Aragón did not, and were stripped of the few regional privileges they had left. A general move towards Castilianisation was to take place from then on. Thus in 1716 Castilian became the only official language for administrative and legal documents, then in 1768 the sole language of education, and in 1799 all theatrical productions in Catalan were forbidden.

Persecution continued on the Spanish side until the nineteenth century and the beginning of the *Renaixença*. The latter was heralded by an *Oda a la patria* written by Benaventura Aribau in 1833, but it really took off in the second half of the century. The origin of the *Renaixença* is supposed to be the European Romantic movement, which tended to glorify the past, both real and mythological. This interest in the past was also reflected in the work of the comparative philologists. This brought about a desire in Catalonia for writers to express themselves in their 'mother tongue', despite the fact that it had hardly ever been used as a literary language for several centuries. An important body of literature was thus produced, and Catalan may be said to have risen from the ashes, for numerous cultural associations and clubs came into existence during this period. Among these the *Jocs Florals* (*Juegos Florales*) were created in 1859 which imitated the Provençal medieval poetry competitions. Newspapers which functioned in Catalan were also founded in the 1880s and 1890s.

This cultural movement coincided, as in the Basque country, with the industrialisation of Catalonia. Both regions were the richest in Spain, unlike their equivalent in France where they were among the poorest. They functioned in a country which was mainly rural, and backward looking, at a time of general instability in Spain as a whole, because of the Carlist wars. All this led to the development of strong regionalist aspirations linked with the desire to protect and modernise local industry. Federalism was the outcome, and indeed the whole Spanish federalist movement was Catalan-inspired, with the Catalan language the pillar to Catalonia's claim to separate status. Whereas Arana had spoken in terms of 'blood and race' as defining a Basque, language was always central to Catalan nationalism, although associated with culture and territory. This was clearly expressed by Enric Prat de la Riba in a book, *La Nacionalitat Catalana*, published in 1892. Prat de la Riba founded a nationalist party, the *Lliga* and became the first president of the *Catalan Mancomunitat*. The latter did not have much power at the time, but it set up the *Institut d'Estudis Catalans* (1907), which eventually codified the language under the direction of Pompeu Fabra (1868–1948), after whom a university has been named in Barcelona. Another difference between Catalonia and the Basque country is that in Catalonia the cultural revival preceded political conscience and action, whereas in the Basque country nationalism tended to precede the cultural revival.

Then, under the Republic (1931–9) Catalan became a co-official language with Castilian, within the context of its autonomous status granted in 1932, but its new status was lost under Franco, when the language, seen as anti-patriotic, was proscribed from all public use. It was referred to as no more than a 'dialect', an inferior version of the national language, and its use was punished by fines and imprisonment. Matters improved slightly after the passing of the Freedom of Expression Law in 1966, which allowed the teaching of Catalan by private organisations and its use in publishing. It was reinstated by the Constitution of 1978. Catalan is the only official language of the principality of Andorra.

The Catalonia speaking area of France, *Rossilló* (Roussillon), was annexed by France in 1659 by the *Traité des Pyrénées*. From then on Catalan was to suffer the same degree of persecution as was meted out to all the other RLs in France. The first step towards the 'Frenchification' of the area was the setting up of French schools. Then, in 1682, knowledge of the French language was declared to be compulsory for anybody wishing to occupy an official position. In 1700, French became the only language ensuring the legality of a document. From then on the Roussillonnais had to learn French to be successful. Finally the 1789 Revolution made French compulsory in the name of equality of opportunity. Marley (1995) quotes, in this respect, an answer to one of the questions of the Grégoire linguistic survey which asked how important to the interviewee was the destruction of their *patois*: 'To destroy it [i.e. Catalan], the sun, the freshness of the nights, the quality of the water, the whole of man would have to be destroyed.'[4] For whereas the Roussillonnais had welcomed the egalitarian promises of the Revolution, their hopes turned to deep disappointment when they realised that equality would lead to the destruction of their language and culture.

Despite this persecution, Catalan continued to be spoken in the Pyrénées-Orientales, to the extent that the survey of 1864 showed it still to be in general use, despite being forbidden in schools. It was Jules Ferry's educational laws in the 1880s which brought about the downfall of Catalan and indeed all the RLs. Its decline was accentuated by numerous shifts in population, the Roussillonnais going to Paris in search of work. This still goes on: Marley states that between 1962 and 1968 one-third of young Roussillonnais aged between 18 and 30 left the region in search of work elsewhere. Moreover, in a centralised state such as France it is normal for workers in the public sector to be sent anywhere in the country where they are needed, so many outsiders have been sent to work in the Roussillon area, which is also an extremely attractive area to retire in.

Another reason for its decline was that when the railway arrived in Perpignan in 1862 it did not link up with Spain which meant that Catalan speakers in France were completely cut off from their counterparts in Spain. They did not, therefore, participate in the *Renaixença*, and Catalan literature did not develop in the same way. It is only since the 1980s that links have been re-established with Catalonia, which has led to the possibility of a literary revival thanks to a readership on the Spanish side of the frontier.

The creation at the time of the Revolution of the *département des Pyrénées Orientales* was already destructive of any sense of identity since it includes a region that was never Catalan-speaking. And destructive illogicalities are still perpetrated in this area since in the new Languedoc-Roussillon region, all institutions relating to Catalan are based in non-Catalan-speaking Montpellier rather than in Perpignan, the traditional capital of French Catalonia. In other words, the French state has denied Catalans both a geographical and an institutional identity. Given that French was the only language used in schools and that schooling has been compulsory for over a century, it is hardly surprising that by the 1970s little or no Catalan was to be heard in the streets of its main town, Perpignan.

Catalan has survived, however, helped by its strong presence in Spain, and has seen an intellectual revival since the 1960s. In 1960 the *Grup Rossellones d'Estudis Catalans* was founded, which favoured a standardised version of the language. In 1967 a splinter group from this more conservative body formed the *Institut Rossellonés d'Estudis Catalans*. In 1968, the *Diades de cultura catalana* were inaugurated and in 1969 the *Universitat Catalana d'Estiu*. Poets and singers also made the language more popular. This led to a movement demanding political autonomy for the region. In 1973 two political parties, the *Acció Regionalista Catalana* and the *Esquerra Catalana dels Treballadors*, put up candidates for the legislative election. In the 1980s various Catalanist candidates stood for election, and in 1985 a new party, *Unitat Catalana*, was formed. Regionalist rather than nationalist, it does not seek independence but seeks to regain some of Catalonia's lost identity.

Catalan is the official language of some 8 million people living mainly in Spain. A 1951 survey estimated that there were 220 000 speakers in French Catalonia, mainly in the *département des Pyrénées Orientales*. EBLUL (1993) puts the number at around 180 000. The *Enquête famille* gives 132 000, while the DGLFLF booklet gives 5 500 000 for all Catalonia speakers, be they in France or Spain, and 126 000 for France. Such figures show a steady decline, even on the Spanish side, hence disquiet there, despite the spectacular progress of the last century and a half.

Moreover two similar official surveys carried out respectively in 1993 and 1997[5] in the *département des Pyrénées Orientales* seem to show further deterioration even during this short period: in 1997 only 55 per cent could understand Catalan, as against 63 per cent in 1993, and only 34 per cent could speak it as against 49 per cent four years earlier. The number who could read Catalan remained roughly the same at 40 per cent as against 39 per cent (Bécat and Sibille 2003: 90–2). Sibille explained earlier on (Sibille 2000) that this difference may not only reflect a drop in speakers over the four years, although that was probably the case, but also a change in attitude: the first survey was carried out at a time of 'euphoria' because of the increase in economic, cultural and human links with Catalonia. The second was carried out during a period of repression under an unsympathetic *préfet* (administrative prefect). The excessive discrepancy between the results of 1993 and 1997 may also be due to the problems associated with self-evaluative surveys. But however these surveys are interpreted, Catalan is clearly an endangered language in France since according to the *Enquête famille* only 30 per cent of those who heard Catalan spoken in their youth have transmitted it to their children.

The terms 'nation' and 'people' are not usually used in France in connection with Catalan speakers, possibly because of the success of the anti-regionalist policies of France. But Catalan is a language which straddles a frontier and is strong in another country, which gives it unknown and untapped potential. The fact that during the Franco period the area welcomed numerous refugees helped strengthen the sense of belonging to a Catalan culture zone. As a result it too had a *Renaixença* movement, although rather later and more modest in scope. This sense of Catalan identity seems to have further increased in recent years, probably thanks to access to the media and publication services based on the Spanish side, and the decreased importance of frontiers in the context of the EU.

The first immersion school opened in Perpignan in 1976. By 2000–1 there were six, with a total of 358 children in kindergarten and the early primary classes. According to a survey carried out in 1997, 62 per cent of the total population of the *Pyrénées Orientales* would have liked their children to learn Catalan in school (Cerquiglini 2003: 92). The actual demand for places was 15 per cent in 1995 and 40 per cent in 2000 (figures given by the Inspection Académique). The problem seems to be mainly a lack of space and finances rather than any lack of demand (see Chapter 5).

## Western Flemish and its replacement by Flemish or Dutch

The main confusion today is between Flemish and Dutch. Are they or are they not the same language? There are good cultural reasons for seeing them as separate entities: the term 'Flemish' is associated with Flemish painters, Flemish–French dictionaries go back to the sixteenth century, and there is a medieval 'Flemish' literature, as well as a distinct popular culture.

There are equally good linguistic reasons for seeing them as varieties of the same language. Duvoskeldt mentions that by the end of the eighteenth century, those living in what would become Belgium and Holland were aware of their linguistic unity.[6] He quotes in particular a Catholic priest stating to the *Assemblée Constituante* in 1790 that 'Nous, dans ce département, nous sommes aussi des Néerlandais, même si nous sommes sous la tutelle de la couronne de France' ('We, in this *département*, are also Netherlanders, even if we come under the control of the crown of France'; Duvoskeldt 2004: 161–70). But although there was a clear sense of the unity of the language, it was not unified as such. There were different varieties, the form spoken and written in the Netherlands being considered the model to follow, the equivalent of the French *bon usage*. Any other form was seen as a corrupt variant, hence the forms spoken in Belgium and France became ostracised, which remains the case to this day.

The relegation of Flemish to the category of sub-variety came from the Flemish speakers themselves, who despaired of ever seeing their language recognised, French having become the sole official language when the Belgian state was created in 1830. As a result, to break their isolation, a group of Flemish-speaking intellectuals decided in 1849 to make common cause with their Dutch counterparts, and organised common linguistic congresses. A dictionary was the result, based on the model of the dictionary produced by the French Academy. This led to a single codified spelling system being adopted in 1864 (the De Vries and Te Winkel system) as against the previously used Des Roches system. From then on, it may be argued, Flemish speakers were to a greater or slighter degree in a situation of diglossia. This was accentuated in 1889 when Dutch, and not its Flemish counterpart (at least as far as the written language was concerned), was proclaimed as Belgium's second official language.

The variety spoken in France is Western Flemish. It occupies a very small area around Dunkirk, not including either the town or the coastal area, called the French Westhoek. It used to be spoken in a considerably larger area, which stopped thirty kilometres north of the Somme. Place-names in northern France clearly indicate the areas where it used to be spoken. There are, for example, more than fifty place-names ending in –*hem* or –*hen* meaning 'house', which is close to the German *heim*. In olden days, Flemish and French speakers lived side by side, hence some places having two names, such as *Atrecht* and *Arras*, *Grevelingen* and *Gravelines*.

Western Flemish started to deteriorate after 1678 when French was made compulsory in all law courts. Then the 1789 Revolution made the speaking of a language other than French anti-patriotic. Finally the *loi Guizot* in 1833 and then the 1850 *loi Falloux* imposed French in the classroom, to the detriment of all others. From then on, only catechism could be taught in Flemish. The result was that by the end of the nineteenth century even the peasants were starting to use French (Walter 1988: 132–3).

During this period, French Flemish speakers gradually lost all contact with their counterparts in Belgium. There was moreover a spelling problem that separated them, since the Catholic Church had remained faithful to the older spelling system of Des Roches for the publication of their catechism books and other religious matters in the vernacular (the official version appeared too 'Protestant' and too 'Dutch'). And when efforts were made between the two world wars to revive Western Flemish, it was the Des Roches spelling system which was used (when the first issue of the magazine *De Vlaemsche Stemme van Vrankryk* appeared, in 1923, it used, in fact, the standard De Vries–Te Winkel orthography, but there was a public outcry and it was immediately reprinted using the De Roches conventions). One priest stated at the time that in 1864 their 'Flemish language was exchanged for a scientific language, a kind of corrupted Dutch' (see Duvoskeldt 2004: 166). The problem was that the Des Roches orthography was no longer suited to the language, which is why another new journal adopted the official orthography in 1929, while the 1931 edition of the Catechism book adopted a mixture of the two.

After the war, catechism was taught more and more often in French and by 1962, the Catholic Church had entirely gone over to French. Moreover an organisation founded to combat the death of Flemish in France organised free evening classes in the standard language, Dutch. This upset the French Western Flemish speakers because they could not recognise in the standard language their own lost identity. This led in the 1970s to the desire to save at least the oral form of the languages, *Westvlaams*, and to try to give it a written form. The first method written to teach the RL was inspired by Robert Lafont and Louis-Jean Calvet's work in that it was seen as part of a decolonising process. It appeared in 1980 under the title *Vlaemsch Leeren*. Another appeared in 1983, *Klap Vlamsch mee de Verscheures* ('Speak Flemish with the people of Verscheures').

After the Savary Memorandum of 1982 (see Chapter 5), an association was founded called *Tagaere Toegaen* ('Let's go forth together') which tried to introduce classes in Western Flemish in schools, but these were not successful, partly because of a lack of teachers, and partly because of a lack of enthusiasm on the part of those who could see no point in learning what they saw as no more than a *patois*.

As a result, the area in which Western Flemish is spoken in France has steadily shrunk. It is said to be spoken by around 80 000 people in the extreme north of France. This figure given in EBLUL (1993) seems high. In *Le Français dans tous les sens* (1988) Henriette Walter preferred not to make a guess but in *L'Aventure des langues en Occident* (1994) she cites a survey carried out in 1984 in Hondschoote, a small town near the frontier, indicating considerable change over the last three generations. According to the survey, Flemish was spoken by 38 per cent of grandparents, 25 per cent of parents were bilingual, but only 2 per cent of children were bilingual. According to the *Enquête famille* just over 10 per cent of those who heard Flemish in their childhood transmitted it to their children.

Western Flemish has no official legal status and no public presence apart from a few local road signs, the result of local initiatives. The teaching of Standard Flemish, i.e. Dutch, is offered in the *Académie de Lille.* (It was included in *Arrêté interministériel* of 8 June 1983[7] which lists the languages which may be examined with the view to obtaining a primary school teaching qualification.) The term *Flamand* remains ambiguous in that it appears on the surface to refer to a RL when it refers in fact to the standard language next door. This is a clear case of a local RL being displaced by its more prestigious neighbour for, despite the local inhabitants seeing themselves as having a Western Flemish identity, they prefer their children to learn Dutch or 'official Flemish', which is seen as more useful. In other words, what is taught is not a RL of France but the official form of the language beyond its borders. This may or may not constitute a RL of France, depending on one's point of view. The same problem applies to Alsatian and Mosellan in relation to German. Some see the disappearance of regional varieties as the death of a language, while others see moving on to a standard form as a sign of moving with the times.

## The problem of Alsatian and Mosellan: varieties of German or separate RLs?

Part of the eastern border of France has traditionally been Germanic in speech. This goes back to the days of the Frankish and Alemanic invasions in the fifth century. Whereas elsewhere in France, the invaders adopted the local speech, while changing it in the process, in these areas the Germanic dialects took over as the language of normal communication. Alsatian and Mosellan (or 'Franconian') are their descendants. There is, however, no unanimity as to whether Alsatian and Mosellan are to be considered 'dialects' of German, 'varieties of German' or RLs in their own right. Nor is there agreement on how to name these languages, the answers given depending on social and political factors.

Linguistically Alsatian comes from Alemanic, and Mosellan from Franconian. Alsatian is spoken in the southern part of Alsace; the northern part, called *l'Alsace Bossue*, speaks Franconian, which is also spoken in half of the *département* of the Moselle (hence it also being called 'Mosellan'), which is part of old Lorraine (hence it also being called Lorrain). Alsatian and Franconian may themselves be broken down into smaller entities (see Philipp 2003).

Alsatian is close to the RLs (or 'dialects') spoken in Switzertland where it is called *schwytzertüsch* or Swiss German and in Baden-Würtenberg. Franconian, also called in France *la langue françique* or *le Platt*, is used in parts of the German Rhineland, Sarre and Luxemburg, where it is called Luxemburgish, and where it functions as one of the three official languages, along with French and German. Alemanic has quite different phonetic features compared to Standard German (or *Hoch-Deutsch*), whereas Franconian is closer to German phonetically but includes numerous specific lexical items.

Alsace became part of France in 1681 and remained so except for the periods between 1870 and 1918, and 1940 and 1945, when it became German. Lorraine became French in 1766. Despite having been part of France for so long their languages remained remarkably well entrenched. Thus Strasbourg, in the eighteenth century, remained an important German-speaking intellectual centre. According to Sibille (2000) they were 'Germans with French nationality'. Even the 1789 Revolution had little immediate impact on the language, only the elite being affected at first. Napoleon is supposed to have said 'Let them speak their language, as long as they can sabre French-style.' But little by little French spread, particularly after the Guizot law of 1833 made primary education compulsory in all *communes* (parishes) of more than 500 inhabitants. The 1850 Falloux law further accentuated the role of French in schools. But the local dialects continued to be spoken, and in some cases written.

It is only in 1918, as a result of the war, that France brutally clamped down on German, by imposing exclusively French in all administrative contexts, which led to many civil servants becoming redundant. Education remained bilingual between 1918 and 1940, but after the war another clamp-down took place, with German for the first time being excluded from education. Not surprisingly, the populations, traumatised by these changes, took refuge in their local RLs, which survived, until quite recently, far better than others.

The creation of a European Community bringing France and Germany into a harmonious relationship, and the importance of Strasbourg in the new European context created a happier situation, which led to the Alsatian and Mosellan dialects declining rapidly. Thus, according to the 1994 Killilea Report, 75 per cent of the population in Alsace over the age of 15 knew Alsatian, whereas another survey carried out in 1997 only gave 63 per cent of the population as speaking Alsatian, of which 86 per cent were over the age of 60. According to the 2003 DGLFLF table only half the Alsatian population now speak Alsatian. Clearly the number of Alsatian speakers is declining rapidly. This is because it is no longer automatically transmitted within the family. This is shown by the fact that EBLUL stated (in 1993) that by 1989 only 36 per cent of those entering primary school in Alsace still spoke the language and in Lorraine only 20 per cent. Even more worrying is the fact that only 17 per cent of the 3- to 10-year-olds interviewed spoke Alsatian (figure quoted by Walter 1994: 327).

The number of Alsatian speakers according to the INSEE/INED *Enquête famille* survey was 548 000,[8] which still makes it the second most spoken RL in France, after Occitan. But the fact that at the beginning of the twentieth century nine children out of ten spoke the dialect with at least one of their parents whereas this figure had dropped to less than half in the 1970s shows that family transmission has reached an all-time low. This figure is now estimated at only one in four, and even then it is used mainly for special occasions rather than in all circumstances. Despite such a decline the level of transmission of the language from the last generation to the present one was 53 per cent which is still the highest of the RLs.

Some statistics, such as those used by the Ministry of Education, simply give the number of German speakers in these areas, hence quite different results, due to the confusion between the concepts of Alsatian, Franconian, and standard German. Since standard German was used as the official written language during the German occupation, there was in the past political and cultural resistance to regarding Alsatian and Lorrain as simply 'German'. And such objections still exist to this day. And yet the claim that German is the written form of these languages appears in both EBLUL (1993) and Killilea (1994). The spokesperson for *Culture et bilinguisme d'Alsace et de Moselle* makes the same claim, comparing the situation of Alsatian with that of Swiss-German.

This is a debatable point from a linguist's point of view, since any language may be written, and indeed Alsatian has been written. In 1999, Robert Grossmann, when Vice-President of the *Conseil régional d'Alsace*, wrote a book entitled *Main basse sur ma langue* ('Hands off my language') in which he vigorously protests at the confusion, and indeed, sees it as a horrible plot to destroy his mother tongue. But this approach is accepted by most forward-looking Alsatians, who see their 'German' language as opening possibilities of employment in German-speaking countries. The situation today in Alsace is, therefore, complex, Alsatian being used as a spoken language (including some radio and television) and German as a written language (education and newspapers). This confusion explains why Alsatian is quoted in the *Atlas de la langue française* as the most frequently taught regional language in France, with 67 000 pupils, whereas it is not even mentioned in Nicole Péry's preliminary report to the Poignant report (*Le Monde*, 4 February 1998).

The reason for this situation is that attitudes towards German have traditionally been determined by political events. Originally, in medieval times, standard German emerged from the language used by the chanceries of the various princes, the impact of printing and the influence of Luther's writing. This formed the basis for a supra-dialectal form of German. The problem in France was that the Germanic-speaking people of Alsace-Lorraine did not participate in its elaboration, having been annexed by the French Crown, and failed to develop, therefore, the same affective links with standard German as other Germanic speakers did. Even so, until the nineteenth century nothing much of a serious nature had been written in what the locals called their 'dialect'. Then suddenly the nineteenth-century written Alsatian took off, mainly in the form of comedies addressing a local audience (i.e. Alsatian written to be spoken) and other minor genres, but also in poetry. German remained, however, the language of 'real' literature. No effort was therefore made to codify the dialects.

With the annexation of Alsace-Lorraine in 1870 there followed a period in which standard German became the only official language. Such intense Germanification was much resented by the inhabitants. This led to an increased use of the dialect in writing, but without codification being felt necessary, each writer using whatever form of spelling best suited his or her purpose. The most influential in this respect were the Matthis brothers (Albert, 1874–1930 and Adolphe, 1874–1944) who adapted standard German spelling to the local context, but there was no compulsion for others to follow suit. Thus, in the early 1930s, the secretary of the *Société des Ecrivains d'Alsace et de Lorraine* could see no need for formal codification, given the level of fragmentation of the dialect. He even stated that no great writing had been produced in the dialect, and that it would appear rather comical if it were. This confirms the low status of the dialect (quoted by Huck 2002: 105).

Finally Nazism is said to have done more for the French cause than any pro-French policy could have achieved. The result was that the oldest members of the population, those who still spoke their 'dialect' and saw it as a form of German, rejected it, which led to its not being transmitted within the context of the family. Only those who saw Alsatian as separate from German could remain faithful to it. This was helped by the fact that Alsatian and Mosellan were – and still are – traditionally referred to by their speakers as *le dialecte*. Then political dissent in 1970s in the aftermath of the May 1968 revolution, led to Alsatian and Mosellan becoming symbols of dissent against French politics and society. A large number of writings appeared in Alsatian and 1975 saw the publication of the first treatise aimed at formalising spelling (M. Urban's *Traité d'orthographe unifiée du dialect alsacien*). A further treatise appeared on the subject, by the same author, two years later.

Codification was meant, according to Urban, to save Alsatian by giving it the status of a language. But many writers reject all notion of codification in the name of freedom. And some maintain that the whole point of a 'dialect' is that it is not written, and that writing it could lead to its demise. It is within this context that the debate as to whether standard German is or is not the written language of Alsatian speakers took place. The present approach seems to favour the concept of the dialect as an oral language and standard German as the normal written language, except in works addressing a very local audience.

A limited but interesting survey was carried out in this respect by J. Broadbridge, as part of her PhD[9] on the perception of the population in the small village of Zillisheim, south of Mulhouse, in the *département* of the Haut Rhin. It was a village where Alsatian could be seen as most at risk. The survey which asked questions such as whether Alsatian was a dialect or a fully-fledged language was carried out by telephone. Part of the population was Alsatian-speaking, and part not. The results of the survey were as follows: 91.4 per cent of the Alsatian speakers and 10 per cent of the non-Alsatian speakers described Alsatian as a dialect; but in answer to the question 'Is Alsatian a fully-fledged language?' 22.9 per cent of its speakers and 36.7 per cent of its non-speakers considered it was, which shows that the concepts of language and dialect are not clearly distinguished in this area.

When asked if Alsatian was a dialect of German, there was considerable reticence to agreeing with this statement, even among the non-Alsatian speakers, stating that its origins were 'other' which included 'Germanic', Alemanic, a mixture, Swiss-German, anything rather than pure German. The idea that Alsatian could be taught through German was vigorously contested by over 82 per cent of the Alsatian speakers although around 23 per cent of the non-Alsatian speakers thought it could be a good idea.

As far as identity was concerned, the language was not seen to be essential to the expression of Alsatian-ness. Even among the Alsatian-speaking interviewees, only just over two-fifths thought that to be truly Alsatian, one should be able to speak Alsatian. Less than a third of the non-Alsatians felt language to be an issue. Alsatian identity seemed more based on the fact of having been born in the area than on language. On the other hand, nearly 40 per cent Alsatian speakers saw themselves as being Alsatian first and French second, whereas only around 13 per cent of the non-Alsatian speakers were of this opinion. This tends to indicate that speaking Alsatian does play a part, even if not a major one, in the identity of the region.

Nowadays the language problem in both Alsace and the Moselle mirrors an identity problem, namely the problem of their 'German-ness' and the place German should play in their culture. Those in favour of considering Alsatian and Mosellan (or Franconian) as full RLs – i.e. separate from German – are in search of a new identity, which precludes the immediate past. As if to prove this point Alsatian theatre – including satire – has witnessed a renaissance since the 1970s, and there are also numerous songwriters and singers using the dialect.

Similar efforts have been made to create a locally based literature and to keep its folk traditions alive. Numerous associations are involved in both cases, such as the *Culture et bilinguisme d'Alsace et de Moselle* and the *Haut Comité de référence pour la langue et la culture alémanique et francique en Alsace et en Moselle*. Clearly Alsace and Moselle try to work together in this respect. These associations are often helped by official organisations such as the *Institut des langues et cultures régionales de Lorraine*.

In Moselle, as in Alsace, the picture remains somewhat gloomy: whereas in 1962 there were 360 000 Mosellan speakers in the Moselle, in 1999, according to a survey carried out by the *Institut national des études démographiques*, there were only 78 000 left. This is still quite a high number compared, for example, to the number of Basque speakers in France. It is not the numbers which are so worrying, but the loss of transmission, which is down to less than 30 per cent, thus placing Mosellan (and Alsatian) in the officially endangered category.

Those who are happy to see German as the written form of their RL, have an eye to the future and the perceived usefulness of knowing German. This is bound to be an important consideration given that many cross the frontier each day to go and work in Germany. Also there are more than 200 000 German speakers in the Alsace area (and some 75 000 Anglophones!). This difference of approach explains the marginal success in the 1980s of schools teaching Alsatian as against German (these were RL classes rather than schools as such – there are no Alsatian or Mosellan immersion schools). These efforts were particularly unsuccessful in the Mosellan area, despite the fact that surveys carried out in the 1980s state that 48 per cent of the inhabitants of Thionville-Sieck spoke Mosellan, and 90 per cent in the area of Sarrebourg-Bitche.

The state was slow in recognising Mosellan. It was not until an *Arrêté* in 1991 that it was recognised as a language which could be taught at secondary level,[10] and not until 2003 that programmes were drawn up for teaching 'les langues régionales d'Alsace et des pays mosellans' in the primary sector[11] (the *Arrêté* also included programmes for Basque,

Breton, Catalan, Corsican and 'Occitan-langue d'oc'). Using the plural form 'langues régionales de ...' avoids the state having to take a position on the German language versus Germanic dialect problem. In other words, straddling the frontiers is at present, on the whole, rather unhelpful for the local RLs of these areas.

## Concluding comments

It is clear that the vitality of a language is not automatically linked with the number of its speakers or the size of the area it is spoken in. Nor is a RL automatically doomed because of poor transmission within the family, since such trends may be reversed, if there is the will to do so. This means adopting suitably robust official policies in favour of the endangered language, particularly in terms of education. The potential success of such policies has been demonstrated in both Catalonia and the Spanish Basque country and acts as an incentive for all RLs. On the other hand, the case of Alsatian illustrates the fact that many factors have to be taken into account when evaluating the position of a RL, since although still the strongest in terms of its vitality, in terms of intergenerational transmission it is now in severe decline.

RLs which are official elsewhere tend to straddle a border. Whether a RL benefits or not from such a position will depend on whether it is seen as 'the same' or not. Thus Catalan and Basque benefit enormously from their official status in Spain, whereas Flemish, Alsatian and Mosellan are dominated by their more prestigious neighbours, and run the risk of being completely absorbed. On the other hand, if the people in the areas where Western Flemish, Alsatian and Mosellan are spoken are willing to see them as variants of the bordering official languages, and willing to learn them as 'their' language, i.e. one with which they feel they have a rapport (which seems to be the case for Flemish and to some extent for Alsatian), this is certainly important in terms of European unity and cross-border understanding.

# 4

# Regional Languages Not Official Elsewhere: Breton, Corsican, Franco-Provençal, Occitan and the *Langues d'oïl*

The reason for making the distinction between RLs which are official or not official elsewhere is that this alters profoundly the dynamics of the problem. This chapter examines those languages which do not benefit from being official elsewhere. They include Breton, Corsican, Franco-Provençal, Occitan and the *langues d'oïl*. This does not mean that none of these are spoken on the other side of the French border. In some cases they are but without having an official status. In a few cases, they do have official status but the number of speakers is so small as to have no significant impact on the RL as spoken in France. Thus the fact that Occitan is the official language of the Val d'Aran is pleasing but does little to help Occitan in France.

The order adopted is alphabetical, with the exception of the *langues d'oïl* which appear last because of their different historic position in relation to the other RLs, having only become officially accepted as *langues de France* – rather than dialects of French – in 1999.

## Breton and the Celtic heritage

The recorded history of France begins with the struggle of the Gauls against the Roman invaders, and, since Victor Duruy made the study of French history compulsory in French primary schools in 1867, school textbooks begin with a chapter on *nos ancêtres les Gaulois* ('our ancestors the Gauls'). For generations of French children 'Gaul' was symbolised by Vercingetorix, the French David fighting against the Roman Goliath, except that in this case David lost. This is, however, part of the national heritage and national awareness, as illustrated in the *bande dessinée*, *Asterisk et Obelisk*.

And yet the Gauls were once invaders themselves. They were Celts and spoke Celtic languages, grouped under the label 'Gaulish'. Very little is known about Gaulish, since the Druid priesthood refused to set down knowledge in writing on religious grounds (Julius Caesar claimed that it took up to twenty years to train a Druid, since all important knowledge had to be memorised). It appears that there were various writing systems, but these were used for unimportant matters or on coins.

Although Gaulish is extinct,[1] one Celtic language is still spoken in France, namely Breton. It is not a direct descendant of Gaulish but of the languages spoken by other Celtic tribes who arrived from Britain in the fifth and sixth centuries, having fled the Germanic invasions. But it is thought that when they arrived in Armorique (*Are morica*, 'situated near the sea'), Gaulish was still spoken, despite the overpowering influence of the Roman Empire.

The geographical area corresponding to Breton was greatest in the ninth century, when it extended from Finistère to Rennes, the present capital of Brittany. By the twentieth century it had withdrawn behind a line from Paimpol in the north to Vannes in the south. This area, the Basse Bretagne, is referred to as the *Bretagne bretonnante* or *Bretagne celtique*. The non-Breton-speaking area is the Haute Bretagne or *région Gallo*, since Gallo, a *langue d'oïl* is spoken there (see below).

Present-day Breton, therefore, evolved from the Celtic language imported from Britain and the Gaulish language already spoken in Armorique which became known as 'Little Britain' (Brittany). In other words, Breton belongs to the Brittonic branch of the Celtic languages which also includes Cornish and Welsh, Breton being closest to Cornish. Many of the inhabitants eventually became bilingual, with Latin and later French as their second language. The varying combinations of the Celtic varieties (including Gaulish) and Latin gave rise to the four major dialectal groups of Breton spoken today: Cornouaillais, Léonais, Trégorrois and Vannetais, with Vannetais regarded as the most influenced by Gaulish. The first three are usually represented by the acronym KLT.

Brittany was established as an autonomous Duchy from 937, when the Normans were defeated outside Nantes. Then in 1491 Anne, Duchess of Brittany, married King Charles VIII of France, thus creating a dynastic alliance which led Brittany to accept union with France in 1532 although this did not prevent Brittany from retaining fiscal, judicial and ecclesiastical autonomy. Even the 1539 Ordinance of Villers-Cotterêts left Brittany fairly unscathed, since Latin was the language used for institutional matters and not Breton, which simply meant replacing one foreign language by another. But the 1789 Revolution abolished the States of Brittany and Breton was seen by the state as an obstacle to becoming a good French citizen. This was the beginning of the decline of Breton.

Originally Breton had not been devoid of prestige, although its aristocracy adopted French early on as a language of general communication in Europe and beyond. Its literature has a long tradition which goes back at least as far as that of French. (Breton is frequently referred to as only being an oral language, but in this, as in many things, Brittany is the victim of negative popular misconceptions.) The oldest known manuscript, a bilingual Latin–Breton treatise of medicine, goes back to the eighth century, and numerous annotations alongside Latin texts have been collected, which testify to a coherent orthography very early on. A Breton/Latin/French dictionary known as *Catholicon* was written in 1464 and published in 1499. This constitutes the first French dictionary, and was meant to be of help to parish priests who, since the thirteenth century, were supposed to use Breton when dealing with parishioners. At this point, written Breton was still fairly standardised and this coherence was to last until the seventeenth century.

It was the influence of the Church which led to several orthographies being used for written Breton, for if the clergy were supposed to use Breton with their flock, it had to be a form the flock could understand. The result was a spelling system for each of the four main dialectal groups. This *breton de curé* (the Breton of priests) became particularly influential since it was also practised in the schools (the *petites écoles*) run by the Church. This was the case even after the 1789 Revolution, plans to install secular schools in all parishes having failed, which left the Church as sole educator. As a result, according to an 1863 survey, three-quarters of the schools in the Finistère were still using Breton as the normal means of communication, and nearly as many in the other *bretonnants* areas.

Some have accused the *breton de curé* of having fragmented Breton, but it has also been argued that these forms were, in fact, standardised forms in that they were the official forms used in writing, including administrative and legal documents. They were also used for writing sermons and for theatrical representations (Le Dû 1996). In other words, these were already supra-parish forms, i.e. abstract entities, in relation to casual speech, which was parish-based, and which Le Dû calls *badume*, meaning 'at home' so as to avoid the word *patois*.

In the nineteenth century a nationalist Celtic movement developed from Romanticism, which led, in 1804, to the creation of a Celtic

Academy, interested in resuscitating Brittany's archaeological past. Inspired by this movement J.-F. Le Gonidec published a *Grammaire celto-bretonne* in 1807 and a *Dictionnaire Celto-Breton ou Breton-Français* in 1821 aimed at bringing some degree of standardisation into the language. To further this aim, he also developed a new unified spelling system, based on his Bas-Léon dialect, 'purified' of any excessive Romance influences and using borrowings from Welsh to update the language. This spelling system was, however, unable to displace the various ecclesiastical versions, and all seem to have been used.

Efforts were again made at the beginning of the twentieth century to move towards a single unified spelling system essentially based on Le Gonidec's, but allowing for variation. Only the Vannetais remained faithful to their own system. Again, between the two world wars efforts were made to come up with a single system, this time with the specific aim of making education in Breton possible. This was because of a growing demand in Brittany that Breton should be taught, particularly in primary schools. The bishop of Quimper and Léon even went as far as to lay down directives to this end, in 1936, which were to be followed in the private Catholic school system. Then the Vichy government in 1941 declared that Breton could be introduced into all schools (by the 1943 *Arrêté Carcopino*). But according to those responsible at the time, for this to be possible, Breton had to be codified. The result was 'unified Breton' (or *peurunvan*) which tried to combine KLT and *vannetais* by indicating in writing the duality of pronunciation. This was symbolised by the ZH sign. Thus *brezoneg + brehoneg = brezhoneg*.

This system had two drawbacks: it was artificial and it was associated with the German regime. It was rejected by the Resistance movement, and also by some of the clergy, in particular Canon Falc'hun, a university man. He suggested in the 1950s a different system based on his work as a phonetician, which became known as 'university spelling'. It was meant to draw a line under the Occupation period and start afresh.

From around 1955 to 1975 there were therefore two competing spelling systems: 'unified' Breton and 'university' Breton (as well, of course, as previous systems such as the most recent form of Vannetais). According to Favereau (2002: 118) the problem was complicated by ideological differences separating the right-wing traditional Breton culture militants and a new, often anti-clerical left-wing Breton movement. It was the latter, in the 1970s, which tried to combine the 'unified system' and the 'university system', thus creating a new 'inter-dialectal' spelling form, which was used for a while. But in the 1980s it was the unified or *peurunvan* system which became the norm because it was chosen by both the *Diwan* schools (Breton immersion schools), and the new state bilingual schools. The Vannetais, on the other hand, tend to use the 'inter-dialectal system'. The Catholic schools tend to use either the 'unified' and the 'university system'. As far as publishing is concerned, two-thirds of writings seem to be published in *peurunvan*, against one-quarter in the 'university' form. The rest follows either the 'inter-dialectal system' or the Vannetais system (see Favereau 2002 for further details).

In 1978 Giscard d'Estaing granted the Bretons a *Charte Culturelle de Bretagne*. This was followed in 1982 by the creation of an *Institut Culturel de Bretagne* and finally in 1999 the *Office de la langue bretonne*. All spelling systems compete for subsidies from these organisations. Hence the publication of a dictionary in 1991 which contains what the authors call a 'multigraphic transcription', i.e. it gives, for each word, all the possible spellings. But it is important to realise that not all words are affected and that the degree of distance between the various forms spoken may be seen either as great or minor depending on whether the person consulted wishes to emphasise common links or differences.

As far as the number of speakers is concerned, it was the educational policies of Jules Ferry that started off a steady decline, but by the 1900s, because of the high birth rate, the number of Breton speakers was still estimated at 1 400 000, the highest figure ever. The Church again played its part in this: in 1902 the *Ministère de l'Intérieur* (the Home Office) decreed that it was forbidden to preach in church in Breton, but priests continued to do so despite risking losing their livelihood (in those days priests still functioned under the *régime concordataire* which meant that they were treated as civil servants and paid by the state) and catechism continued to be taught in Breton until near enough World War Two.

In 1900 the number of monolingual Breton speakers was still half the population in Basse Bretagne, but World War One killed a quarter of all male Breton speakers. This disaster was further compounded by a massive exodus of Bretons to Paris in search of work. As a result, whereas an estimated 75 per cent still knew Breton in 1931, this figure had dropped to 33 per cent by 1951. Despite this, the use of Breton was still present in everyday life until the end of World War Two. According to a 1997 survey carried out by Fanch Broudig (2003) for the FR3 television channel, 31 per cent of interviewees still understood Breton, while 20 per cent said they could speak it either fairly well or very well. These percentages correspond respectively to 370 000 able to understand the language and 240 000 able to speak it. These figures represent a decline in relation to the figures Broudig obtained from a similar survey carried out in 1991. They are fairly close, however, to figures given elsewhere (EBLUL in 1993 and Killilea in 1994). The *Enquête famille* quotes the slightly lower figure of 304 000.

These fairly high figures are completely counterbalanced, however, by those given in terms of the vitality of the language, i.e. its transmission within the family unit. Still according to the Broudic survey, two speakers out of three are over the age of 60, and there are no more than 15 000 able to express themselves in Breton who are under the age of 40. Moreover, even among those who can speak it, nearly 80 per cent of Bretons admit to using Breton less than French, and state that they speak it more with friends and neighbours than within the context of the family. The *Enquête famille* is also very negative, for although nearly 400 000 Bretons remember having heard Breton spoken occasionally by their parents, and just under 300 000 frequently, only 10 per cent of these have transmitted the language to their children.

This point is echoed in the Euromosaïc study carried out by the European Commission (1996) on a number of languages to assess their ability to reproduce themselves. It concludes:

> Both Breton and Sardinian are language groups which demonstrate the virtual retreat of language use within two generations . . . This is characteristic of languages with a low status and a restricted range of institutionalized use which are confronted by rapid change processes . . . In both cases the support required by the various agencies of language production and reproduction in order to confront this intensity of change has not been forthcoming.

This is why most – not to say all – new speakers have to learn it as a second language rather than as a mother tongue.

And yet there has been a revival of interest in both the Breton language and Breton identity. It was not automatically helped in the past by various Breton nationalist movements such as the *Parti autonomiste breton* created in 1927, which became the *Parti national breton* in 1932. Its position was largely rejected because of its readiness to collaborate with the Germans. As a result, Brittany turned to the political left and the *Front de libération de la Bretagne* came into existence in 1968.

Nowadays most Bretons reject violence and since a McDonald's waitress was killed by mistake in 2000 by a bomb which was meant to create material damage only, the movement has gone into hibernation. So nowadays, 'nationalism' is reduced for most people to the development of the Breton language and culture – that is, regionalism rather than sep-aratism. Ties with Welsh, Irish and Scottish Gaelic speakers, which have developed within the context of EU linguistic and cultural programmes, help fight a sense of isolationism.

One of the interesting aspects of Breton 'identity' is that Brittany is traditionally bilingual, Breton–Gallo (Gallo being a Romance language), so Breton cannot, logically, act as a unifying factor for all Bretons. And yet some of its most enthusiastic militants are in areas where Breton has not been spoken since the thirteenth century. This is because the near death of Breton has brought forth a new movement, determined to save it, not only for nationalistic reasons but for its own sake, in order to save the very specific vision of the world linked with it. The members of this movement are the *Néo-Bretonnants*. They stand apart from traditional native speakers (the *Bretonnants*) in that they are usually young (whereas the average age of native Breton speakers is very old), highly educated (the *Bretonnants* are usually fairly uneducated country people), and have learned Breton as a second language. (They resemble in this the middle-class Catalans who brought Catalan back to life in the nineteenth and twentieth centuries.)

For them a codified form of Breton, not linked with geography, is essential to its survival, and the foundation of a *Diwan* in Paris in 2004 backs their point of view. They favour the 'unified' orthography and adopt a purist approach, which rejects borrowings from French in favour of borrowings from Welsh. They promote a strictly positive image of Breton, which contrasts with the negative approach which led to parents not using Breton when speaking to their children, and who saw French as the language of modernity and social progress.

There is supposed to be a fundamental gulf between the Breton mili-tants and the native speakers who do not recognise forms of Breton even slightly different from their own as 'their language'. It is this gulf, according to M. C. Jones (1999)[2] which goes towards explaining why the Breton movement has been more limited than its counterpart in Wales. But such an approach would no doubt be criticised by researchers such as Favereau (1996) who states that the native speakers have now become conscious of the risk of extinction of their language, and have shown a more positive attitude towards efforts made to popularise both the language and culture.

But Jones is right when she states that language is only a part of Breton identity which has enough other markers to survive without the language, much as Irishness has. To this must be added the added prob-lem of Brittany being the seat of not one but two RLs. According to a

survey carried out by Alistair Cole (quoted in Moal 2003), Breton identity is remarkably strong despite the fact such a small proportion of the
population still uses the language: 2 per cent see themselves as Breton
only, 15 per cent see themselves as more Breton than French, 57 per cent
equally Breton and French, 17 per cent more French than Breton, 8 per
cent French, not Breton (1 per cent gave no answer). A clear majority
therefore see themselves as Breton, at least to a certain degree. The aim
of the Breton language militants is to tap into this reservoir of good will
and to persuade more people to send their children to Breton immersion
schools or to bilingual schools.

There is an important network of immersion schools, called *Diwan*,
which have a large attendance, and go up till the *Baccalauréat*. The first
one was created on the Basque *Ikastola* model in 1977. By 2000 there
were 28 kindergartens, 25 elementary schools, 4 *collèges*, which go until
the end of the fourth form, and one *lycée*, which goes to the *Baccalauréat*.
The number of pupils involved was 2251, and these numbers are
increasing. Making Breton a prerequisite of Breton-ness does, however,
create a major problem for the Gallo speakers (see below). For more
details on education see Chapter 5.

## Corsican

Corsica was invaded by the Romans in 259 BC. It came under the rule of
Pisa from the eleventh to the thirteenth centuries and of Genoa from
the thirteenth to the eighteenth centuries (with a brief gap between
1556 and 1559 when it came under French rule). Hence there has been
a long-lasting Italian influence, even though it was often resented.
Corsica was briefly independent in the eighteenth century (1755–67),
thanks to the effort of the Corsican patriot Pasquale Paoli, the island's
hero (he was called the *Père de la Patrie* by Rousseau), who tried to gov-
ern the island according to the principles of the Enlightenment. It was
annexed by France in 1768. In 1789, the Corsican representatives at the
*Constituante* assembly asked for and obtained Corsica's union with
France, at which point some 80 families became ennobled, including
the Bonaparte family.[3] The role of Napoleon and his family in Europe
ensured its continued loyalty to France, and 150 years later, the role
played by Italy during World War Two again strengthened these links.

And yet, thanks to its isolation, the Corsicans retained their linguistic
and cultural identity well into the twentieth century. (According to
Dorothy Carrington (1971) it was possible in the late 1950s to meet
Corsicans who spoke no French. This is no longer the case.) Moreover,

opposition to the French government grew during the second part of the twentieth century, partly because the end of the French Empire meant the end of numerous colonial posts traditionally filled by Corsicans. Ensuing poverty and the lack of success of various governmental projects led to the economic crisis becoming social in 1975. This date marks the beginning of what is known as 'the Corsican problem'.

The catalyst was the government overreacting to the occupation by militant regionalists of a wine cellar in Aleria owned by a repatriate from northern Africa.[4] This led to the death of two policemen which deeply shocked the nation. From then on *la question Corse* became a headache for all ensuing governments, some of which sought a solution in institutional changes. The most important change from a linguistic point of view came with the *Statut Joxe* of 1992, which integrated the teaching of the Corsican language and culture into the state school system. The original decree also contained a reference to the *peuple corse* (the 'Corsican people') as a component of the French people, but this was declared anticonstitutional by the *Conseil Constitutionnel* as being divisive.

Reactions in other areas of France have been mixed. Some RL militants have seen the attribution to Corsica of a special status within the Republic as an unfair privilege and they feel bitter that the Corsicans should have won linguistic concessions through the use of violence, whereas their own democratic efforts have led to considerably less. There is, however, a more positive point of view, namely that what has been done for Corsica may spread to other regions, and that Corsica's fight will, in the end, benefit all. The institutional changes may be seen as heralding the first successful attack on the sacrosanct principle of France as 'one and indivisible' even if the mention of the *peuple Corse* was declared, at present, unconstitutional. The very fact that a government seriously suggested this may be seen as a step in the right direction (for more details see Andreani and Ajchenbaum 2005).

Linguistically, Corsican belongs to the Italo-Romance group. The dialects spoken on the eastern side of the islands are close to those spoken in Tuscany, while those in the south resemble the dialects of southern Italy and share phonetic characteristics with Sardinian. Genoese is still spoken in the town of Bonifacio, but Greek, once spoken in Cargese, has now disappeared. Corsican used to be seen as a purely spoken language, its written equivalent being Tuscan (the relationship between the two languages being similar to that between German and Alsatian). This was, in other words, a typical diglossic situation[5] and Italian continued, in practice, to function as a co-official language alongside French well after 1769. The Corsican elite also continued to attend

Italian universities. But the rise of the French Empire, by providing jobs for all (much as the British Empire did), helped to impose French as the only official language. At the same time, the Corsicans whose links had become stronger with France than with Italy started to develop their own autonomous literature, building on the fact that Corsican poetry had existed since the seventeenth century, or perhaps even before.

This sense of Corsican as an autonomous language (although clearly collateral with Italian) developed to the extent that to say, today, that Corsican is a 'form of' or a 'dialect of' Italian is seen as an insult. And it is true that when walking in a busy town such as Calvi in summer, full of Italian tourists, it is very easy for a foreigner to distinguish between Italian and Corsican speakers. Phonetically the languages are very different. Denominations vary historically, however, with Corsican being referred to as a *langue dite italienne* (as so-called Italian) in a court case in 1859,[6] and as *langue corso-italienne* in another case in 1868. Such an approach is no longer acceptable.

There is no single Corsican language, however. Like most RLs it is fragmented into local varieties, or 'regiolects'. But the militants of Corsican differ from those of most other RLs in not wanting Corsican to be standardised. Instead they want to function within the context of a 'polynomic language', i.e. one which includes all the regional varieties. To quote Marcellesi, a polynomic language is 'a language whose unity is an abstraction and is the result of a dialectic movement and not of simple ossification of a norm, and whose existence is founded on the overwhelming decision of those who speak it to give it a particular name and declare it autonomous of other languages' (quoted in J.-B. Coyos 2004: 113–14).

Education in Corsican schools is therefore based on the local variety, to which are gradually added other varieties to enable the acquisition of at least a passive knowledge of them. Spelling has been elaborated on the basis of Italian orthography adapted to the special sounds of Corsican. The first spelling system to be accepted was set up by D. Geronimo and P. Marchetti in 1970, but militants and educationalists update it regularly. In this system, different spellings are considered acceptable if they form coherent systems. Such a liberal approach is not without its problems, since it by-passes the principle of 'good usage', so helpful and reassuring in education. On the other hand, it avoids the kind of gulf which exists between those who function at the *commune* (or parish) level and those who function at the supra-dialectal or inter-dialectal level (as is the case for the *Bretonnants* and *Néo-Bretonnants*).

As far as the number of speakers are concerned, according to the 1982 INSEE survey cited in the 1994 Killilea Report, 96 per cent of the population of Corsican origin understood Corsican, and it was regularly spoken by some 86 per cent. This represented around 143 000 people. The 1999 *Enquête famille* gives the figure of 122 000, still on the surface an encouraging result. But a 1995 survey carried out by the *Observatoire interrégional du politique* only gave 81 per cent as understanding Corsican, 64 per cent speaking it, 75 per cent being able to read it, and 73 per cent wishing it to be taught at school (figures quoted by Sibille 2000: 33).

This survey, like most, was self-evaluative and therefore not entirely reliable. This may be seen from the results of another survey, carried out in 1998, on fifth and sixth form pupils which gave quite different results: only 72 per cent of the pupils had heard Corsican spoken in the home (60 per cent by parents and 63 per cent by grandparents). But of these only 13 per cent had heard Corsican spoken by their brothers and sisters. Moreover, the parents and grandparents being bilingual, only 39 per cent of the pupils stated they actually spoke the language to their grandparents, 34 per cent to their parents and a rather surprising 22 per cent to their friends. It seems that Corsican, like Breton, is a language which establishes a kind of friendly connivance with friends (figures established by J. Fusina and also quoted in Sibille 2000: 33).

These rather surprisingly low figures are compensated by a desire to learn the language. Thus a survey carried out in March 2004 by the *Académie Corse* showed that the demand for the teaching of Corsican had increased by 17 per cent between 2000 and 2004, with 92 per cent of children being taught Corsican in the primary sector. Corsican is offered as an option open to all since 1999. In 2004–5, nearly 70 per cent of secondary school pupils were studying it in the first and second form, and around 35 per cent in the third and fourth form. In the *lycée* (i.e. beyond the fourth form), the figure had gone from 13 per cent to 20 per cent. And in the *lycées professionnels*, nearly 40 per cent chose Corsican as an option. The *inspecteur pédagogique*, J.-M. Arrighi, also stated that there were always more candidates than places whenever a bilingual class is opened. There are no private immersion schools in Corsica since it is taught in the state system.

The fact that so many wish to learn the language also illustrates that intergenerational transmission is no longer happening enough to ensure the survival of the language. This was shown by the *Enquête famille* which established that transmission from the last generation to the present one was only 34 per cent, which nearly puts it in the endangered category, and one in need of help from the educational system. There has, in fact, been a demand for the teaching of Corsican, along with regional history and geography, since the beginning of the nineteenth century and books were produced to this effect in the early 1920s, which bears witness to the deep-seated awareness of a separate Corsican identity, albeit within a French framework, and the fear, felt very early on, that it could become completely diluted within the French concept of nationhood.

The need to keep Corsican alive was particularly strong in the period between the two world wars, which was characterised by a general renewed interest in regionalism. As a result, Corsican became used for all literary genres. But unfortunately the Corsican intellectual militants were regrouped around two competing magazines, one of which, the basically autonomist *A Muvra*, was suspected of having sympathised with the Italian enemy. This ensured that the movement went completely underground after the war,[7] and so did the whole issue of the language. (The other magazine was more regionalist and close to the *Félibrige*, *L'Annu Corsu*.) It was only in 1955 that the magazine *Un Muntese* tried to gradually relaunch Corsican culture. This explains why Corsican not being included in the 1951 Deixonne law (see Chapter 5) failed to cause much of a ripple in Corsica. It took, in fact, years of struggle on the part of various militant associations to obtain its inclusion in 1974 (Fusina 1999).

Nowadays the Corsican language is clearly associated with nationalism, which became a major threat in 1975 with the foundation of the *Front de libération nationale corse* (FLNC), a terrorist group which regularly targets second homes (as did the Welsh militants). But the killing of a *préfet*, Claude Érignac, in 1998, caused revulsion, both in France and Corsica, which was seen as ungovernable, particularly since the island has always been associated with a local kind of lawlessness, popularised by nineteenth-century romantic writers such as Mérimée.[8]

There are good reasons, however, which explain the gradual development of this state of affairs. One goes back to Napoleon and the Miot Decrees (*Arrêts Miot*) of 1801 and 1802, which gave Corsica a different status to the rest of France, both in terms of administration, justice, finance and customs. This status, which was to the considerable disadvantage of the Corsicans, was supposed to be provisional, but the particularly hated customs barriers set up with 'the continent' only ended in 1912, and others remained even longer. As a result, some Corsicans have felt they were treated as a colony. There is also general dissatisfaction at the lack of help being given to compensate for the expenses incurred for being an island. Nationalism today comes therefore from centuries of bitterness and disappointment, the 1789 Revolution not being seen as having fulfilled its promise of equality with the rest of France. Hence the need for institutional changes.

The metropolitan image of *l'île de Beauté* ('the island of Beauty') is sometimes negative both because of its law and order problems and the fact that it is expensive to run (looking after a population ageing at a worrying rate due to absence of work on the island represents considerable expenditure). Hence a 1996 survey revealed that although 61 per cent of French people wanted Corsica to remain part of France, as many as 24 per cent were in favour of its independence. But while the French view has been canvassed, there has been no similar survey in Corsica.

On the other hand, judging by electoral results, it would seem that less than 15 per cent wish for full independence. Moreover the 1999 *Processus de Matignon*, which aimed at giving Corsica more autonomy, was rejected by referendum in 2003 by 50.98 per cent of the voters, which implies that the great majority of Corsicans see their identity as being both Corsican and French. This kind of dual approach to identity, in which a regional one is compatible with a national one, is at present gaining ground in France.

Politics set aside, the desire to protect and promote the Corsican language and Corsican culture is not restricted to the separatists. Nearly the whole population is now involved. When the signing of the Charter for Regional or Minority Languages was being discussed (see Chapter 5), 5000 Corsicans demonstrated in its favour. It had, unlike in metropolitan France, the broad support of the general public, pressure groups and political parties. Hence the French government making the teaching of Corsican compulsory in all schools and at all levels in 1991. (For more details on education, see Chapter 5.)

## Franco-Provençal or 'Francoprovençal'

Franco-Provençal is the most endangered of the French RLs. It used to be spoken in a large area, which included not only parts of France but also Italy and Switzerland, but it suffered from its main urban centres, Lyon and Geneva, having favoured French early on instead of the local language.

The term was coined in the nineteenth century by an Italian linguist to describe a language which includes traits from both the *langue d'oc* and the *langue d'oïl*, without being a mixture of the two since it has its own linguistic characteristics, hence linguists now prefer to write it in one word, i.e. 'Francoprovençal', to avoid it being thought of as a mixture.

It is not mentioned in EBLUL (1993), but there are some statistics in Killilea (1994), which refer to it being spoken in Italy in the Aosta valley, and in some Alpine valleys in the Piedmont region, and in two communities in the Puglia region, but no mention is made of France. According to the Franco-Provençal specialist, G. Tuaillon, about 1 per cent of the population on the French side still speaks Franco-Provençal, i.e. around 60 000 people, nearly all over 60 years old. Similar figures are given by J.-B. Martin (2002) who reckoned, in 2000, that the total number of potential speakers in all the Franco-Provençal areas to be somewhere between 120 000 and 150 000. But the real problem is not its number of speakers but the loss of its vitality since the INSEE/INED family survey shows that it has the lowest of all the RL transmission rates, around 10 per cent, which places it in the 'moribund' category.

Although Franco-Provençal is a language in its own right rather than a mixture of two others, it is nonetheless extremely fragmented. Moreover, its speakers often do not see it as a language, but only as a *patois* (*Fribourgeois, Savoyard, Valaisien, Bressan, Forézien*, etc). Franco-Provençal is nearly entirely an oral language. 'Nearly' because some texts were written in the *patois* from the sixteenth century on, but only the minor genres were cultivated (comedies, stories, fables, songs, some poems, satirical dialogues, etc.). Many only ever appeared in manuscript form, although during the nineteenth century, under the influence of the Romantic movement, various local scholars, one of which was J.-J. Champollion-Figeac, collected anthologies of these works. Efforts have been made recently to publish them, but this time more for their ethnographic interest than any other.

Franco-Provençal is not formally codified, although in the 1970s the Amis des patois Savoyards worked out a spelling system called *graphie de Conflans* (because that is where they met). The aim was to transcribe texts in a manner faithful to pronunciation. Recently another spelling system was developed by Dominique Stick in *Parlons francoprovençal* which aims at being used for a broader range of varieties. His version rejects the phonetic approach in favour of one taking into account grammar and etymology as being more stable and pan-dialectal. It resembles the new 'classical' or 'Alibert' orthography of Occitan (see below). Both systems are problematic, the latter because it is seen as difficult, and the former because of the vagaries of pronunciation from one area to another.

Franco-Provençal is not formally taught in schools and is not linked with any specific linguistic, cultural or political movement. This is because the older generation had the language drummed out of them at school and, as a result, did not transmit it to their descendants, not wanting to burden them with a linguistic problem. Some now regret this. There is however a yearly *fiesta* which regroups the Franco-Provençal speakers of France, Switzerland and Italy to celebrate their *patois*. These celebrations are organised by each country in turn.

## The *langue d'oc* or Occitan

Occitan has traditionally been the most important of the RLs spoken in France both in terms of the number of its speakers (over 10 million in 1920 according to Jules Ronjat, quoted in Sibille 2000: 39), and the size of its territory (some thirty-one *départements* in France, i.e. a third of the country). To these must be added the Val d'Aran in Spain, where it has been the official language since 1990 and several Italian valleys in the Piémont, where it benefits from some official recognitions since 2000.

The word 'Occitan' is problematic, however, since there has long been disagreement as to whether it refers to a single language or a group of related languages. If geographical criteria are used, the list usually includes (i) Gascon, (ii) Languedocien, (iii) Provençal, (iv) Limousin, (v) Auvergnat and (vi) Vivaro-Alpin (or Alpin Provençal). If linguistic criteria are used, the list includes (i) Nord-Occitan (which regroups Limousin, Auvergnat and Provençal Alpin), (ii) Occitan-Moyen (which regroups Languedocien and Provençal) and (iii) Gascon as a separate entity. Historically too the terminology has often been ambiguous since Catalan writers referred in the nineteenth century to the *llengua llemosina* when referring to the whole of the Oc language and not just to one dialect (Sibille 2000: 35).[9] For some speakers these constitute related dialects or languages, while for others they constitute a fundamentally unified language, depending on whether the wish is to stress similarities or differences. Today's militants all stress the similarities, and their preferred term is 'Occitan'.

The term *occitan* is attested, mainly in Latin, from the end of the thirteenth century and is often attributed to Dante.[10] In the nineteenth century, Mistral and the *Félibrige*, referred to the *langue d'oc*. The use of the term *occitan* remained rare in French until the twentieth century when such terms were popularised by the Occitanist movement, although *Occitanie* and *occitanien* were used sporadically from the eighteenth century onwards. The present-day use of *Occitan* is justified on the grounds that in medieval times Occitan had a unified orthography. *Occitan* is also preferred to *langue d'oc* which may be identified too narrowly with the

Languedoc area, except in official documentation which tends to use the expression *Occitan-Langue d'oc*. The concept of Occitan as a unified language has not, however, automatically percolated down to some of the more elderly users, many of whom still use the term *patois* to describe their language.

Traditional dialectology did nothing to dispel this myth. It was left to modern researchers such as Robert Lafont and others (often regrouped under the label *école de Montpellier* or 'Montpellier school') to destroy such an image, by showing the importance of medieval Occitan in the development of European literature. It was, after all, an international language, spoken by Eleanor of Aquitaine (1122–1204) and her son, Richard Lion Heart, among other famous people, and this all the way to Jerusalem. Nowadays the fact that Occitan is a proper language (and not simply a collection of related *patois*) with a famous literature is fully recognised in most educated circles.

The use of Occitan as a written language competing with Latin goes back as far as French. A unified *scripta* was used for charters dating from the twelfth century and its use spread to all administrative and legal contexts from the thirteenth century onwards. It was also used in scientific contexts such as mathematics, medicine, theology, grammar, botanical studies, etc. It was not until the sixteenth century that French began to take its place on a massive scale. The latest documents date from the seventeenth century. Only in the Béarn did the language (Gascon) continue to be used until 1789, because it remained a small independent state until 1620 when it was finally annexed by France. Until then Béarnais had been the official administrative language.

Occitan's remarkably rich literature goes back to the eleventh century, made famous by its Troubadours in the whole of Europe. Some 2500 poems have survived and over 250 melodies as well as numerous chronicles (Sibille in Caubet et al. 2002: 17–26). But from the fifteenth century literary production went into a decline, Occitan becoming used mainly for the minor genres. There was a certain renaissance in the seventeenth century, but instead of using the old *scripta* writers started to write as they thought fit, which was the beginning of the fragmentation of the written language. It is only recently that successful efforts have been made to return to a unitary system.

The story of how this decline, and the accompanying fragmentation of the language, took place varies from area to area. Thus the Languedoc-Roussillon was brought to its knees in the thirteenth century by the crusade led by the king against the Albigensian 'heretics', after which the whole area was annexed by the French Crown. After that what took place, according to militants, was a form of 'colonisation', much intensified after the 1789 Revolution, which led to the removal of Occitan from all prestigious contexts. Thus although spoken Occitan remained in daily use in rural areas until World War Two, it gradually acquired its *patois* pejorative overtones. After the war, the area was marked by a sense of neglect and depression, which is when Occitan ceased to be transmitted within the family.[11]

Provence, on the other hand, was not colonised and crushed by the state in the same manner. It is true that it was annexed by the king of France in 1481, but with the understanding that the Provençaux should keep the privileges and institutions enjoyed until then. These were not lost until 1535 (by the edict of Joinville), but by then unification was seen as complete. Villers-Cotterêts was fully applied in the area, with the usual consequences for the local language. Thus although the process of domination of French was not as violent as in the Languedoc-Roussillon area, it was just as complete.

In 1859, F. Mistral published a famous poem, *Mirèio*, which marked the beginning of the renaissance of Provençal literature. That same year he founded the *Félibrige*, an association of writers using Provençal, and, in 1904, he was awarded the Nobel Prize. But Mistral and the *Félibrige* made no real attempt to extend the use of a language by then used only by peasants to an urban context. Mistral's poetry remains a celebration of rural life. His Nobel Prize did, however, confer on Provençal a status that later Provençaux were not slow to exploit.

The renaissance of Occitan beyond the limits of Provençal and Mistral's movement began to take place between the two world wars. An important step was taken with the creation in 1945 of the *Institut d'Etudes Occitanes* by Ismaël Girard. A particularly influential academic personality from the 1960s onwards was – and still is – Robert Lafont, a contentious but highly charismatic and influential figure.

Apart from the Languedoc-Roussillon area having a different history from Provence, which led the former to having a more left-wing past than the latter, there have been other sources of discord. The main one has been orthographic. As was mentioned above, during medieval times there was a uniform system of spelling used whatever the local phonetic and phonological particularities. In such a system, a single *grapheme* (i.e. a letter or group of letters) no longer stands for a single sound but for a number of possible sounds corresponding to different realisations of the same morphological or lexical unit (see Sibille in Caubet et al. 2002 for more details). As such it is supra-dialectal, just as French and English are since their orthographies do not reflect differences of pronunciation either.

From the sixteenth century onwards, however, this unified system was replaced by a variety of personalised phonetic writing systems, based on the French system for transcribing sounds (in which [u] is spelt =ou for example). The drawback to such systems is that they are clearly unsuited to a supra-dialectal approach to language. On the other hand, phonetic transcriptions do not demand much previous training whereas a unified system, in which the same letter may correspond to different sounds in different areas, demands considerable training.

Mistral and those who followed him used an orthography which was at least partly phonetic, thus making it unsuitable for the other varieties of Occitan.[12] On the other hand, the orthography developed by Louis Alibert (1884–1959) in his 1935 *Grammaire occitane* was supra-dialectal, being derived from the orthography of the Troubadours in the Middle Ages. In 1945, the *Institut d'Etudes Occitanes* in Toulouse refined the system, and in 1951 Robert Lafont started using it.

The dispute between the followers of these two different types of 'standard' spelling was, for years, mostly destructive, but in 1999 the presidents of the *Institut d'Etudes Occitanes* and of the *Félibrige* signed, in Marseilles, an agreement making both Provençal and Occitan orthographies acceptable, particularly in education. The educational academies of Aix-en-Provence and Nice teach both orthographies (a memorandum sent by the rector of Nice University only allowing for Mistral's version was annulled by the *Conseil d'Etat* in the 1970s).[13] And on the Toulouse side, a *Conseil de la langue Occitane* (CLO) became officialised in 1998 to solve problems of orthography as they occurred.

There are still, mainly on the Provençal side, purists who will not agree with this compromise, which tends to be disruptive since energy is mis-spent solving internal problems. Thus in October 2003, the *Conseil Régional de Provence-Alpes-Côte d'Azur* – known as PACA – passed a motion declaring Provençal and Niçois the RLs of the area. This caused such consternation among the Occitanist movement that another motion had to be passed the following year, stating that 'la langue occitane ou langue d'Oc est la langue régionale de la région Provence-Alpes-Côte d'Azur: le provençal rhodanien, le provençal maritime, le niçard et l'alpin sont les formes régionales de la langue occitane ou langue d'Oc en Provence-Alpes-Côte d'azur.' In other words, Occitan was accepted as the overall label for the varieties spoken in the region. Such disputes are fortunately becoming rare, the concept of a supra-dialectal Occitan being now accepted in most quarters, along with the principle that it has different regional realisations, which constitutes part of its *richesse culturelle*. This is the approach which has been adopted for teaching the language. Thus the new method, *Òc-Ben!*, presents the same material in four forms, namely Gascon, Languedocien, Limousin and Provençal. The teacher is meant to teach students to produce the variety most suited to their area, while helping them to gradually understand the others. This is, in other words, a polynomic approach, similar to the one originally developed by the Corsicans. This approach does not, however, encourage local varieties to expand, on the contrary, uniformity is aimed at through the use of a common orthography.

It is difficult to evaluate the exact numbers of speakers of Occitan. Even EBLUL is uncharacteristically wary in this respect (1993: 15–16): 'There are no official data on the number of speakers. Of some 12 to 13 million inhabitants in the area, it is estimated 48 per cent understand Occitan, 28 per cent can speak it, about 9 per cent of the population use it on a daily basis, 13 per cent can read and 6 per cent can write the language.' These figures are, however, much higher than those revealed by other surveys.

These have been quite numerous. Some were commissioned by the regional councils (the *Conseils régionaux*) and most were carried out by the now defunct *Institut Médiapluriel Méditerranée*, based near Montpellier. These surveys tend to be very sophisticated, since they distinguish between competence, use and transmission of the language. They also examine attitudes and representations of the language, which includes headings such as naming the language, desire to learn the language, the number of people interested in its use in the media, opinions as to whether its use is seen as increasing or decreasing, and degree of attachment to the language, or mere tolerance of it (see Coyos 2004 for more detail).

One survey was commissioned in 1994 by the *Conseil régional des Pyrénées-Atlantiques*; another, in 1997, was commissioned by the *Conseil régional d'Aquitaine* on the use and image of Occitan in the region, while, in 1998, the Languedoc-Roussillon Region commissioned the same. But there is no overall picture of Occitan today since each Conseil régional has its own agenda. Thus Occitan does not appear to be a subject of great interest for the PACA region (Provence–Alpes–Côte d'Azur), since no equivalent study has been carried out for this region, nor for other areas where Occitan is spoken.

Sibille (2000: 38–9) has attempted the following summary of results. In the Languedoc-Roussillon region 34 per cent of interviewees stated they could understand Occitan, of which 20 per cent could understand it easily, and 19 per cent stated they could speak the language, but of these only 7 per cent stated 'with ease' (i.e. fluently). He points out the great differences existing between rural and urbanised areas, the rural areas being linguistically more conservative. Thus in the Lozère 63 per cent could understand it (as against an average of 34 per cent) and 48 per cent could speak it (as against an average of 19 per cent); in the Hérault the figures were 25 per cent for comprehension and 14 per cent for expression. In Aquitaine the average figure for comprehension was roughly similar at 35 per cent. The figures for expression were identical. Adding these results to other smaller surveys and studies leads Sibille to evaluate the number of speakers at 2–3 million, out of a total population of 14–15 million. But most of these are over the age of 50. Therein lies the problem.

As far as transmission is concerned, the results of the INSEE-INED *Enquête famille* study are very sombre since they show that in 1999 only 610 000 persons had heard Occitan regularly during their childhood, and only 1 060 000 heard it used occasionally. According to this report, there could be no more than 526 000 speakers left. This is a very worrying number given the 10 million estimated in 1920. Transmission is only just above the 10 per cent mark, which places it in the 'moribund' category, except that major efforts are being made to revive it, the first being the creation of the *Calandretas*, immersion schools, around which other associations were created to help save both the language and its culture. The first such school appeared in the Bordeaux Academy in 1982. Then, in 1990, the rector of the Toulouse Academy signed an agreement with F. Bayrou, the then Minister for Education, on promoting the teaching of Occitan.

In 2005 there were 31 *Calandretas*. It is still the language most taught, after Alsatian/German (which constitutes a special case), since 72 592 pupils followed Occitan-Langue d'oc classes during the academic year 2003–4. (For more details see Chapter 5.)

The serious plight of the language does not prevent the region having a strong identity and regional aspirations. It sees itself as *le Midi*, and in opposition with *le Nord*, which corresponds roughly to the *langues d'oïl* area, but there are major cultural differences between the south west and the south east. Moreover, whereas a cultural movement developed in the south west in the 1970s, there was no such movement in the south east. Although this movement was at first small, it was very vocal, and touched a nerve among many people and a new interest in the old *patois* developed as a result. They came to be proud of and to take an interest in the reminders of a great past and an affirmation of local identity. This change in attitude led to an increased visibility of Occitan in the Languedoc-Roussillon area, in the shape of bilingual road signs, and the appearance of an extremely popular slogan: *Volem viure al pais* ('we want to live in our country' or 'our area'). This, in turn, acted as a motor for a revival of interest in Occitan in other areas.

The result is that Occitan is now taught both in the private and state systems of education. It is still by far the most important RL in France, both geographically and in terms of numbers. Unfortunately this does not prevent Occitan from being an endangered language.

## The *langues d'oïl*

French developed out of the *langue d'oïl* before it split to give other languages, which saw themselves, as a result, deprived of an autonomous existence. It is not so much that their literary masterpieces, particularly important during the medieval period, are ignored,[14] they are simply included under the label 'Old French'. Thus the *Séquence de Sainte Eulalie*, which dates back to the end of the ninth century, is considered to be the oldest known 'French' literary text, despite containing many Proto-Picard characteristics. So do many other literary texts, such as those of Jean Bodel from Arras, in the thirteenth century, or Froissart, who was from Valenciennes, in the fourteenth century. And the eleventh-century masterpiece, the *Chanson de Roland*, was written in Anglo-Norman, which, according to the editor of a relatively recent edition 'should not lead to prejudice' (Moignet 1969: 10) which implies that the inclusion of local traits should not be seen as an obstacle to the contemporary student of medieval French, since many of the local 'dialects' helped to shape the French language. In other words, although these texts are regionally marked, there was originally no very wide gulf between the various speech areas of northern France.

On the other hand, it seems that by the end of the twelfth century, the language of the Ile-de-France had acquired more prestige than the others, the Ile-de-France being a seat of power and Paris at an important crossroads, and was therefore seen as the desirable norm. Hence Chrétien de Troyes, who was Champenois, wrote in a language which contained very few local traits. This is why Rickard (1974) wrote about the use, in medieval literature, of *Francien*[15] coloured by Picard. Rickard also stated that once Normandy became French in 1204, Norman texts tended to approximate the language of Paris, and that the dialect of Champagne had never differed very much in its written form. As for Picard, he reckoned that many Picard spellings and forms were acceptable alternatives to the written language of Paris. He accepted, however, that vernacular documents tended to contain more pronounced local traits, since they were written for local consumption, but he maintained that even so a strong common element with French was always present. It must be noted, however, that although this seems a reasonable account of what happened, the term *Francien*, coined during the nineteenth century, is no longer considered acceptable, since no proof has emerged so far of the existence of a fully-fledged Francien dialect. There was simply a language, the *langue d'oïl*, marked in different areas by a number of traits.

This does not take into account, however, of the fact that in everyday oral communication and less elevated cultural contexts, varieties of speech continued to develop in their own distinctive ways. The end result is the emergence of a group of languages which have had a development similar to – and yet different from – French.[16] They have sometimes been termed 'sister' languages of French (Dawson (2002: 86) goes so far as to refer to 'Siamese sisters'), or, more recently, 'collateral' languages (Eloy 2004). At the same time, because they are so close to French and because of the prestige of the latter, there has been much interference and language mixing, which has led to them being denied all right to an independent status. This is particularly true from the sixteenth century onwards when the medieval literary tradition fell into decline.

Hence until very recently these languages have been considered either as incorrect French or as *patois*, i.e. of interest only to dialectologists. The 1765 *Encyclopédie* gives a suitably damning definition of *patois*: 'Corrupted language as spoken in the provinces: each has its own *patois* [a list of *patois* follows including Bourguignon, Norman, Champenois, Gascon and Provençal]. The language [i.e. French] is only spoken in the capital' (quoted in Cerquiglini 2003: 138). With such a definition, it is not surprising their speakers had a poor opinion of their language, and that by the Revolution, according to Grégoire's survey, many were keen to give them up. The only ones who did not were the peasants, which further associated these languages with low social mobility and expectations.

Even today many French people think of these languages as varieties of French, in which case it should not be difficult to understand these various forms of speech. Yet this is not so: the present author finds it very difficult to understand shows in Picard, for example. Certain words can be picked up here and there (as when listening to most related languages), but the precise meaning of what is said remains inaccessible to the person uninitiated into the language. The same applies to written Picard. These forms of speech are clearly languages.

The *langues d'oïl* were not recognised by the 1951 Deixonne law and their fight for recognition only dates from the 1970s. The first important step taken in their favour was in 1982 when they were included in the Savary memorandum (*circulaire*) on the use of minority languages in schools, in the sense that the RLs are treated globally, rather than listed separately. Then, in an *Arrêté* in 1983[17] on the recruitment of primary school teachers the term 'regional language' was replaced by 'languages and dialects corresponding to a delimitated area' (*langues et dialectes à extension régionale limitée*) in order to accommodate languages such as Gallo, Norman, Picard and Poitevin, which were actually listed. This led Killilea, in 1994, to state[18] that French governments had been more sympathetic to them than previously, when their existence was simply denied.

This period of expansion in terms of recognition was also marked by the foundation in 1982 of the association *Défense et promotion des langues d'oïl* (DPLO). In 1986 a representative of these languages was appointed to the National Council for Regional Languages and Cultures. They were recognised by the European Bureau for Lesser Used Languages (EBLUL) in 1992, and in 1993 Gallo was added to the list of languages which could be taken as an option for the *Baccalauréat*[19] as from 1995. The *langues d'oïl* were finally recognised officially in 1999 by the Cerquiglini report, which was drawn up in readiness for the ratification of the European Charter for Regional or Minority Languages (signed in 1999 but not ratified to date, see Chapter 5).

They now constitute the newest arrivals on the glottopolitical scene, but there is hardly any official teaching of these languages, apart from Gallo, which is taught within the state system (there are no immersion schools for any of the *langues d'oïl*). There is, in particular, still no official teaching of Picard in France, despite having been recognised by decree in Belgium, along with Walloon, nor of any of the other *langues d'oïl*. A possible reason for the Gallo exception is that it is spoken in Brittany, where language is a major issue (see below).

Delimitating the languages included under this label presents the usual problems. It tends to be done using either linguistic criteria such as isoglosses, or a combination of geographical, historical and political criteria. The danger is both in seeing too many different 'languages' (which leads to destructive fragmentation) or too few, which can eliminate distinctions felt to be important to the speakers. The usual languages listed are: Bourguignon, Champenois, Franc-Comtois, Gallo (spoken in the Romance-speaking part of Brittany), Lorrain, Norman, Picard, Poitevin-Saintongeais, and Walloon (but mainly spoken in Belgium). The 1999 Cerquiglini report lists Bourguignon-Morvandiau, Franc-Comtois, Gallo, Lorrain, Norman, Poitevin-Saintongeais and

Walloon. Champenois was added in 2002. There are, however, major differences in the vitality between them.

The DPLO is made up of all the militant associations which either publish in the *oïl* languages, or teach them. It includes representatives from Champenois, Gallo, Norman, Picard, Poitevin-Saintongeais, and also Morvandiau, but none for Franc-Comtois, Lorrain or Bourguignon.

Another classification recognises five main linguistic zones: (i) the zone including Picard, Walloon, Lorrain, Norman and Champenois;[20] (ii) the Burgundian zone including Burgundian (*bourguignon*) and Franc-Comtois; (iii) the Ile-de-France and areas bordering it which accounts, apart from French, for the Orléanais, the speech used in Touraine, Berry, Bourbonnais and the western part of the Champagne region; (iv) the Armorican zone including Gallo and southern Norman; and (v) the Poitevin-Saintongeais zone (see Sibille 2000).

Research is still much needed in this area to assess which of the RLs still exist and ways of delimitating them. The kind of approach most suited to the problem is illustrated by M. Auzanneau's study of Poitevin-Saintongeais. She points out that the forms of speech used in the area correspond to a continuum – French–Poitevin–Saintongeais – which goes from a relatively neutral French (V0) to a form using maximum number of Poitevin characteritics, termed V4. The cline which goes from V1 to V3 denotes different degrees of 'Poitevin-ness'[21] in increasing order. This enables her to set up a hierarchy of grammatical and lexical characteristics which either have been so strong as to survive into V1, or so weak as to only figure in V4[22] (Auzanneau 1995: 35–63). This is not unlike the classic continuum set up by F. Carton which goes from Standard Language to local *patois*, with forms in which either dominates in between (Carton 1981: 15–28).

Determining the number of speakers for these languages is difficult linguistically since isoglosses can only give clear answers where there are clear bundles, which is not always the case. Hence maps show these boundaries in dotted rather than full lines. Another major problem is due to the fact that these RLs function on a continuum going from regional French, i.e. French coloured by the local RL characteristics, to full-blown separate RLs. Those interviewed can hardly be expected to give answers which are consistent with one another, since their answers will depend on where they place themselves subjectively on this continuum.

Bearing this in mind, the most up-to-date and reliable source of information is the *Enquête famille*. It established the unexpectedly high figure of 204 000 speakers, with a transmission rate slightly above that for

Occitan at around 28 per cent. The highest figures are for Picard, with an average of 29.9 per cent, or 1 265 000 speakers.

The reason why such large numbers of speakers have been ignored in the past is because of their status as 'dialects' of French. But whether they are considered to be 'dialects' (i.e. politically not important) or 'languages' (i.e. worth fighting for), these languages present an educational problem in so far as they have infiltrated standard French. This has led to some of the poorest results in French for the *Baccalauréat*. This is why there are people who favour teaching the *langues d'oïl* to help children distinguish between them and French. This represents the minimalist approach to the teaching of these languages. But there are also those who equate language and culture and who would like the *langues d'oïl* to be taught for their own sake, since transmission is no longer automatically happening at the intergenerational level. This could be termed a maximalist approach. But whatever the reason for teaching them, the problem of orthography still has to be solved.

Codification of the *langues d'oïl* presents the usual problem of deciding whether to use a unified orthography in which a single grapheme may correspond to different realisations depending on the variety of language spoken, or one more closely linked with the pronunciation of a particular variant, using French orthographic conventions as a basis. The former is more difficult since it has to be learned, but it allows for a broad readership. The latter makes for ease, but is possibly dangerous since it makes the *langues d'oïl* look too much like French, which has led many writers to add various signs, such as apostrophes and diacritics, to counterbalance the problem. Another drawback is that a system which emphasises local diversity, limits the field of readers. Between these two poles, numerous other personal systems have been developed.

Dawson (2002), a Picard specialist, has pointed out, however, that highlighting the difference between the many systems in existence disguises the many points they have in common. He argues that these languages, not being 'big' languages, do not need intense codification, their lack of uniformity being part of their charm. For him such languages should remain polynomic and polygraphic. But a minimum of consensus is required for their teaching to be possible. It seems that the Feller–Carton system (Feller being Walloon and Carton Picard) provides a reasonable compromise, with its use of the French system for transcribing sounds, and a representation of morphological factors which has been simplified (see Dawson 2002 and Carton 2004 for further details).

The *langues d'oïl* are associated with regional identities, which unfortunately do not always correspond with the new administrative regions.

There is one case in which a *langue d'oïl* actually links up with an identity problem: Gallo, spoken in the Haute Bretagne. Gallo is the most recent form of speech to have been recognised as a language. Although this recognition is still limited mainly to its militants and linguists, Gallo is now taught in some schools (see figures in Chapter 5).

The problem in Brittany is that there is not one but two RLs, only one of which, Breton, equates easily with Breton identity. Indeed the term 'Gallo' was traditionally used unflatteringly by Breton speakers in the Basse Bretagne to refer to the non-Breton speakers of Haute Bretagne, seen as responsible for the advance of French into their territory and the corresponding decline of Breton. As for the users of Gallo themselves, they refer to their language as a *patois* or even 'deformed French'.

This creates a problem for Gallo speakers, estimated by the *Enquête famille* to number around 28 300. They may adopt one of three possible positions. Either they become ardent *néo-Bretonnants*, which many have done (the centre for the revival of Breton is Rennes, where Breton had not been spoken since the ninth century). Or they may reject their Breton identity in favour of a French one, which could allow Gallo to play a part. A third position is a Breton identity without reference to the Breton language, but only to Breton culture. This last solution is very popular as may be seen from the enormous success of Breton Celtic festivals. (See Manzano 1996 and Nolan 2006 for a study of Gallo.)

The clash between the first and second position happens when Breton nationalists try to reclaim areas lost since the end of the ninth century, when Breton was spoken most extensively (it was spoken along the coast all the way to Pornic, in Nantes where whole districts spoke Breton, Rennes, St-Malo etc.). Hence bilingual signs appear in these regions, and particularly in Nantes, a development not always welcomed by the non-Breton speaking locals who have their own militants to counterbalance such claims (see Blanchet in Manzano 1996).

## Concluding comments

Breton has risen from the ashes thanks to the use of Breton in education, a move inspired by the Basque example. This education has now spread from the private sector (the *Diwan* schools) to the state system, and the problem of deciding what constitutes Breton now seems on the way to being resolved.

Occitan is the most spoken RL and in the largest area, but it has a low density of speakers. Moreover, a number of disagreements between the various adherents of specific varieties weakened its position in the past, but matters have greatly improved in recent years on that score. Its main strength is that it can boast a literature with an international reputation. It is also relatively easy to learn when starting from French, like all the Romance languages, compared with Breton or Basque.

Corsican has been protected by being spoken on an island. However, poor employment prospects have meant that most Corsicans of working age have had to seek work on the continent, which constitutes a severe threat to both language and culture. On the other hand, an original approach from the start to spelling and regional variation removed one common obstacle to the development of the RL. But it was intense political activity – including violence or at least the threat of violence – on the part of the Corsican militants which led to Corsican being taught in the state system at all levels, thus making it the RL best protected by the state. In other words, the Corsicans have achieved what the other RLs are still aiming for.

Franco-Provençal, although still spoken, is the weakest of the French RLs, since it has few speakers, few militants and the lowest rate of intergenerational transmission. Nor does it figure in the educational system or the media. Sadly, it seems to have reached the 'moribund' state. This is no doubt due in part, on the French side, to its main urban centre, Lyon, not having adopted it when Latin fell into decline.

The *langues d'oïl*, on the other hand, have just entered the glottopolitical scene. Among these, only Gallo is officially taught. Although Walloon and Picard benefit from having been officially recognised both in France and in Belgium, everything is still to be done for their revival to have a chance of success. Their official recognition in France represents nonetheless a remarkable change of fortune for languages which were, until very recently, seen as no more than dialects of French.

In other words most of the RLs are fighting back and, as a result, institutional changes have taken place, which are acting in their favour. These are the subject of Chapter 5.

# 5
# Revitalising the Regional Languages of France

Although in decline for years, the RLs have refused to go away, and there is now some state recognition in the shape of teaching subsidies, some presence in the media and cultural events, and also some important institutional innovations. There are a number of reasons for this change of heart. The Algerian war and decolonisation in the late 1950s and early 1960s gave rise to the idea that the French regions had also been the victims of 'colonisation' and that what the French state had rejected, namely their language and culture, was no longer to be despised but admired and saved. This was, at least, the view of the strongest political RL militants.

Then, in 1968, it was the political, social, and economic domination of Paris which was questioned. This led to a beginning of decentralisation, with the creation of the 'regions' in 1982. This move to decentralisation was further accentuated in the 1980s when new European economic regions emerged, since they ignored national frontiers. One such region is the trading triangle linking Toulouse–Montpellier–Barcelona, with Perpignan in the middle: this was to have important consequences for Occitan and Catalan, which work closely together. In addition, the new political emphasis on Brussels and Strasbourg further emphasised the importance of the regions, in contrast with the tradition of centralisation. Hence there is now hope on the part of the RL militants, and also a wider sympathetic public, that something could still be done to stop their disappearance. This chapter examines what has been achieved so far.

The first section assesses the problems and factors involved, including the levels of RL transmission, when trying to revitalise the RLs. These may differ from language to language. The rest of the chapter deals with efforts made in recent years to help them survive. Any account of the legal and institutional changes that have taken place has to start with the 1951 Deixonne law, since it was the first law to allow the RLs into the classroom. Others followed with equally important consequences (section two). These have been mainly in the field of education, particularly private education, with the state feeling it had to follow suit (section three). The same applies to the media (section four). This, in turn, coincided with a general move towards administrative decentralisation, which now allows for the expression of a certain amount of regionalism, or pluralism (section five). The state even went as far as signing the European Charter for Regional or Minority Languages, but various Jacobin forces came into play at this point which stopped it being ratified. But the very fact of signing did imply some recognition on the part of the state (section six). How far these efforts at revitalising the RLs are likely to be successful is discussed in the concluding comments.

## Relevant facts and figures

It is interesting to note how geographically stable the RLs have been throughout the centuries. It is true that Basque and Breton have receded from a territorial point of view and that Poitevin-Saintongeais has shifted from being a *langue d'oc* to becoming a *langue d'oïl*. But on the whole there has been remarkable stability through the ages.

Linguistic areas rarely coincide with political borders, and as a result a number of RLs straddle the borders. Where they have official status in the other country, as is the case for Basque and Catalan, they may be strengthened by the knowledge that at least they will not completely disappear from the linguistic map. From a practical point of view, they benefit from the publication of materials in the RL, particularly educational, access to the media, and contact with a language used for all functions. This may not always be the case, however, if the official language 'next door' is closely related but different from the RL in question, which runs the risk of being absorbed by its more prestigious neighbour. This is clearly the case for Western Flemish, Alsatian, and possibly Mosellan, which have resisted better for complex historical reasons, but are now in decline, while German is on the increase, which means they are now in a very ambiguous position.

Few of the surviving RLs are completely devoid of links with corresponding languages beyond their frontiers, although they may not have official status: Occitan has links with areas of Spain and Italy and affinities with Catalonia. Franco-Provençal is spoken in Switzerland and Italy, and one of the *langues d'oïl*, Picard, in Belgium. Breton has links with Cornish, and a little more distantly with Welsh, and generally the broader Celtic group. Such links strengthen the RLs in question and help to establish beneficial social links across borders. They need to be taken into account when planning their revitalisation. (Corsican clearly has linguistic links with Italian, but tends on the whole to be in denial on this matter. It may be assumed, however, that the language benefits nonetheless from these links.)

RL militancy became associated, in most cases, with regionalist movements at a time when national decentralisation became the order of the day, i.e. from the 1960s onwards. Clearly decentralisation should help, at least in the long term, since elected regional bodies have to take into account the wishes of their electorate (see below). This depends, of course, on the electorate being committed to the RLs. Certainly more people today than ever before seem to think that speaking a minority language is no longer incompatible with being French. The question is whether this change of heart has come too late, and what can and should be done. This in turn depends on the role to be attributed to the RLs within the French context. There are no clear answers so far on this fundamental question, nor a convergence of views.

The importance of the RLs to the identity of those who live in the area where the RLs are spoken varies greatly. There is a cline which goes from those for whom the RL is fundamental to their identity, to those for whom other cultural markers are more important, while others reject the very concept of regional identity in favour of simply being 'French'. For them, the RLs symbolise the past and have become irrelevant in the new context of the EU. They therefore prefer their children to learn a 'useful' language, such as English, rather than a RL. Bearing in mind that their parents' generation was told that speaking a RL was something to be ashamed of, it is hardly surprising that the levels of intergenerational transmission should be extremely low, as may be seen from the results of the *Enquête famille*. Revitalising the RLs promises, therefore, to be an uphill struggle on both these counts.

The results shown in Figure 1 show the alarming drop in the number of children who heard their parents speaking a RL in the course of the twentieth century. Figure 2 shows the number of adults who have *not* transmitted their RL to their children (e.g. 90 per cent did not transmit Franco-Provençal, i.e. transmission was only of the order of 10 per cent). It is symptomatic that of all the languages other than French transmitted within the context of the family, it is English which comes out on top.

Figure 3 shows the situation in greater detail, differentiating, as in Figure 1, between 'habitual' as against 'occasional use' of the language

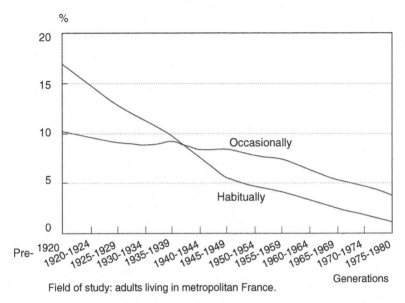

Field of study: adults living in metropolitan France.

*Figure 1* Proportion of adults whose parents spoke to them in a RL either habitually or occasionally (adapted from *Enquête Famille 1999*, INSEE).

by one or both parents of the respondents. (It must be noted, however, that the questionnaire did not use the term 'occasional' but 'et aussi', i.e. 'and also' or 'additionally', which was interpreted by the researchers as implying 'occasional', an assumption which may or may not be justified, depending on each case.) The third column, which deals with transmission to the next generation, again distinguishes between cases where only one or both parents have transmitted the language.

Clearly all the RLs in France are endangered languages, Franco-Provençal being the most at risk. Occitan and Breton are also very much at risk, despite having survived nearly intact into the twentieth century, both in their written and spoken form. Catalan and Basque, being official languages in Spain, do not come into the same category. Nor do Alsatian, Mosellan or Western Flemish because of their ambiguous relationship with German and Dutch respectively. Finally, one of the most surprising factors thrown into light by this survey was the unsuspected importance in terms of both numbers and transmission of the *langues d'oïl*, which appear in Figure 3 in third position.

These figures do not, however, tell the whole story. Basque, for example, shows up very badly in Figure 3, and yet its importance as a leader in the

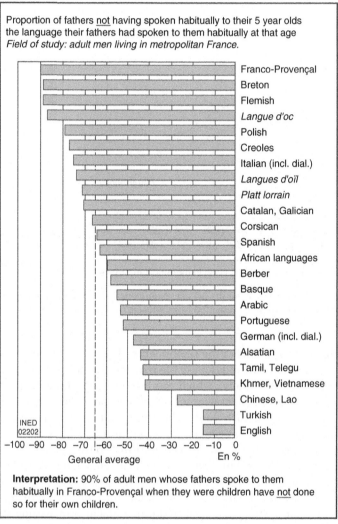

Proportion of fathers <u>not</u> having spoken habitually to their 5 year olds the language their fathers had spoken to them habitually at that age
*Field of study: adult men living in metropolitan France.*

**Interpretation:** 90% of adult men whose fathers spoke to them habitually in Franco-Provençal when they were children have <u>not</u> done so for their own children.

*Figure 2*  Linguistic erosion over one generation (adapted from *Enquête Famille 1999*, INSEE).

revivalist movement cannot be overstated. Moreover, although the study of natural transmission is important in showing language regression, it does not take into account institutional efforts, in the domain of the media and education, to bring the RLs back to life, or at least to stabilise their position. Important efforts are being made nowadays in this direction, although these seem to be more successful for some RLs than others.

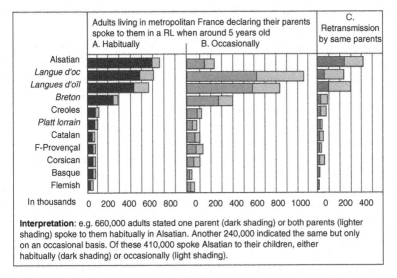

|  | Adults living in metropolitan France declaring their parents spoke to them in a RL when around 5 years old | | C. Retransmission by same parents |
|---|---|---|---|
|  | A. Habitually | B. Occasionally |  |

Alsatian
*Langue d'oc*
*Langues d'oïl*
*Breton*
Creoles
*Platt lorrain*
Catalan
F-Provençal
Corsican
Basque
Flemish

In thousands  0  200  400  600  800    0  200  400  600  800  1000    0  200  400

**Interpretation:** e.g. 660,000 adults stated one parent (dark shading) or both parents (lighter shading) spoke to them habitually in Alsatian. Another 240,000 indicated the same but only on an occasional basis. Of these 410,000 spoke Alsatian to their children, either habitually (dark shading) or occasionally (light shading).

*Figure 3* RLs transmitted in childhood and retransmitted to the next generation (adapted from *Enquête Famille 1999*, INSEE).

## The Deixonne law and other milestones in RL education

The Deixonne law (loi no. 51–46 du 11 janvier 1951) was the first law to allow the RLs into the classroom. It was voted nearly unanimously by the *Assemblée nationale*, probably because its main aim appeared to be to help teachers cope with linguistic interference between the RLs and French in the classroom. (It was also said to be a reward for some of those who had fought in the Resistance movement during World War Two.) Article 2 of the law allows 'teachers to use local forms of speech in primary school and in kindergarten each time this could be useful in the context of their teaching, in particular of the French language'. Moreover, the law only allowed for one hour of language teaching per week and one hour devoted to the local culture and literature, and this only as an option. Teachers in teacher training colleges (*écoles normales*) were to be trained to give such classes, but only 'whenever possible'.

One of the first problems encountered when drawing up the Deixonne law was how to name the various RLs (the term 'Regional

Language' being recent). The law uses different terms depending on the context. When referring to them generally it uses the expression 'l'enseignement des langues et dialectes locaux' (i.e. the teaching of local dialects and languages). It refers more specifically to *parlers locaux*, i.e. local speech, in the context of the teaching of the RLs at nursery school and primary level (this was to counterbalance the Falloux law of 1851 which stated that all teaching must be in French). *Langue locale*, i.e. 'local language', is used to refer to the teaching of RLs beyond the *Baccalauréat* level, i.e. at university. Another problem was which languages the law would apply to. The answer, in 1951, was only Basque, Breton, Catalan and Occitan.

The law itself was unclear in many respects. It did not, for example, define what was meant when referring to 'language', 'literature', 'folklore' and 'local art forms'. Nor did it define its ultimate aims. Finally, everything in the law was optional. In practice it simply gave permission to those committed to the RLs to teach them, as long as nobody in authority objected. Not surprisingly it adopted a non-legalistic turn of phrase, which has been commented upon since. Thus, stating that the 'pedagogical instructions will be sent to the rectors to authorise teachers to have recourse to local speech' has not got the same weight as 'teachers are allowed to have recourse to the local speech' (see Hammel 1996: 37).

Originally the law had been intended to be more robust. More particularly, it had been planned that the RLs would be taught as optional subjects not only in the primary sector but also at secondary and university level. This was because the law was watered down by the *Conseil de la République* (the second Chamber under the Fourth Republic) and the *recteurs d'académies* (France is divided from an educational point of view into *académies*, i.e. 'regions', each with a 'rector'). Moreover, lack of enthusiasm and the dragging of feet on the part of the educational bodies involved led to delays in the implementation of the law. Even when it was implemented, not all parents got satisfaction in their demand for their children to be taught the local RL, hence the existence of a body of litigation between academies and dissatisfied parents (there is another body of litigation of a different nature concerning refusal to deliver letters addressed in the local RL, Breton in particular; see Pontier 1997: 42).

Nonetheless, the Deixonne law marked the first positive move in favour of the RLs. Although at first it only covered Basque, Breton, Catalan and Occitan, others were gradually added during the course of the following thirty years. Alsatian was added in the form of German in 1952 (see section three below) and Corsican in 1974. Then an *arrêté* of 8 June 1983[1] on the organisation of examinations to be passed to qualify as a primary school teacher gave a much longer list: German (in the Nancy-Metz and Strasbourg academies); Basque (Bordeaux academy); Breton (Nantes and Rennes academies); Corsican (academy of Corsica); Flemish (Lille academy); Gallo (Rennes academy); *langue d'oc* (in the academies of Aix-Marseille, Bordeaux, Clermont-Ferrand, Grenoble, Limoges, Montpellier, Nice and Toulouse); Norman (academies of Caen and Rouen); Picard (academies of Amiens and Lille); and Poitevin (academies of Limoges and Poitiers). Creoles are also accepted, not only in the *départements d'Outre Mer*[2] but also in the academy of Aix-Marseille.

Other languages were added in the context of subsequent decisions in terms of languages which could be taken for the *Baccalauréat*. Thus the *langues régionales d'Alsace* and *langues régionales des pays mosellans* were added in 1993 to be applied in 1995 (*arrêté* of 15 September 1993) (Mosellan had already been integrated into secondary education by a previous *arrêté* in 1991). In other words, different RLs and languages were added bit by bit, in the context of a multitude of decrees and *arrêtés* (Eysseric 2005). Many of the texts do not actually list the RLs covered, which means that all now stand a chance of being included.

The next milestone after the Deixonne law was the *loi Haby* (75–620, 11 July 1975), since it allowed for the optional teaching of RLs at all levels, i.e. primary, secondary and tertiary, on the condition that there was a demand. This constituted more or less a revolution within the context of the Ministry of Education, although in practice a 'demand' was not automatically followed by a positive response. This led in 1981 to some RLs becoming for the first time eligible subjects for the CAPES (*Certificat d'aptitude à l'enseignement secondaire*), the main secondary school teaching qualification. These RLs include Basque, Breton, Catalan, Corsican and Occitan. Unlike other academic subjects, they cannot at present be taken as a single subject for the CAPES, but only in combination with another. The only exception is Corsican, which may be taken as a single subject, which makes Corsican a special case. Alsatian comes under the CAPES for standard German, with the 'dialect' as a possible option. The latter does not contribute to the candidate's success or failure, but the qualification obtained includes the mention 'Alsatian', which enables the candidate to teach optionally in this language (*arrêté*, 24 August 1993). Similarly, Western Flemish comes under the CAPES for Dutch, but with no special option in the RL.

Matters are therefore extremely complicated, and have to be examined language by language. In this context, the French have adopted the kind of piecemeal approach usually associated with British linguistic policies.

The 1982 and 1983 *circulaires Savary* constitute the third milestone. The 1982 Memorandum (*Circulaire* 82–52) stated three important principles. The first was that the state declared itself committed to the RLs and their cultures. The second was that the teaching of the RLs and their cultures should be given a proper place in the educational system and in particular in the national curriculum. The third was that such teaching should be optional both on the part of teachers and pupils. The 83–547 memorandum of 30 December 1983 suggested experimenting with a bilingual French–RL education system, called *système paritaire* (see section three below).

Another sign of progress for the RLs in the secondary system was their elevation from being merely optional subjects, adding points to the *Baccalauréat*, to being classified first as a third 'modern language' and then as a second 'modern language', thus giving them the same status as foreign languages.

Finally, decree no. 2001–733 of 31 July 2001 created an academic council for the RLs, the *Conseil académique des langues régionales*, to promote the teaching of RLs and their cultures and to advise rectors of educational academies including one or more RLs (Aquitaine includes both Basque and Occitan). It is mainly a consultative body, although it is also involved in the development of pedagogical materials. Its efforts seem unequally divided among the various RLs, since nothing, so far, has been done for Picard, for example.

Most of the legislation in favour of the RLs accumulated since 1951 has been regrouped in the new *Code de l'éducation* and the new *Code rural* (which affects agricultural secondary schools) which became law in 2005.[3] An *arrêté*[4] was added in May 2005 allowing all candidates to take an optional oral examination as part of their examinations, without having followed a course on the subject.

So far, these codes only refer to the RLs being 'authorised' to be taught, with the one exception of Corsican, which is taught within the school timetable in all nursery and primary schools. The new code is quite explicit on this point since it states that 'regional languages and their culture *may be taught* at all educational levels according to the modalities defined by agreement between the State and the local authorities' ('un enseignement de langue et culture régionales *peut* être dispensé tout au long de la scolarité selon les modalités définies par voie de convention entre l'État et les collectivités territoriales où les langues sont en usage' (article L312–10)). The main problem has been that, in practice, what happened depended on the good will – or otherwise – of the local *recteurs d'académies*, to which must be added the negative effect of the new article 2 of the Constitution (see Chapter 1), frequently quoted in opposition to the ambitions of the RL militants. This has led to some desperate actions: Yannig Baron went on hunger strike in 1998 to obtain two and a half Breton teaching posts, and in 2001 the president of the Catholic association *Dihun Breizh*, also went on hunger strike for the same reason.

There has been, however, a significant shift towards a more tolerant and flexible approach to language since, previous to 1951, any mention of a RL within the classroom was illegal and could lead to the teacher being sacked. Many consider that this change is still not sufficient to ensure the RLs' revival, given their very endangered status. Those who oppose the RLs see them as a threat to the unity of the state. As a result, politicians are torn between allowing the RLs to progress (see the 1975 Haby law and the 1982 and 1983 Savary memoranda) and keeping them out (see the legal cases against the integration of the *Diwan* schools into the state system, see below). Progress in this context has, so far, been linked with the Socialists being in power, whereas the Jacobins (who belong mainly to the right but also include members from the left) – particularly in the shape of the *Conseil d'Etat* and the *Conseil Constitutionnel* – constantly aim at limiting the success of their efforts. Many in government also tend to play a game of hide and seek, partly no doubt because the electorate is also divided on the subject.

Certainly the last forty years have been full of electoral promises in respect of the RLs, of which only a few have been honoured. There have also been over fifty pieces of proposed legislation in their favour, which have never even been debated in parliament. It has therefore been left largely to individuals to fight for their survival. This is true particularly in the field of education and the media (see below), where the state has grudgingly followed in their footsteps. But the very fact that it has done so is encouraging in itself.

## The development of RLs in the private and public sectors

'Immersion schools' symbolise the RLs' great fightback. They were the Trojan horse which first introduced RLs into the educational system in a meaningful way. They are private schools, set up by parents, in which the RL is solely used in kindergarten and to a slightly lesser extent at primary level, when French is gradually introduced. The aim is for the children to be perfectly bilingual by the end of primary school. They were founded using a loophole in the 1901 Law on Associations.

The first immersion schools were Basque and called *Ikastolak* ('schools' in Basque). There are now a number of *Ikastolak* which form a federation called SEASKA (meaning 'cradle'). The first school was a kindergarten which opened in 1969; the first primary school opened in 1975, the first *collège*[5] in 1980 and the first *lycée* in 1984. By 2003, the SEASKA schools included 2678 pupils, of whom 2064 were in kindergarten and primary education, 464 were following courses in eight *collèges* and 150 in a *lycée*. Thirty-eight educational establishments were therefore involved.

In 1976, a Catalan immersion kindergarten was founded in Perpignan, by the *La Bressola* ('cradle') association. A primary school followed in 1981, at Arrels (founded by the Arrels association), and further primary schools in 1983 founded by *La Bressola*. By 2003 the *Bressolas* had 430 pupils in ten kindergartens and primary schools.

In 1977, the *Diwan* association (meaning 'young shoot') founded the first Breton immersion kindergarten. The *Diwan* schools were the most successful from the start. The kindergarten was followed in 1980 by a primary school, in 1988 by a first *collège* and in 1994 a first *lycée*. In 2003, the *Diwan* association was responsible for the education of 2760 pupils, of whom 2033 were in thirty-one kindergartens and primary schools, 564 in six *collèges* and 163 in a *lycée*.

In 1979, the *Calandreta* association (meaning both 'lark' and 'apprentice') opened its first schools in Pau and Béziers. By 2001, the *Calandretas* were responsible for 1069 pupils in twenty-two kindergartens and primary schools and 72 pupils in a *collège*. One of the distinguishing features of the *Calandretas* is the effort put into training its teachers. This led to the opening in 1994 of a *Centre de Formation Pédagogique Calandreta* in Béziers.

Finally, a small associative movement was formed in Alsace in 1990 at the instigation of Richard Weiss. It is called the ABCM[6] – Zweisprachigkeit association. The schools do not follow the principle of full immersion, but are bilingual. Three bilingual kindergarten classes were opened in 1991. Although at first the languages used were German and French in equal proportions, in 1996 it was decided to increase the German element by 10 per cent to take account of the local dialect where it exists. By 2003, ABCM had 524 pupils distributed among eleven kindergartens and primary schools. The results are represented in Table 2, adapted from the *Rapport au Parlement sur l'emploi de la langue française 2005*, itself based on the DESCO survey of March 2004.

In 1983, the success encountered by SEASKA and its *Ikastolak* led the then Minister for Education, A. Savary, to introduce bilingual French–RL

Table 2 Immersion schools run by the associative movement 2003–2004

| | Schools* | | Collèges | | Lycées | | Total | |
|---|---|---|---|---|---|---|---|---|
| | Pupils | Establishments | Numbers | Establishments | Numbers | Establishments | Numbers | Establishments |
| Diwan | 2033 | 31 | 564 | 6 | 163 | 1 | 2760 | 38 |
| SEASKA | 2064 | 29 | 464 | 8 | 150 | 1 | 2678 | 38 |
| Calandretas | 997 | 22 | 72 | 1 | | | 1069 | 23 |
| Bressolas | 430 | 10 | | | | | 430 | 10 |
| ABCM | 524 | 11 | | | | | 524 | 11 |
| Total | 6048 | 103 | 1100 | 15 | 313 | 2 | 7461 | 120 |

* 'Schools' refers to both kindergarten and primary education

classes.[7] The system put in place was a *système paritaire*, which means that the same number of hours must be spent teaching in each language.

The first bilingual school to be set up by the state was for Basque in 1983. Each class was to have two teachers, one per language, whereas in the immersion system there is normally only one. A slight advantage was given to French in these schools: teaching in Basque only starting in the second year of kindergarten. Learning to read is also first in French and then in the RL. An association was created, *Ikas–Bis* (meaning 'to learn two', i.e. languages), to promote bilingual teaching in the state system. The same model was adopted for Breton, also in 1983, for Catalan in 1993 and for Occitan in 1999, albeit with some minor alterations: the principle of having two teachers was dropped for Breton in favour of bilingual teachers, and for Catalan RL teaching starts in the first class of kindergarten.

Alsatian constitutes a special case within the system. As mentioned previously, it was excluded from the Deixonne law, but in 1952 a decree was passed setting up optional German classes in the final years of primary education in those areas where Alsatian was the normal means of communication. Then in 1972 permission was given to introduce German experimentally. This was generalised to the whole primary system in 1988. In the 1980s matters changed dramatically since 'German', in its dual form of spoken 'Alsatian' and written standard German, acquired in 1983 the status of being both a foreign language and a RL of France. Official texts drawn up in 1982 and 1988 allow for the use of 'Alsatian' proper in kindergarten and its use for the teaching of German.

From 1990, and probably inspired by the example of the ABCM, the focus moved to establishing bilingual education (13 hours in French, 13 hours in German per week). An agreement (or *convention*) was signed on 18 October 2000 between the state, the region and the *départements* of Alsace and Moselle generalising early education in the RLs (dialect and German) and its continuation in the secondary system. It has been pointed out by Botherel-Witz (in Cerquiglini 2003: 39) that demand is lowest in the most dialectophone areas. This could possibly be due to the speakers of Alsatian not equating their language with standard German.

There are also private religious schools, mainly in the Catholic sector, which have also taken on the fight to save the RLs. This is hardly surprising in areas such as the Basque country and Brittany where catechism was traditionally, and until recently, taught in the RL. Thus in Brittany, in 2001, Catholic schools accounted for 2113 bilingual pupils, of whom 2004 were in kindergartens and primary schools and 109 in secondary education. In the Basque country, there were 1450 pupils in bilingual Catholic classes, of whom 1170 were in kindergartens and primary schools, and 250 in *collèges* and 30 in a *lycée*. And in 2000, the

private religious sector in Alsace was responsible for the bilingual education of some 150 pupils (Petit 2001). The success of the bilingual
education system may be assessed from Table 3 (adapted from the one in
*Rapport au Parlement sur l'emploi de la langue française*, 2005).

The schools run by the associative movement, be it SEASKA, *Diwan*,
*Bressolas* or *Calandretas*, are mainly all free (unlike the religious private
schools), hence they face numerous financial difficulties (the *Bressolas*
are the only ones not to be completely free). Unfortunately the 1850
Falloux law does not permit local authorities to give funding beyond a
certain level, even if they wish to. This leaves the individual schools
having to raise money by whatever means they can, such as local fairs,
etc., which is hardly satisfactory. These schools are also secular, like
those in the state system. This has led to the belief, in some quarters,
that they should be integrated into the state system (others, however,
fear loss of independence and being gradually destroyed from within).

A first step was taken in this direction in 1990, under the then
Minister for Education, Jack Lang, when *La Bressola* signed an agreement
associating Bressola and the state. According to this agreement the
teachers would be paid by the state. Basque signed a similar agreement
in 1994. But in 1995, François Bayrou maintained that the agreement
was illegal, and replaced it by a new form of agreement (or *Protocole
d'Accord*) which made them 'associative schools' under the 1959 law on
associative contracts (*contrats d'association*). Such schools may have their
teachers' salaries paid for by the state, but only if they have already been
running successfully for five years. The agreement is between the state
and individual schools and not the association representing them. This

*Table 3*  Bilingual education in both the state and the private sector (including only
establishments having signed agreements with the state) for 2003–2004

|  | Schools | | Collèges | | Total | |
|---|---|---|---|---|---|---|
|  | Numbers | Estalishments | Numbers | Establishments |  |  |
| Basque | 4335 | 91 | 1253 | 18 | 5588 | 109 |
| Breton | 6286 | 134 | 535 | 26 | 6821 | 160 |
| Catalan | 968 | 23 | 139 | 3 | 1107 | 26 |
| Corsican | 2497 | 40 | 657 | 13 | 3154 | 53 |
| Occitan* | 3062 | 80 | 337 | 8 | 3399 | 88 |
| Alsatian** | 10 549 | 202 | 1005 | 70 | 11 554 | 272 |
| Mosellan*** | 68 | 3 |  | 68 | 3 |  |
| Total | 27 765 | 573 | 3926 | 138 | 31 691 | 711 |

* Occitan is labelled *Occitan-langue d'oc* in the original table
** Alsatian is labelled *Langues régionales d'Alsace*
** Mosellan is labelled *Langues régionales des pays mosellans*

*Protocole* enabled *La Bressola* to survive financially and open three new schools in four years. It also brought with it important teacher training advantages, and the right to recruit teachers in Spanish Catalonia, when none can be found in France. Basque, Breton and Occitan have all benefited from such agreements.

To summarise, the 95–086 Memorandum of 7 April 1995 which regulated the teaching of the RLs proclaimed 'the State's commitment to promoting the teaching of the RLs'. It recognised three modalities: the immersion schools, which are private and may sign an agreement of association with the state, bilingual education in both private and public establishments, and the teaching of the RLs in a special stream within the normal state system. Although bilingual schools may be either private or state, they are mostly state schools. There are also RL classes in the normal state system, but these teach the RLs for only 1–3 hours per week. The aim, in this case, is not so much to teach a language, but to create an awareness of the languages and their culture (official texts refer to 'la sensibilisation à la langue et aux cultures régionales'). They act, in other words, as a 'taster'.

Although the agreements passed between the state and the associative movement put the associative schools in the same category as other private schools, it still leaves them with considerable financial problems, since they are free, and the help they receive only covers part of their costs. As a consequence, in 2001, the *Diwan* association set in motion in 2001 a process intended to integrate their schools fully into the state system. This was done under a Socialist government, when Jack Lang, who was very sympathetic to the RLs, was Minister for Education.[8] An agreement was duly signed by Jack Lang and Andrew Lincoln who represented the *Diwan* on 28 May 2001 which gave them formal recognition and laid down a protocol for their integration.

This was a step too far for many Jacobins in the educational system. On 2 October 2001 six unions and various *associations laïques* called upon the *Conseil d'Etat* to outlaw such proposals on the grounds that they were anti-constitutional. This episode may be termed the Jack Lang *débâcle*. As a result, on 30 October 2001, the agreement passed between Jack Lang and Andrew Lincoln was rejected by the *Conseil d'Etat* as being incompatible with the texts which define the state educational system. Lang was not too discouraged at that point, and in March 2002, he negotiated a new contract with the *Diwan*, still with the intention of integrating the *Diwan* into the state system. The problem was that by then 71 per cent of the *Diwan* staff declared themselves opposed to integration, whereas the majority of delegates to the Diwan General Assembly had been in favour. This led to terrible conflict and Andrew Lincoln's resignation.

While all this was going on, the *Conseil d'Etat* passed judgements which went far beyond what was expected. On 25 November 2002, the *Conseil d'Etat* stated that not only were the immersion schools illegal, but so were the bilingual ones, despite their having existed within the state system for over twenty years. This was on the grounds that it was not clear whether exact parity between French and the RLs was being respected or not. In the case of the bilingual schools, this was only a temporary distraction, since the problem was easily resolved by drawing up more accurate timetables, but as far as the immersion schools were concerned, it placed them outside the state system for years to come.

Since the main argument for not integrating the *Diwan* is article 2 of the Constitution, the only way to solve the problem would be to amend the Constitution. Until very recently this would have been inconceivable. And yet in November 2002 a proposal put before the *Assemblée Nationale* for such an amendment was defeated by only 50 votes to 39, which indicates a marked change in opinion, possibly because France is now part of a larger entity, namely the EU.

Moreover, however inadequate the present situation may seem to the RL militants, particularly in terms of the lack of any real obligation on the part of the state to teach the RLs, the results are impressive if one bears in mind that fifty years ago there was no RL teaching at all. Table 4 shows the total numbers of children having benefited from at least some teaching in the RLs in 2003–4. The right-hand column gives

*Table 4* Total numbers of children having benefited from at least some teaching in the RLs in 2003–2004

|  | *Primary* | *Collège* | *Lycée* | *Total 2003–4* | *Total 2001–2* |
|---|---|---|---|---|---|
| Basque | 7699 | 2820 | 855 | 11 374 | 9351 |
| Breton | 23 507 | 6550 | 948 | 31 005 | 16 576 |
| Catalan | 9107 | 1648 | 388 | 11 143 | 11 175 |
| Corsican | 24 677 | 7377 | 2377 | 34 431 | 30 784 |
| Gallo | 1505 | 250 | 249 | 2004 | 1761 |
| Occitan* | 57 297 | 17 617 | 3855 | 78 769 | 67 549 |
| Alsace** | 83 499 | 28 697 | 3173 | 115 369 | 83 159 |
| Mosellan** | 4591 | 42 |  | 4633 | 4454 |
| Total | 211 882 | 65 001 | 11 335 | 288 728 | 224 809 |

* listed as *Occitan-Langue d'oc* in report
** *Langues régionales d'Alsace* and *Langues régionales des pays mosellans* refer to the teaching of German with elements of the local 'dialect'

the numbers for 2001–2. Comparison between the two columns shows an encouraging increase for all the RLs (same source as for previous tables).

## The RLs and the media

Progress has been less spectacular in the media than in education, but progress has nonetheless been made, although sometimes indirectly. Thus, although Decree no. 90–66 of 17 January 1990 on the cinema and audio-visual industries was meant to help the production of 'French works', it covered works in both French and in the RLs. The same provision applies to songs: the law demands that 40 per cent of all songs on the radio should be in 'French' which includes the RLs. The prescriptive *loi Toubon* (1994) (Chapter 1) explicitly states in article 21 that prohibitory regulations relating to the use of languages other than French do not apply to the RLs. Indeed it was when this law was discussed, that the idea of French as the sole permitted language encountered serious opposition for the first time. On the other hand, some of its articles have been used against the RLs, even though this was not, supposedly, the intention of those who drafted it.

The problem is that although article 11 of the *Déclaration des Droits de l'homme et du citoyen* of 1789 guarantees freedom of expression, it contains a rider specifying that this right may be limited where it contradicts other constitutional provisions: 'The free communication of thoughts and opinions is one of Man's most precious rights; every citizen may therefore speak, write, and publish freely, except where such freedom constitutes an abuse to freedom in cases determined by the law' ('La libre communication des pensées et des opinions est un des droits les plus précieux de l'homme; tout citoyen peut donc parler, écrire, imprimer librement, sauf à répondre de l'abus de cette liberté dans les cas determines par la loi'). This gives the legislator the right to limit such freedoms so that they do not contravene other laws, such as, for example, article 2 of the present Constitution. Hence a clash between these two principles.

The RLs seem to be winning the battle at present, at least where the media are concerned. Thus Law no. 2000–719, which modifies Decree 90–66, makes a number of statements which allow for the use of RLs in radio broadcasts, since they are now seen as part of the French 'patrimoine culturel et linguistique dans sa diversité régionale et locale' (as part of France's 'cultural and linguistic heritage in all its regional and local diversity') (article 2). This is, moreover, part of the explicit mission of the France 3 (FR3) television station. Other articles are similar to the ones contained in the 1990 decree mentioned above. But private radio or television stations have to sign an agreement with the *Conseil supérieur de l'audiovisuel*, guaranteeing the 40 per cent of time spent using either French or the RLs.

Furthermore, the law on the freedom of communication passed in August 2000[9] states in article 3 that the state-funded media have a duty to promote the RLs and their cultures. This was reiterated in another law in 2004 which mentions the need to promote the RLs[10] (including those spoken overseas, not dealt with in this context), while another one states that some financial help may be given to publications in the RLs, such as the press.[11] (Eysseric (2005) comments on the fact that this help is very limited, but the *Rapport au Parlement sur l'emploi de la langue française*, 2005, stresses the positive nature of such a law.)

The same legislative progress has been made in the context of the production of audiovisual works, including the cinema industry. Thus Decree no. 92–1273 allowed subsidies given previously only for works in French to be allocated to works in the RLs. Decree no. 95–110 also reiterates that the expression 'original works in the French language includes since 1990 works in the RLs'. In all later decrees on various aspects of help to be given to the arts, the RLs are specifically included.

In other words, since 1990 official texts governing such matters now include the RLs. The next step is obviously to examine what has happened on the ground. As far as radio broadcasting is concerned, the answer is very little. According to the 2005 *Rapport au Parlement sur l'emploi de la langue française*, the France Bleu network of radio stations broadcasts in most RLs, but the time allocated to them is pathetically short (it is measured in minutes per day for the various forms of Occitan, except for Toulouse which accounts for one hour, one hour per day for Basque, just over two hours for Breton, including both stations, over five hours for Corsican, over six hours for Alsatian. Picard only accounts for nine minutes per week. Much more needs to be done in this field.

As far as television is concerned,[12] in 2004, France 3 Alsace devoted some 80 hours during the course of the year to 'Alsatian' (German + Alsatian dialect), France 3 Aquitaine-basque around 55 minutes per week to Basque, France 3 Aquitaine-occitan around 35 minutes per week to Occitan, France 3 Méditerranée around 30 hours in the course of the year to Provençal, France 3 Sud-catalan et occitan some 21 hours per week to Occitan and about 6 hours per week to Catalan, France 3 Corse a good 100 hours in the course of the year to Corsican. The report is less clear on France 3 Ouest-breton since, although it gives 56 minutes per week for two specific programmes, it mentions news bulletins and a magazine programme, but without stating their duration. As in other contexts, Corsican emerges as an exception, and so does Alsatian for quite different reasons. The Languedoc-Roussillon also seems more active in this area. However, the general results remain poor, which is serious given the importance of the media in the spreading of a language.

The Ministry for Culture, on the other hand, is playing an important role on the cultural front, giving support to efforts such as those of the Centre dramatique occitan de Toulon, and to films such as Philippe Carese's *Liberata*. Moreover, the *Librairie des langues de France* facilitates the translation and publication of literary works. The DGLFLF also gives what it can to organisations involved in promoting various linguistic and cultural activities associated with the RLs. The problem is that much more financial help is needed than is available.

## Impact of the process of decentralisation

It may be assumed, although this is not always the case (see the case of Scots in Chapter 5), that RLs will do better under a decentralised system, in which local wishes can be better expressed. This is certainly the case in France, where successive governments for years resisted any move to decentralisation as contrary to their Jacobin ideals. It was only the economic need for administrative divisions larger than the *département* which, in 1955, led to the creation of *régions de programme*, which regrouped the *départements* into larger units for the development of the major economic and social programmes typical of modern times. In 1960, these *régions de programme* became *circonscriptions d'action régionale*. In 1964, eight *métropoles régionales* were designated to counterbalance the overshadowing effect of Paris, to which another five were later added. The *régions* were born in 1972, with the 1973 regional reform giving special status to Paris and its region on the one hand, and to Corsica on the other. In 1982, twenty-two new 'regions' were created. These regions are not exactly the same as those set up in 1955, nor do they correspond exactly to the old provinces, despite often adopting their name.

The new regions are important because, for the first time, they each have their own elected assembly, the *Conseil régional*, which is responsible for the economic, social, scientific and cultural development of the region. The important element here is of course the 'cultural' element and how it is defined. The other body is the CESR (*Conseil économique, social et régional*) which is made up of personalities and representatives of important organisations, and is consulted by the *Conseils régionaux*. Thus a new administrative tier has been added which may be lobbied by pressure groups such as those demanding the teaching of the local RL. What is regrettable, however, is that there is sometimes a lack of correspondence between regional and linguistic borders, such as the Picard language and the Picardie region. Another problem is that the state has simply devolved many of its traditional responsibilities to the regions, without providing them with the necessary funds.

The creation of the regions is, however, clearly beneficial to the RLs since it allows policies for individual RLs to be set in motion, without the whole of France having to agree. Their creation has also highlighted regional specificities which had remained hidden under the highly centralised system which had prevailed until then. One of the problems for the RLs is that they have to knock on too many doors: the *Conseil régional*, the *Rectorat* (for educational matters only) and the DRAC (*Division régionale des affaires culturelles*).[13] The latter deal with publishing, music, dance, theatre, art, cinema, museums and so on, but not only for the RLs. Success for the RLs depends, therefore, on good cooperation between the education department, the media and the DRAC, as in Corsica, but this is not always the case.

Some of the *Conseils régionaux* and the CESR, for their part, are being extremely positive at present towards the RLs, which bodes well for the future. Thus in Alsace an agreement has been signed in 2000 for the period 2000–6 between the *Education nationale*, the *Région* and the two Alsatian *départements*. On the other hand, no such agreement has been signed in favour of Mosellan since bilingualism is not so highly considered in the Moselle, and the numbers involved are fewer.

In Brittany, the state and the *Région* co-finance the *Office de la langue bretonne*, created by the region in 1999 to promote the use of Breton in public and social life. In December 2004, the *Conseil régional* unanimously recognised the existence of two RLs, Breton and Gallo, and, in February 2006, signed an agreement with the *Diwan* association to advance the teaching of Breton.

It is in the *département des Pyrénées-Atlantiques*, which is part of the *Région Aquitaine*, that plans for promoting the RLs are most advanced, as a result of an agreement signed in November 2004 with the Interior Minister, which created an *Office public de la langue basque*. This comprises the state, the region, the *départements* and others seeking to find how best to promote the transmission and use of Basque. The *Région*

*Aquitaine* is also currently developing plans for the promotion of Occitan. Similarly the *Région Languedoc-Roussillon* unanimously adopted in Feburary 2006 an ambitious plan to develop and promote Occitan.

The regions therefore constitute the most important new players in the game and the RLs have much to gain from their support. Unfortunately, not all are so positive towards their linguistic heritage, or at least adopt a different approach. Thus PACA (the Provence Alpes Côtes d'Azur region) does not do much for Provençal, and only accepts very grudgingly that Provençal is part of Occitan. But the majority of regions with RLs have adopted a positive stance. Politics have played a major part in this: there has been a different mood towards the RLs since the left won nearly all the regions in 2005. The RLs now have elected supporters in positions of (relative) authority and enjoy what the CESR for Aquitaine described, in December 2005, as a *capital de sympathie* not felt at the national level (see section six below), hence policies in their favour.

One of the justifications for spending money promoting the RLs has been economic. Thus, in December 2005, Aquitaine CESR stressed in its report the importance of the economic potential associated with the promotion of local languages and cultures. The report also refers to the fact that although the government failed to ratify the Charter for the Protection of Regional or Minority Languages, there have been enthusiastic French representatives at all levels in all the organisations involved in promoting European plurilingualism (Euromosaïc, MERCATOR, European Bureau for Lesser Used Languages, etc). Helping the RLs goes hand in hand with a pro-European approach.

## France and the European Charter for Regional or Minority Languages

The European Charter for Regional or Minority Languages was promulgated by the Council of Europe in 1992. It derives from a number of initiatives taken mainly by the European Parliament (EP) during the late 1970s and 1980s demanding protection for RLs and MLs and cultures. Thus the First Arfé Resolution in 1981 resulted in the creation of the European Bureau for Lesser Used Languages (EBLUL) in 1982 and the Second Arfé Resolution of 1983 led to the establishment of an 'official' budget to support Community languages and cultures (it was later declared unlawful). The 1987 Kuijpers Resolution demanded concrete measures to save and promote RLs and cultures, and support for the Council of Europe's proposed Charter for Regional or Minority Languages.

The Charter itself can be traced back to the public debate on RLs and minority languages at the Palais de l'Europe in 1984, when the Standing Conference of Local and Regional Authorities of Europe established a committee of experts to prepare a draft European Charter for Regional or Minority Languages. The Charter was adopted by the Standing Conference in March 1988 and was favourably received by the Parliamentary Assembly of the Council of Europe in October 1988. An expert committee was set up to advise on the form to be accorded to the document, and it reported in April 1992. In June 1992 the Committee of Ministers of the Council of Europe voted to accord the Charter the legal form of a Convention, thus making it legally binding. Only France, the UK, Cyprus and Turkey abstained, while Greece voted against it. The Convention was opened for signature in November 1992 and came into force in the countries having signed and ratified it in March 1998.

On 7 May 1999, the French Minister for European Affairs signed the Charter for Regional or Minority Languages, with what was presumed to be the full approval of the President, Jacques Chirac. The reason for this change of heart was the different approach towards the RLs and their cultures which had developed over the years. Moreover, the French government was under heavy pressure from the EU to sign. Finally, although in principle far-reaching, in reality the Charter was drawn up in such a way as to make it easy for states to agree to it, since it is a kind of *à la carte* convention, with states being allowed to sign up for certain sections only. And in the case of France, the RLs already benefited from the strict minimum required by the Charter.

But natural as this must have seemed to the government at the time, it took the whole nation by surprise, and sparked off the old debate between Jacobins and Girondins.[14] It even brought to the fore a suggestion of communitarianism (*Communautarisme*). Expressions such as the 'Balkanisation of France' were bandied around in the press. Passions ran high. Hence the *Conseil Constitutionnel* being asked to judge whether ratifying the Charter was compatible with the French Constitution or not.

On 15 June 1999 the *Conseil Constitutionnel* ruled that the Charter was doubly incompatible with the French Constitution. It was incompatible with article 1 which states that France is *une et indivisible* and with article 2 which states that the language of the Republic is French. Ratification of the Charter would require changing the Constitution. It could not, therefore, be ratified.

Another problem, of a quite different nature, was due to the publication in 1999 of the Cerquiglini Report. This had been commissioned by the French government prior to the ratification of the Charter, but instead of the expected six or seven RLs to be given protection by the Charter, it listed 75 (now 77). The main reason for the 75 languages was the inclusion of all the languages spoken in 'Greater France' which includes the DOM-TOM.[15] (To do otherwise would have been to classify the latter as overseas French 'possessions', an unacceptable concept today.) These account for some 55 languages. The 20 languages left include not only RLs but also minority languages (MLs) not territorially based, but considered 'traditional' or 'historic languages of France', terms which appear in the Charter's preamble. It is on such grounds that Dialectal Arabic and Berber were included, since they were spoken historically in the ex-French Algerian *départements* by French citizens who, for social, economic or political reasons (this was particularly the case with the *harkis*), settled in France without ceasing to be French citizens.

Cerquiglini also pointed out that the distinction between the language of immigrants and the traditional languages of France is further complicated by the fact that the French Republic recognises the *droit du sol* or *jus solis,* i.e. children born in France of immigrant parents can claim French nationality. Which again implies accepting more languages as 'indigenous'. (But not languages such as Italian which are not endangered languages, being official elsewhere.)

Finally there are problems associated with the traditional RLs because of their association with territoriality, which goes against the constitutional principle of France being 'one and indivisible'. Hence the lawyer Guy Carcassonne, when preparing the case for signing the Charter, maintained that the RLs of France were part of the French heritage as a whole rather than belonging to their region of origin: thus Breton belongs to the whole French nation, rather than to the Bretons (in the same way as the Alps belong to all the French rather than those who simply live there).

Cerquiglini said much the same in his report, adding that the various RLs are spoken in areas other than their place of origin (mainly Paris) because of modern social mobility. He also pointed out that for a variety of reasons the concept of the 'territory of a language' is difficult to define scientifically. He therefore suggested that when signing and ratifying the Charter it would be necessary to insist on the notion of 'minority languages' rather than 'territorial languages', the latter being incompatible with the concept of the French state. Hence the present use of the term *langues de France* instead of RLs or MLs. This clearly marked a change of approach to the whole problem. Reactions to the report were mixed. Some RL militants saw it as a stab in the back, because it seemed to turn their case into ridicule. Others saw it as a ploy to enable the Charter to become constitutionally acceptable.

There have been important consequences to the drawing up of the Cerquiglini Report and the signing of the Charter, even if the latter has not been ratified. One was to examine the vexed question of what constitutes a 'language', which led to all the *langues d'oïl* becoming officially 'languages'. Another was to look more closely at the languages of immigrants long established in France, where they have developed their own particular 'French' characteristics (Dialectal Arabic and Berber for example). These are now considered to be French 'minority languages' (MLs) and are regrouped with the RLs under the all embracing title of the *langues de France*. Thus the recently created *Association Universitaire des Langues de France* includes representatives both of the RLs and the MLs. It is nonetheless a fact that it is the 'traditional' RLs which are, at present, at the forefront of the fight for survival.

Surprisingly, the Charter's supporter are not all regionalists. For example, Claude Sicre, one of the founder members of the Occitanist Rap group Fabulous Troubadors, has stated that he is anti-regionalist, maintaining that the debate should be about cultural decentralisation, i.e. cultural democracy, which should lead to cultural plurality. Others are simply exasperated by the whole debate, which they see as an artificial problem. In particular, they see the *Conseil constitutionnel* as being out of touch with French society which has increasingly evolved *de facto* towards a certain kind of multiculturalism. It has been argued that multiculturalism can coexist with the nation-state as long as it is not synonymous with communitarianism.

France is, on the surface, a volatile country and one in which great debates (and revolutions) take place. They usually concern the nation as a whole in that they figure largely in all the media and are much discussed at a personal level (matters are quite different in this respect in Britain). These debates (and revolutions) are themselves a source of unity and show democracy functioning at a popular level. It is true that they usually fizzle out, but not without leaving behind some permanent changes, often of a rather minor nature but also sometimes of major importance, if only in the long term. It is a succession of such minor changes that have defined the evolution of the country as a whole. This certainly applies to the debate on the Charter, which has led, not only to changes of attitudes among an increasing proportion of the population (although still a minority), but to important institutional innovations.

Two initiatives, in particular, were the result of the *Conseil constitutionnel*'s damning report, presumably meant as consolation prizes for the RLs. Firstly an *Observatoire des pratiques linguistiques* was created in 1999 under the aegis of the DGLF. It is responsible for coordinating research both on regional or other varieties of French (such as *le français des banlieues*, i.e. street French) and all the MLs. Two projects which have benefited from help from the *Observatoire* include a large-scale project on French accents and the INSEE/INED *Enquête famille*.

The second important initiative was renaming, on 16 October 2001, the DGLF (*Délégation générale à la langue française*) the DGLFLF (*Délégation générale à la langue française et aux langues de France*). This is important because the DGLF is part of the *Ministère de la culture et de la communication* and as such is responsible for putting into practice governmental linguistic policies. Now that it is the DGLFLF, it also responsible for reporting on both MLs and RLs and encouraging research in this sphere. Thus the yearly *Rapport au Parlement sur l'application de la loi du 4 août 1994 relative l'emploi de la langue française* (i.e. the Toubon law) now includes a section on *les langues de France*. This is important both symbolically and practically since money is involved, although it is mainly allocated to the DRACs. Renaming the DGLF the DGLFLF also gave *de facto* recognition to the RLs which is very important, particularly since it employs staff specifically allocated to the promotion of the *langues de France*.

## Concluding comments

Despite their status having greatly improved, the RLs still have no legal status as such, but they are nonetheless recognised by the state which accepts that it has responsibilities towards them in certain domains. The main problem is that there is, in practice, no legal compulsion for the state to promote the RLs, particularly if financial commitments are involved. This is particularly clear in the field of education, where enormous progress has been achieved at all levels, thanks to efforts made in the private sector, which were then adapted and adopted by the state. Problems remain, however, because there are plenty of loopholes to prevent the RLs from being taught.

Thus, in 1996, an association of parents demanded that Breton should be reinstated for their children, after their Breton teacher had left. The *juge administratif* stated that there was no obligation for the state to provide such teaching, quoting both the Deixonne and the Haby law, which both stress its optional character.[16] In another case in which an association sought permission for their children to write their answers for the history and geography papers for the *brevet* (similar to our GCSEs) in the local language, the parents were told that no official text compelled the educational system to provide for such an option.[17]

Similarly, in 2002, parents in the Alsace-Moselle were told that although the law allows for bilingual education, it does not make it a right.[18]

It would not be accurate, however, to presume that objections are only judicial. They also come from the public. In 2001, a primary school teacher in Alsace was prevented from teaching a nursery rhyme, in French, German and Alsatian, which he did each week, because of complaints from a Francophone mother, who felt the general atmosphere of the class was too Alsatian, too German. The inspector of the *Education nationale* asked the teacher to apply for a bilingual post elsewhere (reported in *L'Éime Prouvençau*, no. 41, May–June 2001).

Another problem is the inequality of treatment of different RLs. There are two RLs which receive better treatment from the state than the others, namely Corsican and Alsatian. In the case of Corsican, this is due to political imperatives. Where Alsatian is concerned, this extra help may come to be a poisoned chalice for those who do not consider standard German to be the written equivalent of Alsatian. Some of the new regions, created in the context of France's move towards decentralisation, are also more sympathetic to their RLs than others. At present the *département des Pyrénées-Atlantiques* in the Aquitaine region is cited as a role model in terms of the extent of its commitment to saving the Basque language

Finally, financial problems affecting the associative school network brought about the idea that these schools should be integrated into the state system, since, like the state schools, they are free and secular. The constitutional *débâcle* arising from the *Diwan*'s request for such a change of status, has made clear that although France is moving away from its traditional Jacobin approach, such options still lie in a far distant future.

As far as the media is concerned, everything necessary has been done from a legal point of view to make the RLs' introduction into public life possible, albeit that this is based on the rather surprising premise that 'French language' 'includes' the RLs. But in practice, much remains to be done. The best hope for future progress must be the *Conseils régionaux*. The problems for them are in all cases financial, to which must be added in some cases lack of interest and commitment.

Finally, although for many the non-ratification of the Charter for Regional or Minority Languages was a great disappointment, the representatives of EBLUL were right when they declared at the time that it was the signature and preparation for signature and ratification that were important. The RLs certainly get as much help as if the Charter had been ratified, and the importance of renaming the DGLF the DGLFLF cannot be overstated. Whether this will be enough to save the RLs is another matter.

# Part III

# The Regional Languages of Britain

# General Presentation

If the person in the street were asked what are the RLs of Britain, the answer would probably include Welsh, Scottish Gaelic and Irish Gaelic (or 'Irish'). Some may add Cornish, which they may think is extinct. Others may add Manx, although the Isle of Man is not strictly speaking part of the United Kingdom. All of these are Celtic languages. Some, particularly if living in Scotland, may add Scots, a collateral language of English. Finally, they may add the form of French spoken in the Channel Islands, which, again, like the Isle of Man, is not part of the United Kingdom.

Books on the subject usually include Irish seen in the context of Ireland as a whole, since Irish in Northern Ireland cannot be properly assessed on its own. They usually refer to the manner in which the Celtic languages came to develop from Western Common Celtic. They also tend to discuss extinct languages, such as Cumbric and Pictish, of which too little remains for definitive conclusions to be drawn. Norse and Norn, and Flemish in Wales, may also be discussed, either because of the influence they may have had on surviving languages, or as interesting anomalies in their own right.

The only non-Celtic language normally discussed in the context of the RLs of Britain is Scots (or 'Lallans'), to which Ulster Scots must now be added, although its linguistic credentials are often in dispute. Scots and Ulster Scots are the only Germanic languages, other than English, claiming separate linguistic status. All other forms of speech of Germanic origin come under the general heading of 'English dialects', much in the same way as, until quite recently, the *langues d'oïl* came under 'French'. The English dialects tend to be looked upon with fondness, particularly since the Romantics made them fashionable, and there is a genuine desire to preserve them, but so far no major move to promote them in the public domain.[1] As a result, they will not be discussed in this context.

And yet some of the English dialects could be considered linguistically as separate languages, if only on the grounds of a lack of mutual intelligibility with English. This may be illustrated by the fact that a group of GPs and consultants were lectured recently on the Geordie dialect, the absence of knowledge of which was found to have caused problems between patients and newly arrived medical staff. This followed the publication of a successful pamphlet called *Nip to Gut Rot or Glossary of Yorkshire Medical Terms*, which explains to newly arrived doctors in Doncaster what the locals mean by *ows thissen*, i.e. 'and how are you, doctor?' Workshops on the way mining, farming and shipbuilding have formed distinctive Geordie words and phrases are also being offered.[2]

The absence of people fighting for their cause is no doubt partly because the identity they represented until the end of the Empire was superseded by a sense of Britishness. Nowadays, however, according to the 2001 census, only 48 per cent of the people living in England described themselves as 'British', 35 per cent in Wales and 27 per cent in Scotland, so this may well change in the future. The lack of militancy is also due to the fact that non-standard varieties of English were considered unacceptable in education and public life, at least until the Beatles and Harold Wilson (among other famous people) made an element of regionalism acceptable in certain limited contexts. But since devolution, the English are having to redefine their identity, which may explain a possible resurgence of interest in English dialects. Thus a recent article in *The Guardian* (23 March 2006) stated that thousands of children in Norfolk are to be taught the county's dialect at school, as part of a project to promote the much maligned local accent: 'Derided by city slickers and mocked in adverts for "bootiful" Bernard Matthews turkeys, Norfolk's mother tongue will be recorded and practised by pupils in 11 schools after Friends of Norfolk Dialect, or "Fond", was awarded a £24,600 grant to introduce understanding and appreciation of the vernacular.'

This hardly amounts to a linguistic policy, as such, and it may either be a passing phase, or the beginning of something big. But whatever the future may hold, so far English dialects have not been claiming any particular status, and are not, therefore, included in this study. Also excluded are the languages spoken in the Channel Islands and the Isle of Man,[3] since they are not part of the United Kingdom. And no mention is made of the numerous community languages spoken in Britain since they are not regional languages as such. The only languages included are those marked for protection in the context of the Charter for the Protection of Regional or Minority Languages, signed in 2000 and ratified in 2001. These include Welsh, Scottish Gaelic (or, simply, 'Gaelic'), Irish Gaelic (or, simply, 'Irish'), Scots and Ulster Scots, to which Cornish was added in 2002.

The amount of protection this guarantees to the RLs depends on whether the RLs have been signed up for Part III protection or merely Part II. Part III contains specific undertakings in relation to the specific fields of education, justice, public services, the media, cultural activities, and economic and social life. States ratifying the charter are required to sign up to a minimum of 35 of the articles in Part III, which entail minimum undertakings in respect of education, justice and administration. Three Celtic languages, Welsh, Gaelic and Irish, benefit from Part III support because they are well documented, are still spoken by sizeable numbers of people and have been overtly linked with nationalist movements.

Part II sets out the general principles and aims which each country must accept in their entirety for all the RLs and minority languages in that country. They are essentially pious statements of intention concerning recognition and promotion rather than real guarantees. But granting a language Part II protection does at least mean recognition of its existence. Scots and Ulster Scots come under this heading, with Ulster Scots, unlike Scots, receiving considerable financial help from the British government for purely political reasons. Cornish is the only Celtic language to benefit from Part II rather than Part III protection, but this, in itself, is a miracle, since at the time of ratification it had been assumed that Cornish was dead. It was only added a year later as a result of a government commissioned report on the subject, which concluded that it had become, once more, a living language.

The Celtic languages are the oldest known to have been spoken in the British Isles, although others must have been spoken prior to their arrival. Their origins are, however, open to dispute for the period preceding the introduction of writing, which was brought to Britain with Christianity.[4] The most commonly accepted theory is that the Celtic languages were imported into the British Isles around 500 or 600 BC, although some maintain that they were *in situ* at a much earlier date. Another area of dispute is whether the Celtic speakers who went to Ireland did so by passing through Britain or went directly from the Continent, which is the most widely held view.

What is certain is that the Celtic languages developed from Western Indo-European, and that in the British Isles, they may be sub-divided into the Brythonic or P-Celtic in Britain and the Goidelic or Q-branch in Ireland.[5] The P and Q labels correspond to a particularly important phonological difference between the two branches: the [k] in the Q-branch (also called Goidelic, or Gaelic) corresponds to a [p] in the P-branch (also called Brythonic, Brittonic, or British). Thus Irish *ceathair* gives Welsh *pedwar* meaning 'four'. The P-branch includes Welsh, Cornish, Breton and the extinct Cumbric. At one point it may have been spoken over the whole of Great Britain, from where it spread to Brittany at the time of the Anglo-Saxon invasions in the fifth and sixth centuries.

The Q-branch includes Irish Gaelic, Manx[6] and Scottish Gaelic. When and how the Q-branch was brought over to Scotland is another area of debate. But certainly there was a period when the language spoken in Ireland and Scotland differed but little, particularly in writing. In all cases, there may have been sub-strata which affected how the P- and Q-branches emerged and developed. Pictish in particular remains a mystery in this respect (see Price 1984, 2000).

Some of the problems involved in describing the British RLs are different from those associated with the French RLs. There are, in particular, fewer problems involved in assessing the numbers of speakers, and their age, because there are no constitutional constraints on the kind of questions asked in demographic censuses. These started very early in Britain, the first general survey dating from 1801. The first linguistic question appeared in the 1851 census for Irish (but only as a footnote), in 1881 for Gaelic and 1891 for Welsh. From 1891 all censuses contained linguistic questions in Wales and Scotland. The reason a question was included earlier in Ireland than in Great Britain was the need to find out how many children had to be catered for in the new national schools, created in 1831–2 with the specific purpose of eradicating the Irish language.[7]

Interestingly, one of the reasons given nowadays for including questions on language, race and religion is to ensure fairness of treatment between the various communities which make up Britain's multicultural society, whereas in France the same questions are forbidden, also in the name of equality.

It is also easier to discuss such matters from a political point of view since the English language, unlike French, is not seen as an untouchable pillar of the nation. In Britain the RLs were destroyed for pragmatic reasons, not on the altar of ideals, hence there are few problems of principle in trying to revive them. And finally they are limited in number to six as against the official French approach – not adopted in this book – of including all possible minority languages both indigenous and imported, spoken both in the mother country and its dependencies abroad.

This does not mean that assessing the RLs in Britain is easy. The same problems apply in Britain as in France when analysing censuses and surveys which are self-evaluative, since the answers given will depend on the prevailing political climate. As a general rule, respondents tend either to exaggerate or denigrate their linguistic capabilities. This was particularly the case in the Irish censuses before independence, when answers depended on how best to undermine British intentions.

More recently, Price (1984: 59) has commented on the unexpected increase of 10 per cent in the number of Scottish Gaelic and English bilingual speakers between 1961 and 1971, and the even more astonishing number of monoglot speakers recorded in 1971. They numbered, according to the census, 477. The Census Office, having found such a figure surprisingly high, decided to investigate these cases further. Of 109 monoglot speakers traced, 46 had stated in 1961 that they were bilingual and 33 had then declared they did not speak Gaelic. It was argued that some of the bilinguals may have become monoglot in old age, reverting to their first mother tongue, and that some of those who did not speak it originally acquired it, which should have made them bilingual rather than monoglot. Price concludes that whatever the explanation, such figures, however useful, should not be taken at face value.

Disparities may also occur according to how the questions are worded. Thus asking whether a person 'can' speak a language is not the same as asking if a person 'does' speak a language. For the 2001 census, it was decided that 'can' would be adopted in all cases. Since previously in Wales the word 'does' had been used, this probably depressed the actual number of Welsh speakers. Similarly, in a trial run to include a question on Scots, when asked 'Can you speak the Scots language?' 33 per cent of those interviewed answered 'yes', whereas when asked 'Can you speak Scots (e.g. Doric, Lallans, Buchan)' the proportions dropped to 17 per cent. The result was that Scots was simply not included in the last census.

Another associated problem is the uncertainty associated with what 'knowing a language' means, even when there are no political or emotional issues at stake (which is rather hard to imagine, language being such an emotional subject). Linguistic questions in censuses have become far more sophisticated in this respect: whereas in the 1891 census, the data collected indicated the numbers of persons aged two years old and over who were monoglot in Welsh, Irish or Gaelic, recent

*Map 5*   Language communities in the UK

censuses have asked very much more sophisticated questions, distinguishing in particular between both oral and written comprehension
and production. This makes modern British censuses far more sophisticated tools than what had been known so far, and very much more
reliable than French surveys. But being self-evaluative their results are
still not entirely reliable.

An advantage of British surveys is that they often correspond to
administrative constituencies, which means that it is possible to draw
maps indicating percentages of speakers of a particular language in a
particular area. It is then possible to see at a glance where languages
have receded or progressed. (See, for example, J. Aitchison and
H. Carter's *A Geography of the Welsh Language 1961–1991*.)

One of the drawbacks of the British censuses is that they have often
been worded slightly differently in England, Wales, Scotland and Northern
Ireland. In some cases, for example, the population has been divided into
different age groupings. In other cases, the various possible categories of
people with some form or other of linguistic ability have been collated differently (there are sixteen possible combinations of the four basic language

abilities – namely spoken and written comprehension and production – some of which are meaningless[8]). Finally, consistent practice has not always been followed with previous censuses, often in the name of improvements, which makes it difficult to assess changing trends. The population may, for example, be categorised differently in terms of age and social class, and the administrative divisions may vary, hence there are problems comparing their results (see MacKinnon 2003: 250–61). They represent, however, an invaluable tool for assessing the vitality of a language, and whether certain policies, such as educational policies, are making a difference or not. They also make it possible to draw a far more accurate picture of their position at any one time than it is for the French RLs.

The present plight of the British RLs is blamed on the imposition of English through the centuries at all levels. This was sometimes done with good intentions (in the name of equality and progress) and sometimes bad (in the name of power and control). Other minority languages throughout Europe suffered the same fate, and their representation in organisations such as the European Bureau for Lesser-Used Languages helps to focus their efforts in trying to re-establish their place in society. A move towards a Europe of Regions is also supposed to help their case. It will be interesting, in this connection, to see whether devolution in Britain is indeed bringing improvements to the RLs concerned. Even where there is no devolution, as in Cornwall, the fact that Cornish militants were able to establish links with the other Celtic languages and with EU organisations has been of paramount importance.

The RLs in this section are classified according to the political entity they belong to. Chapter 6 examines the RLs spoken in England and Wales, since they come under the same legal system. This obviously means Welsh, which has become a role model RL, but also Cornish which has made an amazing comeback. Chapter 7 examines the indigenous languages of Scotland, namely Scottish Gaelic and Scots, in what is, for some, a trilingual situation. And Chapter 8 deals with the language issue in conflict-torn Northern Ireland, where Irish Gaelic and Ulster Scots both have a part to play.

# 6
# The Regional Languages of England and Wales[1]: Welsh and Cornish

Although Wales may be said to constitute a nation, England and Wales come under one heading, because prior to devolution Wales had been deprived of its own institutions ever since the Act of Union of 1536. Laws passed in England normally applied to 'England and Wales', and many still do since the Assembly is subordinate to Westminster. Even post-devolution, the concept of an 'England and Wales' unit lingers on. The 2001 census was problematic in this respect since it did not allow for 'Welsh' to appear in the nationality box, whereas it allowed for Gaelic, seen as a possible ethnic group in Scotland and Ireland, and also seen as a possible ethnic group in Northern Ireland.[2] In other words Wales was traditionally seen as closer to England than Scotland and Ireland, and it was this absence of separateness from England which led the Welsh language to becoming all important in defining Welsh-ness. Hence Gwyn Jones (1977) asserted in a radio lecture: 'The disappearance or severe contraction of Welsh as a living tongue would be a national and human disaster, and to many Welshmen it *would* be the end of Wales – their Wales.'

Welsh has been the most successful of the Celtic languages in surviving intact, despite the odds. One reason for its survival is its long literary tradition, another is having adopted, after the Reformation, the new state religion which functions, by definition, in the vernacular. Finally, the fact that the population did not have to leave Wales in search of work, as the Irish and Scots had to do, was also extremely important. Welsh has now achieved official status, even if its use in all contexts does not constitute an individual right.

Cornish, on the other hand, is the language which has suffered most from the English conquest, and there is no likelihood at present of devolution for Cornwall, despite there having been petitions for a Cornish Assembly. On the contrary, it has been regrouped with Devon into an area called 'the Region of South West England', which denies Cornwall any specifically Cornish identity. And yet there have been Cornish revivalists ever since Cornish ceased to be spoken, at the end of the eighteenth century, and in the last half of the twentieth century they managed to revive the language, the only national symbol available to them, to the extent that the government added Cornish to the languages listed for protection under the European Charter for Regional or Minority Languages a year after it was originally ratified, which is a measure of their success. This means that it is no longer classified as a dead language. (Much the same applies to Manx, except that in Mann,[3] being an independent state, progress has been far more rapid.) These are impressive achievements, although only time will tell whether they will have a long-term impact or not.

# Welsh

### Historical development

Welsh developed from Brythonic, from which derive the terms 'Britain' and 'British'. It is the only language in Britain to have had an unbroken history until now. It was the advance of the Germanic tribes which isolated the Brittonic-speaking kingdoms of the north, west and south west. This led to the development of Cumbric in southern Scotland and north west England,[4] Welsh in Wales and Cornish in the south west as separate languages. They were all known as 'Welsh', which has been understood to mean 'foreigners' but also can mean 'Romanised'.[5]

Linguistically, the beginning of Welsh (and also Cornish and Breton) may be dated from when Brythonic, an inflected language, lost its final syllables. This is why in Latin inscriptions containing Brythonic names, these are considered to be in Welsh if they have lost their final syllable. Similarly, the Welsh term *Cymry*, meaning 'fellow countryman', comes from the Brythonic *Combrogi*. Janet Davies (1999: 7) has pointed out that the adoption of this term marks 'a deepening sense of identity'.

The earliest examples of this phenomenon date from the seventh century AD. The first text in Welsh is an account of a law suit written on one of the pages of a Latin manuscript of the Gospels, which probably dates from the eighth century, but Welsh literature as such is said to go back to the sixth century, because five Welsh poets were referred to in Nennius's[6] *Historia Brittonum* ('history of the Britons'). (Although the latter was composed around the ninth century, it dates them as having lived in the time of a king who lived between 547 and 559.) Of these Aneirin and Taliesin's work were saved, in altered because modernised form, in thirteenth-century manuscripts. They are known as the 'Early Poets'.[7]

These poets mark the beginning of a rich literary tradition, unbroken to this day. Its prestige goes a long way to explaining the survival of Welsh. It was also the language of the law, until annexation by England. Indeed it was used in all domains, including medicine, science and astronomy. Codification of the laws of Wales, in particular, survive in 42 texts, six of which were in Latin, written down between 1250 and 1500, with passages displaying a 'distinctively earlier flavour' (see Janet Davies 1999). In other words, Welsh in the Middle Ages was a fully developed language and one to be proud of.

Wales was incorporated into England in 1536. The aim of the Act of Union of 1536 was not so much to destroy the Welsh language, as to give the Welsh the same legal rights as those enjoyed by the English. Indeed this had been requested by the Welsh gentry. But for this to be possible, there had to be a certain amount of uniformity across the realm, so English was made the official language of the courts and of all public office. This had a catastrophic effect on the language since it created a bilingual ruling class in Wales, fluent in English. This caused a state of diglossia to develop, with Welsh becoming a marginalised second-class language. Welsh gradually ceased to occupy a core position, as the gentry gradually gave up using Welsh on a daily basis. This spelled the end of 1000 years of cultural unity.

Logically, anglicisation of the gentry should have been the death of Welsh, but the language was kept alive by the new state religion, Anglicanism, and later, Non-conformism. One of the consequences of Henry VIII breaking with Rome in 1534 was the replacement of Latin by English as the language of worship. Since most Welsh people spoke no English, but went over to Protestantism, Welsh replaced Latin as the language of worship. For although the Act of Union of 1536 made English the language of public office for reasons of state, much as *Villers-Cotterêts* did for French three years later, in the case of religion, worshipping God the right way was seen to be the main issue, not the language used. This led in 1547 to the publication of the first book in Welsh, which contained the Lord's Prayer, the Creed and the Ten Commandments, a mere thirteen years after the break with Rome. Other works, not necessarily of a religious nature, were also printed in Welsh thereafter, including a Welsh–English dictionary and a first grammar of Welsh.

In 1563 an Act was passed by Elizabeth I[8] providing for the translation of the Book of Common Prayer and the Bible into Welsh. The Book of Common Prayer appeared in Welsh in 1567, as did a translation of the

New Testament, by William Salesbury. 1588 saw the publication of the translation of the Old Testament, as well as a revised version of the New Testament. Thus a complete version of the Bible appeared in Welsh thirty-three years before the English 'Authorised Version' or 'King James Version' (Price 1984: 99). William Morgan, the translator, may be considered the first great figure in the history of the Welsh language, having produced a splendid text in poetic and exalted language, which rapidly became a model to follow.[9] The importance this gave to Welsh in terms of its status and dignity cannot be overrated. Also the fact that the Bible was translated into Welsh so early on is unique in relation to the other RLs, both in Britain and in France, and goes far towards explaining its advantage over the other Celtic languages.

Writing dictionaries and grammars and translating the Bible (John Davies revised it in 1620) led to a pragmatically achieved form of codification, which lasted until World War Two, by which time it was felt to have become archaic. The problem then became not so much codifying the language, but modernising the system in place. Price points out that:

> the fact that Welsh acquired at this time a literary language that was both firmly based and generally accepted was to prove of inestimable benefit. There is certainly room for debate about the extent to which literary Welsh might be brought closer to the spoken language, but Wales and the Welsh language are spared the bitter quarrels that have all too often sprung up among the partisans of rival systems in the case of such languages as Breton, Occitan[10] or Basque, where there is no common literary language and no agreement as to the principles (orthography, dialectal or inter-dialectal basis, and so on) according to which such a common language may be established. (Price 1984: 100)

These works were all printed in England until the first press was set up in Wales in 1718. By then, some 300 books had already been published in England. These covered all kinds of subjects, such as politics, gardening and others, but the most popular subject was religion. Price reckons that by the 1980s some 20 000 books had been published in Welsh.

Another great figure in the history of the Welsh language was Griffith Jones who founded in 1731 informal schools to teach ordinary people to read the word of God in Welsh. These were set up for children and adults alike, and it was reckoned that in six weeks they could learn to read. More than a quarter of a million people were taught to read Welsh over a period of twenty years, which had the effect of democratising the language. The move away from the Church of England towards Non-conformism also accentuated this tendency since Non-conformity (Methodists, Congregationalists, Quakers, Presbyterians, Baptists) tended to be associated with the lower echelons of society. This was because before the Toleration Act of 1689, the Puritans from which these sects emerged were subjected to the kind of persecution which led the more wealthy and certainly the more ambitious back to the Church of England.

The reason for leaving the Church of England in the first place had been its change of attitude towards Welsh. The Church had originally promoted the use of Welsh in the interest of converting the population, but this was seen by many purely as an expedient, only to be used until the Welsh had learned English. Their argument was that learning English would be in their interest, since it would give them equality of opportunity with English speakers. There were also some Non-conformists who shared that view. This led, in 1674, to the foundation of the Welsh Trust, financed by both sides of the denominational divide, to teach English. This work was continued by the Society for Promoting Christian Knowledge (SPCK) founded in 1699.

But the majority of the Non-conformist clergy were Welsh speakers and functioned in Welsh. They felt that saving souls was more important than learning English, and Wales was, after all, a mainly Welsh-speaking country. The earliest map of the distribution of the language is for 1750 and is based on the returns of curates, vicars and rectors throughout Wales concerning the use of Welsh or English in services (Rees Pryce 1978 quoted in Aitchison and Carter 1994). It shows that the completely Anglicised areas were still very restricted and that no major inroads had been made into Welsh since the Middle Ages. The Act of Union had not so much displaced Welsh geographically but progressively limited the domains in which it was used (Aitchison and Carter 1994). The huge majority of the population remained monoglot.

This led the clergy to persuade the Welsh Trust to spend money publishing both religious and non-religious works, as long as they were uplifting, in Welsh. Moreover, although the SPCK, like the Welsh Trust, established English-speaking schools, in some districts they functioned in Welsh, particularly in the north. In other words education was seen as a way of promoting social benefit very early on in Wales (and Britain in general). The aim was not so much the destruction of Welsh, which continued to be spoken in the home and at chapel, but to introduce bilingualism as a factor for social progress. Interestingly, the kind of debate this problem aroused predates similar ones which took place during the French Revolution between the Jacobins and the Girondins. Promoting English may be seen as a Jacobin position which predates the Jacobins.

In all of these discussions Welsh was seen not so much as an end in itself but as a means. There were, however, some people interested in the language *per se*[11] and in its culture, which led, in the eighteenth century, to intense interest in a Druidic past, of which the Welsh poets were the more modern descendants. This interest became more marked as Wales started changing from an economic and social point of view. Agriculture became mechanised in the course of the eighteenth century, and by the 1770s the development of the great iron works in Merthyr Tydfil brought about a new urban society, which made Welsh the first RL to become a language used in an industrial and urban context, unlike Irish which became limited to the *Gaeltacht*.

Edward Williams (1747–1826),[12] among others, feared at that point the loss of Welsh traditions, hence his reigniting interest in the Druidic past, which is the origin of the *Eisteddfod*, a congress in which bards come together to compete in literary and musical prowess. The first took place in 1789, after which they petered out because of the effects of the French Revolution, but were revived in 1815. This had the great advantage of making the people feel better about a language which had slid down the social scale, in all except the religious domain. The *Eisteddfod* concept still plays a major role in Wales today.

Problems for Welsh worsened in the course of the nineteenth century because of the Industrial Revolution, and the opening up of the coalfields. By the 1870s South Wales was the most important industrial region on earth, and had a cosmopolitan population similar to the kind of population mix typical of a town such as Chicago. In the early days, Welsh was successful in that incomers working in the mines tended to learn Welsh, and some of today's native Welsh speakers are descendants of these early immigrants. Maintaining Welsh as the normal language of daily communication was also helped by movements of population from Welsh-speaking North Wales to South Wales, the rural population from the north seeking jobs in the south, and introducing Welsh where often few spoke it. Improvement in the traditionally difficult access to the north for those working in the coalfields also helped to create a new sense of Welsh identity throughout Wales. This new sense of identity came to be symbolised by the adoption of a national anthem composed in 1868.

In other words, the strength of Welsh was due to Wales having jobs for all. There was no need, as in Ireland or Scotland, for its population to migrate. The problem was that in the end Wales did not have enough Welsh speakers to fill all the jobs available. It is this which brought about the downfall of the language, for between the 1890s and 1914 large numbers of English workers had to be brought in. This had a devastating effect, to the extent that names of streets were changed to English names across Wales, the English being unable to pronounce the Welsh ones. By the 1900s, when Cardiff had become one of the busiest and most cosmopolitan ports in the world, it used English as a lingua franca. This led to the paradoxical situation in which, according the 1911 census, Welsh had never had so many speakers (977 366) but was only spoken by 43 per cent of the population, whereas in 1901 it had been spoken by half the population. Also by the late 1890s Welsh was used in some contexts but not others. It was used in the home, but no longer as the main language of the coalfields. It was still used in chapel, but no longer much in public life. Wales began to see itself as part of the British Empire, in which English was the language all understood. It had become part of the British nation.

English also made inroads in the rural areas because of education, which was in English, which was, in most cases, how most parents wanted it to be. As in 1789 in France, they wanted to be rid, at least partly, of their language, so that their children had a better chance of success. But Welsh continued to be acquired at home and in chapel (in the same way as Basque and Breton were maintained by the Catholic Church). Then came the traumatic episode known as the 'Treachery of the Blue Books'.

What happened was that in 1846, a commission was set up to make sure that enough was done for the children of the 'labouring classes' to be able to acquire English. This led in 1847 to the publication of the *Report of the Commissioners of Inquiry into the State of Education in Wales*.[13] The report highlighted the gulf which separated the English-speaking upper classes and the Welsh-speaking lower classes. The Welsh language was associated with poverty and ignorance, and a barrier to progress, and also with immoral behaviour on the part of the lower classes. The basis of the accusation was a large number of letters sent mainly from Anglican clergymen, who maintained, as one put it, that 'morals were generally at a low ebb, but want of chastity is the giant sin of Wales' (quoted in J. Davies 1999: 44). There was a clear implication that Non-conformist meetings were used as an excuse for illicit sex, which considerably exacerbated relations between the Anglican Church and Chapel, and had the effect of inspiring the Non-conformists to prove their extreme respectability.

This also pushed some people towards rejecting Welsh in favour of English, assimilation being seen as the only way of removing English contempt. Others, on the contrary, rejected English in disgust, which marked the beginning of linguistic nationalism.[14] The task of the new language nationalists was formidable given the ever increasing number of children being educated through the medium of English. This was not new, since it went back to the seventeenth century, but the Education Act of 1870 had made matters much worse for Welsh since it set up a complete network of elementary schools to which attendance became compulsory in 1880 (roughly the same date as in France). Secondary education was introduced in 1889, which further increased the impact of English. Welsh was never actually forbidden,[15] as the RLs were in France, but other pressures were brought to bear, apart from the social pressures mentioned above. Thus, the Revised Code of 1861 instigated that teachers only collected their full salaries if they could prove their pupils had made adequate progress, particularly in English. There was therefore no gain in teaching Welsh, and since the Education Act of 1870 maintained the same financial incentives, Welsh gradually disappeared from the timetable. As a consequence, it also started disappearing from areas where it had survived intact until then.

Some Welsh educationalists reacted against the educational appropriateness of teaching monoglot Welsh speakers only through the medium of English. This led the schools inspector Dan Isaac Davies to set up in 1885 a Society for the Utilisation of Welsh in Education, the proclaimed aim of which was to improve the teaching of English. His approach was probably wilfully ambiguous in the sense that it appears to use the RL to help its monoglot speakers acquire the national official language, whereas it was probably meant as a covert form of defence for Welsh. (The French Deixonne law was similarly ambiguous nearly three-quarters of a century later.) This society came to be known as the Welsh Language Society or *Cymdeithas yr Iaith Gymraeg*. The same title was chosen in 1962 for the foundation of a society to revive Welsh in Wales, out of respect for Dan Isaac Davies.

Davies also submitted a Royal Commission's report, which recommended capitation grants for schools which taught Welsh and the use of bilingual books. The weakness in what was granted by the state was that everything was optional, but it had the advantage of granting Welsh a presence in at least some schools. Welsh also became a possible subject for examination in the secondary sector from 1895, just about a century before the same happened for Breton in France. Education has therefore been both a force opposed to Welsh, and one which let it in by the back door.

No such progress was made in law and administration during the nineteenth and early twentieth centuries. (Since 1889, English was the sole language of the newly formed local authorities.) One of the problems was the complete lack of interest on the part of most politicians. Thus David Lloyd George, despite being Welsh and a dedicated Welsh speaker, did nothing to help Welsh survive at a time of rapid decline, for he had far more pressing social reforms to introduce. Nor did the Labour Party since it was internationalist in its early days. Then came the blow of World War One, in which 40 000 young male Welsh speakers were killed. And finally the economic crisis of the 1920s which led the Welsh to emigrate for the first time, usually to England or America. A press nearly entirely in English and the glamour of an English-speaking cinema completed the move towards general Anglicisation.

And yet the end of the nineteenth century had been seen as the 'Golden Age' of Welsh, because of its large number of speakers. Dan Isaac Davies had predicted in 1885 that by 1985 there would be three million bilinguals in Wales. This was wildly optimistic, since according to the 2001 census, the numbers were 575 460 being able to speak it and 222 077 having some skill or combination of skills other than the ability to speak it (138 416 comprehension of spoken Welsh, and 83 661 oral comprehension plus an ability to read or write, or read and write) (see Dunbar 2003a). This makes a total of just under 800 000 able to understand it, which represents an improvement of 2 per cent on ten years previously.

These figures are a long way from Dan Isaac Davies' prediction of three million. Moreover, the gross figures are misleading in that they cannot expose the real problem, which is the lack of intergenerational transmission within the family. But where he was right was in introducing the concept of bilingualism as a basis for Welsh-ness. The very fact that by 1911 only 43 per cent of the population spoke Welsh, whereas the population as a whole felt Welsh, meant it was time to rethink what is meant by being Welsh. In the past Welsh-ness had always been defined by language, and yet from then on there were two languages in Wales, Welsh and English. This created in the 1920s and 1930s unprecedented stress for the Welsh, faced with the death of their defining national marker, which led some Welsh militants to some drastic actions, as well as legal ones.

Among the legal initiatives, there was the launching by Ifan ab Owen Edwards of the Welsh League of Youth in 1922 (*Urdd Gobaith Cymru*) which organised Welsh-speaking summer camps, which were very successful. Then in 1925 came the launching of the National Party of Wales (*Plaid Genedlaethol Cymru*), whose aim was mainly to re-establish the use of Welsh. Its first president was the controversial Saunders Lewis, who set fire, along with two accomplices, to a bombing school, which had been set up, despite objections from the locals, in an area judged to be essentially Welsh in language and culture. All three gave themselves up to the police and stood trial in Caernarfon in 1936. They requested to use Welsh for their case, but this was contemptuously rejected. When the jury failed to agree on a verdict, the case went to the Old Bailey, which sent them to prison for nine months. This turned the culprits into martyrs overnight. They received a hero's welcome on their return to Wales, and a petition was launched seeking to repeal the language clause in the 1536 Act of Union. This led to the Welsh Courts Act of 1942 which allowed for Welsh to be used in any court in Wales by any party or witness who considers that otherwise they would be disadvantaged. It also led to the Education Act of 1944 which enabled Welsh-medium schools to be opened.

These achievements fell far short of the demands of the Welsh nationalists and language militants. One of the problems they encountered after World War Two was that Saunders Lewis, the founder of the Welsh Nationalist Party in the 1930s, had supported Franco and other right-wing dictators (much the same had happened in Brittany). Another more important reason which explains why, after the war, nobody seemed to care about the fact that by 1951 only one person in three spoke Welsh, was the seriousness of the social problems which characterised the post-war period. Although the Welsh had a great political representative in Aneurin Bevan, the Welsh Labour politician showed little interest in Welsh given the pressing social ills he had to deal with as Minister of Health (1945–51). It was therefore left to individuals to take up the fight.

### The fightback

The 1960s and the decades which followed were quite different in character. They were marked by the end of the British Empire on the one hand, and a worldwide new approach to human rights on the other. It is in this context that a number of events took place which mark the revival of Welsh. Some actions were small but symbolic, such as the Beasleys, from Llangennech, refusing to fill in their tax returns in English and to pay their taxes. An important incident was the Liverpool Corporation flooding a valley in which there was a completely Welsh-speaking village, Trewerin,[16] in 1960, which caused such an outrage as to mark a turning a point in the history of the language. Numerous protests followed, such as stopping traffic, and major demonstrations took place in 1965 when the reservoir was opened. Defacing road signs and painting onto them their proper Welsh spellings was also popular. This led in the

1970s to official bilingual signs being put up. They are now part of the landscape. More recently there has been a campaign run by *Cymuned* (civil rights activists) for a return to Welsh topographical names. This is part of a worldwide movement in this direction (cf. the renaming of Ayres Rock in Australia as Uluru, its Aboriginal name).

The various governments in place could not afford to ignore such a movement. It led, in 1964, to the establishment a Welsh Office with a Secretary for Wales, in which Welsh issues were to be discussed, particularly those appertaining to the Welsh language. It was based in Cardiff, and brought with it hundreds of jobs. For the first time, speaking Welsh became a positive asset when applying for such jobs. This innovation was followed by the first Welsh Language Act in 1967 which allowed for Welsh to be used in all official contexts, although English was to be retained as the language of the courts, in accordance with the language clause of the Act of Union of 1536. A particularly important move was the creation of a Welsh television channel in 1982 (see below), and in 1988 an advisory body, the Welsh Language Board, was set up to recommend further linguistic legislation. The success of the Welsh medium schools was also fairly spectacular (see below).

As a result of these successes and the fact that the language militants were still not satisfied, Westminster passed three more Acts which further enhanced the status of Welsh: the Education Reform Act of 1988, the second Welsh Language Act of 1993, and finally, as a result of a successful referendum held in 1997 on the establishment of a Welsh Assembly, the Government of Wales Act in 1998. The Education Act of 1988 made Welsh a core subject in Welsh-speaking schools and a foundation subject in non-Welsh-speaking schools (see below for more details). The Welsh Language Act of 1993 gave statutory recognition to the Welsh Language Board founded in 1988, and established the principle that in the conduct of public business and the administration of justice in Wales both Welsh and English should be treated equally. Jobs in the public sector, for example, have to be advertised in both languages. It therefore imposed a degree of compulsion. The Government of Wales Act 1998 gave devolved government to Wales in the shape of the Welsh Assembly.

The Welsh Assembly, in which more than half the members are Welsh speakers, has proved very supportive to the language. Ron Davies, the Secretary of State, pledged in 1998, at the *National Eisteddfod*, that both languages would have equal status in the Assembly, which they now have. The percentage of the Assembly business carried out in Welsh was only 10 per cent in the early days of the Assembly, but it is hoped it will increase, although this presents a problem of principle for those members of the Assembly returned mainly by English-speaking communities. But whatever the percentage, making it possible for Welsh to be used is making a statement about its worth. Moreover, well before that, there were also a number of councils which either functioned in Welsh only (e.g. Dwyfor), or provided either a fully bilingual administration (e.g. Gwynedd) or an element of bilingualism (e.g. Dyfed). All depends on the density of Welsh speakers in place and their degree of commitment towards the language.

The results of these dramatic institutional changes over the years could first be first measured in 1991 when the census showed the first rise in the number of Welsh speakers in a century. The 2001 census is more encouraging still: whereas the 1991 census gave 18.7 per cent of the population as able to speak the language, in 2001 the figure was 20.5 per cent. This shows the importance of sympathetic linguistic policies when trying to save a language. It may be argued, of course, as some do, that these are not 'natural' speakers, and that their accents are not totally 'Welsh'. But all languages change, usually for reasons of interference from others, in this case English, and to condemn the result as not 'real' Welsh would be to condemn the language as a whole.

The problem is that it still does not give official status to Welsh, in so far as its use is not compulsory. The right to use Welsh in law courts is allowed 'as long as due notice is given'. This clearly does not give Welsh the same weight as English (Aitchison and Carter 1994: 113–14). It does not create the right for a court to function entirely in Welsh, only the litigants and the witnesses. Moreover, although the Act stipulates that every public body which provides for a public service must prepare a 'scheme' specifying the measures it proposes to take as to the use of Welsh, this obligation is qualified by the words 'so far as is both appropriate in the circumstances and reasonably practical'.

Another problem which has been well analysed by Robert Dunbar (2003a) is the fact that the Act does not give any individual right to Welsh. If individuals are discontented at the failure of an official body to carry out an approved scheme, they have to complain to the Welsh Language Board, which may (but only 'may') then undertake an investigation. If there has been failure, the Board will then contact the public body concerned and demand the faulty situation be remedied. If this meets with no success, the Board can then address a complaint to the Welsh Assembly, which will then take whatever measures it chooses, which may be implemented through the courts. At no point can the individual concerned do anything of his own accord apart from alerting the Board to the problem enountered. The fact that the Welsh Language Board is at present a 'quango' (i.e. a quasi-autonomous non-governmental organisation) is also seen as regrettable and even undemocratic. This has resulted in unfortunate rifts among the militants between those willing to function within the system and those who won't.

In other words, to use Dunbar's words, the model followed is not an 'individual rights model' but an 'administrative enabling' or 'planning based' model. Those who want more need an individual rights model, for as things stand at present, if the Board does not to want to investigate a complaint, nothing compels it to do so. In an 'individual rights' model the individual can follow complaint procedures, going through the courts if necessary. It would purely be the complainant's decision.

Another problem which worries language militants is the lack of any compulsion on businesses to follow suit. They complain that this allows for a bilingual situation, in which English will continue to be the language of economics, which, by definition, means the dominant language. But both the 1993 Language Act and the Welsh Language Board represent important steps in the right direction. Welsh now has a degree of visibility in the public domain since all official forms have to appear in both languages and as a result a knowledge of Welsh has widened job opportunities. It acts as a model for other RLs, particularly Scottish Gaelic, and is the envy of most.

Apart from the areas of law and administration, education and the media are the other areas in which recognition of a RL is of major importance. The Education Act 1988 is, in this respect, the culmination of years of efforts. The first improvement came with the official guidelines issued in 1907, which allowed for the use of Welsh in primary schools and in kindergartens. Then the 1927 official *Welsh in Education and Life Report* expressed worries in relation to deficiencies in the teaching of Welsh. The tone was by then far removed from that of the Blue Books. In the mid-1940s, Welsh was widely used as a medium of instruction in primary schools where Welsh was still the predominant language. Elsewhere, efforts to teach Welsh to monoglot English speakers varied according to the local authority. But all this was done on an *ad hoc* basis. Then the 1944 Education Act established a major change in obliging local education authorities to provide Welsh-medium education in primary schools where sufficient demand existed.

As a result, 1947 saw the opening of the first state Welsh medium school, designated as such. Others followed in quick succession. Its original aim was to teach children from Welsh-speaking families to be educated in their mother tongue, but they rapidly attracted a majority of pupils from

English-speaking Welsh homes. These days, in some parts of Wales, over 95 per cent of pupils in Welsh medium schools come from non-Welsh-speaking homes.

Development of these schools has been rapid. By 1974 there were 61 designated Welsh primary schools. By 2001–2 there were 442 Welsh designated schools with a total of nearly 51 334 pupils (about 27.2 per cent of all primary schools, and 18.2 per cent of all pupils) (Dunbar 2003a). By the following year, the number attending Welsh-only or main medium education had risen to 51 977.[17] There were no primary schools where no Welsh was taught.

By 2001–2[18] (Dunbar 2003a) there were 53 secondary schools, with 38 817 pupils (about 22.5 per cent of all secondary schools and 14.4 per cent of all pupils) in which more than half the foundation subjects were taught wholly or partly in Welsh. By the following year the number of children being educated in these schools had risen to 39 458. There were no secondary schools where no Welsh was taught.

The development of a Welsh medium nursery school system is probably the most important of all since, given the partial break in intergenerational transmission, they are the only ones to lay the linguistic foundations necessary for children to be able to progress further in the educational system. By the time the Nursery Schools Movement (*Mudiad Ysgolion Meithrin* or MYM) was founded in 1971, there were already 68 such schools. By 2005, the movement was responsible for some 600 classes and 435 mother and toddler groups. In December 2004 it received a grant of £1 million from the Welsh Assembly. Neither parents nor children need to speak Welsh in order to be able to attend, the aim being for children to play, learn and socialise through the medium of Welsh.

The expansion of nursery and primary Welsh medium schools was particularly rapid in the Cardiff area, creating new Welsh native speakers, in the same way as the immersion schools have done in France. The difference here is that they belong to the state sector (even the first 1939 private Welsh medium primary school was integrated into the public sector). The problem so far is that despite their success, their pupils tend to abandon their language when they get back home, or play with their friends. Aitchinson and Carter have commented on the fact that 'Welsh is a plant which has been growing energetically but which has not yet produced a deep and extensive root system' (quoted in J. Davies 1999: 81).

As children from these schools reached secondary school age, pressure built up for Welsh medium secondary schools. The first opened in 1958. Some of these use only Welsh, while others have a more bilingual approach. The Education Act of 1988 made Welsh a core subject in the National Curriculum in all Welsh medium schools. The proportion of Welsh taught as a second language in non-medium primary schools varies from county to county, but all children are exposed to some Welsh. From 1999 all secondary schools were to offer Welsh as a second language up to the age of 16. This had important implications in term of the numbers of teachers and resources required if all GCSE and A level subjects are allowed to be sat using the medium of Welsh.

The major problem for those educated in this way is the lack of adequate provision at university level, although this is now slowly improving. The fact that there are very few courses offered in Welsh in scientific subjects has an obvious deterrent effect in terms of sending children to all-Welsh schools.

Moreover, such developments have not been without attracting controversy. Originally the Welsh designated schools were opened in areas where little Welsh was spoken, since it was assumed that Welsh would be used in the others. As a result, the former county of Gwynedd, a strongly Welsh-speaking area, had a policy of sending children to either Welsh medium secondary schools or English medium secondary schools, or bilingual schools, depending on their linguistic ability in each of those languages. The Local Education Authority was, however, taken to court by a parent who wished his child, a native speaker of Welsh, to be taught through English. He alleged racial discrimination when this was refused. The case fell through on a technicality, leaving the situation still unclear, but the principles involved are reminiscent of the Jacobin attitude, except that the Jacobin concept of equality has been recast as 'anti-discriminatory'.

Similarly, the Dyfed Local Education Authority tried to categorise schools according to the language of each community. It ended up with 188 mostly rural primary schools categorised as Welsh-medium. This was challenged by a pressure group, Education First, claiming this was discriminatory to non-Welsh speaking children in the area. In this case the county's decision was largely vindicated (Awbery 1998: 160–1).

Groups of academics in Aberystwyth and Bangor also established a movement called the Language Freedom Movement, active in resisting all moves to integrate Welsh into the curriculum: a clear case of Jacobinism. On the other hand, the adult education sector is thriving. Courses were set up, inspired by the renaissance of Hebrew in Israel. Some of these courses are very intensive such as the eight-week course held yearly at Lampeter. Welsh reality television also had a kind of 'Big Brother' programme, with twelve people isolated in a remote village in

North Wales for eight weeks to learn Welsh, filmed as they attempted to come to grips with the language. The first series was voted 'Best Light Entertainment' in the 2003 Welsh BAFTAs.

The reasons for adults wanting to learn Welsh are varied. Some want to help their children whom they have sent to Welsh medium schools, others may be part of a mixed marriage, or, having moved to Wales, may wish to become accepted by Welsh society, while others may simply wish to improve their chances on the job market. As many as 1 million people are said to be learning, or interested in learning, Welsh. This represents a remarkable success for the campaign to make Welsh popular, particularly when one considers that devolved government for Wales was turned down in 1979 partly because of the fear of 'Welsh taking over'.

Equally important in the spreading of a language is the media. Its oldest form, publishing, goes back to the sixteenth century, but the problem is that given the market forces which prevail today, publishing in Welsh is not a particularly attractive financial proposition, hence a need for subsidies and general help. The Welsh Joint Education Committee has been active in this sphere since 1954, and specific counties such as Cardiganshire started subsidising the publication of books for children even earlier. A Welsh Books Council was instituted in 1961 specifically to give grants to publishers. In 1997, 636 books were published in Welsh, on all kinds of subjects, including lighter subjects such as home hairdressing (Awbery 1998: 163). Interestingly some new publishers have appeared on the scene, who publish, to quote Janet Davies, 'material considered too titillating or too extreme by the other presses' (1999: 90). This seems an encouraging departure, whatever one's opinion on 'titillating material', since it implies a normalising of a language which has tended to be associated with the lofty spheres of religion and poetry (one-third of books published for adults are on poetry), to which must now be added educational books. One of the gaps still seems to be books for older children and young people, who tend to turn to English at this stage, thus endangering the Welsh revival project.

The periodical press seems less healthy, compared to its golden age in the nineteenth century. There is no daily newspaper in Welsh, although there are weeklies covering current affairs. But the 1950s saw the launching of a host of new periodicals covering all kinds of topics, including scientific ones, thanks to the financial help received from the Welsh Arts Council, founded in 1967. The only periodicals not needing help are the neighbourhood newspapers, By 1998, there were 56 of these, with a combined circulation of around 52 000.

Most important are the new media, however, namely radio and television, both for spreading a language and codifying it. Welsh-speaking radio broadcasting developed early on in the 1940s and 1950s in the context of the official BBC. In 1953, Wales was given its own Broadcasting Council. At this point, its members asked for more hours to be devoted to Welsh, which met with opposition from the majority of non-Welsh speakers. This problem was resolved in 1978 with the creation of an all-Welsh station (Radio Cymru) and an all-English one (Radio Wales). By the 1990s Radio Cymru was broadcasting from 6 a.m. to 12 p.m. Local radio stations also broadcast in Welsh.

Problems were not resolved as easily where television is concerned. Indeed it took a hunger strike in 1979 for a Welsh channel, S4C, to be created. And yet when the BBC started transmitting in 1952, it offered a series of Welsh programmes. Similarly when Television Wales and West started broadcasting in 1958, programmes in Welsh were included. By the 1960s the two channels together were broadcasting some 11.5 hours per week. These were, however, at off-peak times. Demand grew for a fully Welsh-speaking channel, which was promised by the Labour government in 1974. The following Conservative government, elected in 1979, went back on its promise to that effect, endorsed when in opposition. This caused an outrage, and the president of *Plaid Cymru*, Gwynfor Evans, went on hunger strike, addressed numerous rallies, and helped to create an atmosphere of fear on the part of the British government.

As a result, Sianel Pedwar Cymru, or S4C (Welsh fourth channel) went on air in 1982. Its core funding is guaranteed by the Broadcasting Acts of 1990 and 1996. According to the 1991 census, 50 per cent of Welsh speakers looked at a particularly popular soap opera, *Pobl y cwm*, i.e. 'People of the valley', and the figure quoted for 1996 for the same programme was 82 per cent (Awbery 1998: 162). In 1998 a new digital channel was launched, which supplies 12 hours per week. S4C has an output of 154 hours per week, with between 35 and 40 in Welsh. The other programmes are usually bought from outside Wales. Subtitling in English has been a way of extending the reach of the channel, and making it useful for those learning the language. According to S4C's annual report for 2004, there was an upturn in viewing figures (the first in many years) and a £34.4 million profit was made from commercial investment.

Again this has been an area in which progress has been marked by controversy, with those in favour of Welsh radio and television clashing with those against, who object to the development of what they see as sectarianism.

The demographic position is an interesting one in that it illustrates that simply looking at figures in the abstract does not paint a true picture, and that the percentage of the population able to speak a language gives a better picture. As far as numbers of speakers are concerned, the last adult monoglot Welsh speaker is said to have died in the 1960s, but Janet Davies states (1999: 71) that monolingualism in Welsh among small children continues to be high, and seems to be on the increase thanks to the Welsh medium education policies in place. This alone places Welsh in a quite different category to the other RLs in Britain.

The latest census return is very encouraging in that it shows, for the first time, an increase in the number of Welsh speakers, after a century of decline. In 1901, just under 50 per cent of the population claimed to be Welsh speaking, while the 1991 census gave only 18.7 per cent. But the 2001 census gave the figure of 20.5 per cent of people in Wales who said they could speak the language (around 600 000), and 28 per cent (around 800 000) ticked the box to say they could understand it. But while the use of Welsh is on the rise in urban areas, such as Cardiff, and the Anglicised south east, it is declining in some of its traditional 'heartland' or 'core' areas in the north and west. Some feel that this is the real problem. The conclusions drawn by Huw Lewis, Chair of the Welsh Language Society, are as follows: (i) 'The reality that faces the language in communities across Wales is very different.' This has important language policies consequences. (ii) 'We must accept that we can only safeguard and develop the Welsh language by implementing far reaching holistic policies, in fields such as housing, planning status, education and transport.' This brings up some important problems in terms of the legality of such policies (see below). (iii) 'Half-hearted, bit-part solutions will never be enough – you can't half save a language.'

These conclusions were echoed by Rhodri Williams, chairman of the Welsh Language Board: (i) 'The decline in the western counties is something which the Board has been aware of for years. Even though it is important to welcome the increase in the south-east, it is also imperative that we all work together to halt any further decline in the western counties.' This refers to the fact mentioned earlier that Welsh in the newly Welsh-ified south is still a plant with very shallow roots, which develops in school, and can be dropped in adulthood. Its transmission to the next generation is far from assured. And (ii) 'In the face of substantial decline in the fortunes of minority languages in every part of the world, it is immensely gratifying to be able to announce that the Welsh language is on the up.'[19] Which is why most writers refer to being able to be speak in terms of 'modest optimism'. One optimistic pointer is that the 1992 Welsh Office survey revealed that where both parents are Welsh speakers, 81 per cent of the children are also fluent. Since the figures are lower for older age groups, this suggests a greater determination to pass on the language than in relatively recent times (Awbery 1998: 166).

The reason optimism has to be modest, however, is clear if one examines Aitchison's and Carter's maps giving percentages of the population speaking the language. Whereas the 1971 map shows over 80 per cent of Welsh speakers in all the 'core' areas, and few or none in the Anglicised south and east, the 1991 map shows only very small and very few pockets of purely Welsh-speaking areas, while there has been a dramatic increase both in the south and in the east. In other words the Welsh-speaking population may have increased, but it is widely diluted.

This is partly due to an influx of English speakers. It started in the 1960s with the buying of holiday homes (which were sometimes burned down by language militants, adding to the other forms of pressure brought to bear on the British government which, in turn, no doubt helped increase the visibility of Welsh). Many made these houses their retirement homes, thus bringing English into often purely Welsh speaking areas. The areas where cottages were cheap were the rural areas, hit by the rural exodus to the south, thus increasing the numbers of Welsh speakers there. Some also settled in Wales, in search of a more environmentally friendly lifestyle. Whatever the reason, the influx was huge,[20] and often into the core areas (the chair of the Gwynedd County Council's Housing Committee referred to the threat posed by between 90 and 100 per cent of all homes put on the market being sold to outsiders[21]).

This brings in the whole problem of what it is to be Welsh. Those who feel that Welshness is defined by the language[22] wish to slow down the in-migration from England, by monitoring, for example, the purchase of houses in Wales, and only allowing this to happen where the Anglophone expresses a willingness to learn Welsh (which some do). There have also been complaints that English people retiring in Wales are a weight on the community. This kind of statement, associated with *Plaid Cymru*, has brought accusations of racialism against the English. This is true, but, on the other hand, the only way to save Welsh is for the whole population, including the Anglophones, to become bilingual. The accusation of racism can clearly be countered by that of respect for your host's culture. (Except that some English speakers see Wales as a mere extension of England. Clearly the debate is never ending.)

The problem for the language is that not all Welsh people feel that to be Welsh you have to speak the language. Some castigate those who create jobs for which a knowledge of Welsh is necessary, protesting that this is blackmail. The writer Byron Rogers, for example, maintains that such policies exclude the vast majority from these jobs, and that just as a similar majority used to be dispossessed for lack of fluency in English, the same is happening again the other way round. He concludes 'Dispossession in our own country is for us a very old experience, it is just that in its time it has taken many forms' (Rogers 2003: xiv). He thus fulfils Saunders Lewis' prophecy, made in 1962 in a famous radio broadcast. He stated that the way things were going, Welsh would be dead by the twenty-first century, unless it became an official state language, used in all public domains. But he warned that this would encounter not just external opposition, which he thought would not be too problematic, but opposition from the Welsh themselves: 'The opposition – harsh, vindictive and violent – would come from Wales' (Aitchison and Carter 1994: 42). He is not alone, since many fear that Welsh is divisive, and goes against Wales' historical cosmopolitanism. Some of its militants, such as Saunders Lewis, have also been associated with right-wing nationalism in Europe.

Janet Davies (1999) herself mentions in her introduction that for the majority of the people of Wales, the language has only a marginal impact and that she felt no less Welsh as a child when she did not speak the language compared to now when she does. She points out that pessimism comes from those who lament the disappearance of a monoglot population and a disappearing way of life. From her bilingual standpoint, Welsh has a future, albeit a different one. For Welsh to survive, it is necessary to prove that its knowledge is life-enhancing. Unfortunately she does not say how.

One suggestion is to channel some of the underused energies of the often disaffected young into Welsh cultural events, of the pop music and other lower-brow varieties. This is indeed happening at present, since there are numerous pop groups functioning in Welsh (they appear to be particularly popular in Eastern Europe). On a more negative note, it is also well known that being a native speaker of Welsh creates for its speakers – particularly in North Wales – a sort of freemasonry, with Welsh as a secret code. Many have experienced, in this respect, the tendency to switch from English to Welsh if an English intruder comes in.

Another important positive aspect of the Welsh revival is the creation of new employment. According to research carried out at the Cardiff University Economic Unit, at least 2000 jobs have been created in the Cardiff region, which means that the young do not have to leave Wales in search of work, particularly if they are interested in working in the media. Teaching is another wide open field. This may explain why English speakers in Wales seem to be becoming less worried about Welsh than they used to be, and why many send their children to Welsh medium schools and try to learn it themselves. Welsh medium schools are also considered to be more academic. Welsh has therefore become more acceptable to the majority of the population. This is illustrated by the fact that membership of the nationalist *Plaid Cymru* has considerably broadened over recent years. Although knowing Welsh was never a condition to joining, the party nonetheless tended to attract mainly Welsh speakers. Nowadays membership includes many people who would traditionally have been regarded as foreigners. Not only have many originally English people joined, but also numerous Americans have joined up, and at least one Muslim, at the time of writing.

## The Cornish revival

### Historical development

Cornish and Welsh could not be more different in terms of their history. And yet, historically, the Cornish people and the Welsh spoke the same language. It was the victory of the West Saxons at the Battle of Dyrham in AD 577 which effectively split the southern Britons into two peoples. Their common language is thought to have started diverging from the end of the seventh century. The gradual advance of the Anglo-Saxon kingdom of Wessex also resulted in population movements from Dorset and Devon into Brittany and Galicia in northwestern Spain. In Brittany their speech survived as Breton, and it was the maintenance of trading and cultural links between Brittany and Cornwall, from the sixth to the sixteenth centuries, which helped Cornish survive. Some now claim to have resurrected such exchanges.

Those who stayed in Britain found their domain gradually reduced, until its boundary became fixed in the tenth century at the Tamar, after their expulsion from Devon in 936, where it has remained ever since. Cornwall was regarded nonetheless as a separate province, although subordinate to the English Crown, but with separate ecclesiastical provision in the earliest period. A sympathetic attitude to Cornish characterised the pre-Reformation Church. Cornwall also retained at first some of its own institutions, namely the Stannary parliament, which had its origins in 1198 and 1201 when the Cornish and Devon tin interests were separated. This developed into a separate Cornish parliament maintaining Cornish customary law (Cornwall was divided into four areas, each electing six men to the Stannary parliament). Further royal charters confirmed the constitution and powers of the parliament, including veto over English legislation.

Although the influence of the Stannary parliament waned over the centuries, this semi-independence continued even after 1337 when Cornwall was annexed *de facto* and became the Duchy of Cornwall. Indeed, there followed a period marked by some stability for Cornwall and its language, hence present-day militants wishing for the term 'Duchy of Cornwall' to be retained, since it illustrates its separate status from England.[23] This period of relative stability came to an end with the advent of the Tudors (Henry VII, 1485–1509) who constantly interfered and eroded Cornwall's semi-independent status.

The first major rebellion took place in 1497. It was triggered by the imposition of what was considered to be both an immoral and illegal tax, and the confiscation of the Stannary charters and the suspension of the Stannary government. A peaceful march to London ended in the slaughter of an estimated 2000 people (the English reports give 200), mainly of men of marriageable age, thus dealing a demographic blow to a language that had already been badly affected by the Black Death in the 1340s.

The second major rebellion was caused by the Reformation, when the imposition of the English Prayer Book caused an outcry in Cornwall, where Latin was the language of religion and Cornish the language used in all other domains. The Cornish people objected their lack of knowledge of English. But in England this was seen as a stand against the Reformation, and something to be crushed at all costs, which it was, in 1549, when the Crown ordered the slaughter of 10 per cent of Cornwall's male population (900 were killed in front of Exeter cathedral, an event which was commemorated in 1999). These risings have been compared to the Jacobite risings of 1715 and 1745 in Scotland, with similar implications for the language, the most destructive being the imposition of English as the language of religion.

It is true that from 1560 catechism and sermons, the Lord's Prayer, the Ten Commandments and the Apostle's Creed, were allowed in Cornish where English was not understood, but this was not sufficient to give a solid base to the language, as the translation of the Prayer Book and Bible had done for Welsh. As a result, whereas there had been a rich Cornish literature before the Reformation, mainly of a religious nature, which included in particular famous miracle plays, this ceased nearly completely with the Reformation.[24] All the monasteries and places of learning were destroyed, and Cornish soon started a slow decline. The Reformation also reduced substantially the traditional ties with Brittany, isolating the language from all external contact. It continued, despite its demographical decline, to be developed as a literary medium throughout the seventeenth and eighteenth centuries. Indeed there has never been a total absence of literary and intellectual interest in Cornish, from the time of its decline to the present day, which is what has made its revival possible.

The next important influence in Cornwall was Methodism, first brought there by Wesley in 1743 (according the 1851 census there were only 14 per cent Anglicans in Cornwall), but the Cornish language was by then too weak for a Methodist preaching tradition in the vernacular to become established, as it had done in Wales and in the Isle of Man. Moreover, Cornwall having been until then the most industrialised area of Britain, this had brought a steady influx of incomers, which further accentuated its decline.

Despite this, educated people continued to write in Cornish, labelled subsequently 'Late Cornish'. They were the first to become concerned about the fate of their language, being well aware of the reasons for its demise, namely loss of contact with Brittany, loss of the miracle play tradition, the dismissive attitude of the gentry, and increased contact with outsiders. The lack of a Cornish Prayer Book is also blamed (Payton 2000: 114). But Cornish continued to be used for the Lord's Prayer, the Creed and, on a more prosaic level, for counting, particularly of fish, one of the two mainstays of the economy, the other being mining. It has also been reported that at the very end of the eighteenth century, when travellers going to America stopped in Falmouth, they had the impression they were in exotic surroundings because of the different language spoken there (Gauthier 1995: 89–90).

Thus although the last reputed monoglot speaker of Cornish, Dolly Pentreath, died in 1777, the language continued to be written, and spoken at least in 'bits', particularly amongst the lower classes. It also seems that Dolly was not quite the last speaker. Some claim it was John Davey, a schoolmaster near Zennor (1812–91), who is said to have kept his knowledge of Cornish alive by speaking to his cat (but he was, of course, bilingual). He also wrote a short piece of original verse. Other nineteenth-century speakers have also been mentioned. This sad state of affairs may be contrasted with the estimated 38 000 who spoke Cornish in the fourteenth century, when the number of its speakers was at its peak.

### The revival of Cornish

To whomever the title of last speaker of Cornish should go, its survival from the late eighteenth century onwards was due to what have been termed 'semi-speakers', and specialists who collected what remained of the spoken language. Almanacs and pamphlets about Cornish continued to be produced, and lectures continued to be given, ensuring that Cornish remained a living part of Cornish culture.

One of the first academics to take an interest in Cornish was Edward Lhuyd (1660–1709), an Oxford scholar involved in a comparative study of the Celtic languages. He visited Cornwall in about 1700 and recorded all he could of the Cornish language, including its sounds, having discovered it was still spoken in some twenty-five parishes. Jacob George, for his part, produced a *Memoranda of Old Cornish Words still current in Mousehole and Newlyn* in 1858.

The most important in terms of the modern revivalist movement was Henry Jenner (1848–1934), a Cornishman working at the British Museum, who developed a passion for the language, and toured Cornwall collecting its remnants. Jenner's 1904 *A Handbook of the Cornish Language* represents the first effort at full reconstruction. He based the legitimacy of its revival on the fact that there had never been a time when there had been no person in Cornwall without some knowledge of the language. He also established the principle of Cornwall as a Celtic nation, and even became a bard in both Welsh and Breton, which illustrates the closeness of these three languages even in the twentieth century. In 1907 he inaugurated a Cornish *Gorseth*, similar to the Welsh *Eisteddfod*, which became a yearly occasion from 1928 on. Jenner was seen as the father of the Cornish revival.

Another major figure was Robert Morton Nance (1873–1959) who founded, with Jenner, the Old Cornwall Society in 1920. It started producing a journal, *Old Cornwall*, in 1925, which has survived to this day, the aim of which was to collect 'the fragments of the past' in order to regenerate Cornwall's national identity, culture and language. It contains frequent Cornish-language articles. A youth movement was established, called *Tyr ha Tavas* (Land and Language), and it also produced a literary magazine, *Kernow*, which only lasted from 1934–6, but was to have an important influence. Nance also published *Cornish for All* in 1929.

It seems that revivalists such as Jenner and Nance wrote Cornish – the written tradition never having died out completely – but probably had little initial speaking ability before World War One. But in the interwar period, the revivalist movement aimed to bring back to life the spoken language as well. Hence A. S. D. Smith produced *Lessons in Spoken Cornish* in 1931. A dictionary was produced by Nance shortly afterwards.

The establishment of *Gorseth Kernow* and the beginning of church services in Cornish in 1933 encouraged such an enterprise, as did the writing of a number of plays by Nance and Peggy Pollard. By the 1930s at least twelve people were able to speak the language, including Nance's daughter who had been brought up to speak the language, and who may be considered as the revival's first 'native Cornish speaker', A new magazine, *New Cornwall*, was started in 1952 and lasted until 1973, which carried articles of contemporary interest, some of which were in Cornish. 1967 saw the foundation of a Cornish Language Board (*Kesva an Tavas Kernewek*) to bring the language, through education, to a much broader public and to organise classes and examinations, while increasing Cornish consciousness. This led, in the 1970s, to the organisation of gatherings 'to chat' in Cornish (*Yeth an Weryn*), throughout Cornwall.

Music has also played an important part in this revival. The first broadcast in revived Cornish was a programme of choral music in 1935, after which singing in Cornish became very popular. This general interest in Cornish spread to a much wider circle in the 1970s, i.e. at the same time as other RLs benefited from a revival of interest. This period saw the appearance of Cornish language camps, Cornish language walks, and at this time a number of young families started to use Cornish as a language in the home. An organisation called *Dalleth* ('Beginning') was founded in 1979 to support bilingualism in the home. In 1981 a children's periodical *Len ha Lyw* ('Read and Colour') was founded to support early language acquisition. Texts then started to be published in Cornish by a number of publishers. Formal church services in Cornish increased. They include in particular, Christmas and Harvest Festival services. There have been a number of religious publications in Cornish: vespers in 1935, a hymnary and psalter in 1962, editions of Mark and John in 1976, the Book of Common Prayer in 1980, and in 2002 the New Testament.

There are, however, practical problems associated with Cornish, which emerged mainly in the 1980s, since there are now at least three varieties of revived Cornish in use. Previously, when the Cornish Language Board (*Kesva an Tavas Kernewek*) was created as an examining authority in 1967, it had the backing of all speakers who were happy to see it operate using Nance's version of Cornish, 'Unified Cornish'. But, by the 1980s, the circle of Cornish speakers had broadened considerably, and therefore more thought was given to pronunciation and then to orthography and its relationship with pronunciation. It was then that differences of opinion arose.

Originally Jenner had based his revival of Cornish 'where it had left off', and his spelling and pronunciation were influenced by the tradition of speaking of the last semi-Cornish speakers. Nance, on the other hand, wanted a return to the literary language used in medieval literature, in order to build on what was well documented, namely Middle Cornish.[25] Where faced with a void, he supplemented the language with words drawn from Late Cornish or even Breton or Welsh. From this emerged 'Unified Cornish', the pronunciation of which was supposed to derive from Late Cornish. It was this form which became the norm for the

*Gorseth Kernow* annual ceremonies, and was the language used by revivalists during the interwar years.

It was during the 1980s that a number of academic Celticists attacked Nance's 'unscientific' reconstruction (see Price 1984). This led to much heated debate and research, and an important new version of Cornish was developed by Ken George, which he named 'Common Cornish' (*Kernewek Kemmyn*). It was similarly based on the Middle Cornish period (c. 1500), but where George's system differs from Nance's is in the estimation of how Middle Cornish must have been pronounced, which he worked out using computer programmes. This in turn affected spelling. Common Cornish was adopted by the Cornish Language Board in 1987, and the bulk of recent literary output has also been in this form. But the Language Board also administers examinations in Unified Cornish, and its membership includes users of both.

Other revivalists, on the other hand, had come to the conclusion that Jenner's suggestion that revived Cornish should be based on what had survived from Late Cornish was the correct one. This led Richard Gendall and others, in the 1980s, to adopt a new Modern Cornish (*Kernuack*) version based on the Late period, and with Late period pronunciation. This was derived in part from the Cornish accent still present in the forms of English spoken in the far western part of Cornwall. The justification for this was that the non-standard sounds used in English correspond to Lhuyd's sound descriptions of Cornish of the 1700s. Gendall also allows for borrowings from English for words such as 'telephone' and 'television' (on the grounds that language borrowing is natural), which is rejected in the other versions (on the grounds that when speaking Cornish one should not be obliged to constantly break into English). Those in favour of Modern Cornish set up a Cornish Language Council (*Cussel an Tavas Kernuack*) in 1986 to encourage the study of Cornish from all periods.

Another academic, N. J. A. Williams sided, in the 1990s, with Nance's Unified Cornish, on the condition that it was improved. This was done by keeping Middle Cornish as the foundation of the language, while shifting the emphasis to the later period. *Agan Tavas* (Our Language), a group dedicated to defending Unified Cornish against Common Cornish, responded enthusiastically (Payton 2000).The result was called Unified Cornish Revised (UCR or *Kernowek Unys Mandys*). This had the effect of bringing Unified Cornish closer to Modern Cornish, which appears to have brought about much-needed cooperation and compromise: Unified Cornish is clearly 'purer' but Modern Cornish is probably more the result of the natural development of the language.

Nowadays revivalists are at pains to point out that the differences between Modern, Unified and Common Cornish are minor and do not impede mutual intelligibility. But this problem, as is the case with so many RLs, remains a stumbling block to its development in the educational field and in terms of official documentation. Indeed it is one of the aims of the new official *Strategy for the Cornish Language*[26] (see below) to find a way forward in this respect.

It is interesting to note that there are two different forms of campaign taking place in Cornwall, one for linguistic recognition, the other for more political and constitutional autonomy. *Mebyon Kernow*, 'The Party for Cornwall', was founded in 1951 and has won seats over the years on all tiers of local government in Cornwall. It has also contested parliamentary seats and is campaigning for a Cornish Assembly. In 1974 when the Stannary was symbolically reconvened for the first time in centuries to assert the independence of Cornwall in relation to the Crown, the militants claimed they did not mind being 'British' but they refused to accept that they were 'English'. They maintained that they were never legally annexed (whatever a 'legal annexation' may be – it seems a bit of an oxymoron) and that Cornwall had a special legal status. To illustrate this point the Stannary parliament sent a letter to Prince Charles asking for £20 billion in respect of excess taxation paid between 1337 and 1837. Seemingly, during that period, the inhabitants of Cornwall were subject to double taxation, as if they were foreigners. Therefore they were foreigners. If, on the other hand, they were English, and it had all been a mistake, then Prince Charles was to reimburse the excess taxes they had paid during that period. Nobody really expected Prince Charles to pay up. It was just to make a point, although the letter stated that the money, when repaid, would go towards helping the regeneration of the language (see Angarrack 1999).

Although language and language rights were and are an important part of the arguments for greater political autonomy, those campaigning traditionally for linguistic recognition were not necessarily involved in the political campaigns. The quest for linguistic recognition was directed at Europe, with the appointment of a representative to the European Bureau of Lesser Used Languages' (EBLUL) UK Committee in the 1980s and the later establishment of a sub-committee for Cornwall. This was followed by a long campaign for recognition under the Charter. This campaign was successful since Cornish was first officially recognised as a living language by EBLUL in 1993 and in 1994 by the Killilea Report, and the Charter in 2002–3.

The campaign for the revival of Cornish has also been remarkably successful in terms of the increase over the last few years in its number of speakers. It was reckoned in 1981 that there were some 40 effective speakers of Cornish, but numbers have greatly increased since then according to the MacKinnon Report commissioned by the British government and published in 2000.[27] It would appear that by then 171 persons were using Cornish in family life, 20 children were acquiring the language as 'native speakers', and 85 were acquiring knowledge of the language within their families. MacKinnon's study suggested around 300 effective speakers of Cornish (of whom 30 were in the London area). This figure was based on the numbers passing the Cornish Language Board examinations at the highest level, together with language bards received previously. His study also revealed that 459 were learning the language, of whom 126 were under the age of 16. EBLUL, which tends to be rather optimistic, mentions several thousand as having some knowledge of the language, while the *Strategy for the Cornish Language* document, published in 2004, states that there are around 300 effective speakers, and around 750 learning the language through adult education classes and correspondence courses. In other words, whatever figures are believed to be the most exact, Cornish has become once more a living language, albeit an extremely fragile one.

As the British government was unaware of the existence of Cornish as a living language at the time of ratification of the European Charter for Regional or Minority Languages, it was not included in the list of languages to be protected. This led to protests on the part of the language speakers, backed by such people as Andrew George, MP. There were also many protests on the part of the political/constitutional/ethnic rights militants. This led to a commission being appointed to study the issue, which in turn produced the MacKinnon Report, referred to above. Its conclusions led to Cornish being added to the Charter as a language to be given Part II protection (the announcement was made in November 2002, and the decision was officially ratified in March 2003). Matthew Clarke, of the Cornish Language Fellowship, claimed that this was 'the most important day in the history of the Cornish language'.

This appears to be the case, since implementing the Charter has meant an obligation on the part of officials to initiate discussion within the Cornwall County Council and with Cornish language organisations in Cornwall to ensure that the views of those wanting to learn and use the language are taken into account. So far this has led to the setting up of a steering group which produced the 2004 *Strategy for the Cornish Language* after wide public consultation. The latter was the basis on which funding was allocated. Funding of £600,000 over three years was made available early in 2006 by government, to be used to employ a Cornish Language Development Manager (now in place) and administrative support, as well as for the funding of projects. The Cornish Language Partnership, which includes representation from all tiers of local government, other statutory bodies and the languages NGOs, is the new organisation which will drive the delivery of the strategy over the next three years.

The 2004 *Strategy for the Cornish Language*[28] states what is already in place and its vision in terms of targets for the future. As far as education is concerned, there is some form of teaching the language in twelve primary and four secondary schools, on a voluntary basis, both on the part of teachers and pupils. Recently two language colleges have begun teaching Cornish as part of the curriculum (in Hayle and Penrice). New interactive CD Rom learning tools have been published. And in 2003 100 pupils from primary schools piloted in 2003 Cornwall Education Authority's 'Sense of Place' initiative by performing songs in Cornish on St Piran's Day. According to the Head of Modern Languages for the County, the problem is that interest at a serious level remains small. The aim is therefore to introduce more 'taster' classes and to produce better teaching materials in order to develop a broader appeal. The *Strategy* document also recognises that there is a need to raise standards of teaching and teaching qualification in Cornish. But this problem and others such as shortage of teachers and teaching materials, endemic in the case of most RLs, have not prevented those responsible for the *Strategy* document from formulating the most ambitious of ultimate aims: the provision for learning the language from pre-school through to university and adult education.

Another expressed aim is making Cornish more visible in public life, as a 'valued and visible part of Cornwall's distinct culture and heritage'. One aspect of this visibility is through the use of bilingual signage on and in public buildings, on letterheads and promotional materials, on websites, and by promoting the use of historic Cornish names for towns and streets. This does not mean only established street names or names of buildings, but names for new ones (Kerrier District Council, in particular, has a policy on designating Cornish language names for new streets and public buildings, and Penwith is following suit).[29] The *Strategy* document also mentions developing Cornish branding and other commercial opportunities which the language offers for business, in marketing products and developing new products, including in publishing and in tourism: Cornish is seen as desirable from an economic point of view through the development of local distinctiveness.

Certainly progress is being made, bearing in mind the language's very low starting point (links were established with the Isle of Man for advice, since Manx too started from a similar point). Not only are there now native speakers where there were none, but there is a clear commitment on the part of official bodies to contribute to the general effort: not only has Cornwall County Council adopted a policy of support for the language, but all the district councils and 38 town and parish councils have done likewise. The Heritage Lottery fund now has a policy on heritage languages, which includes Cornish, and Cornish is also represented on various bodies at EU level.

Much more needs to be done in terms of broadcasting, since the latter is limited to a brief news programme on Radio Cornwall on Sundays, but film and video materials are being developed (in 2000–1, a film, *Bitter Sweet*, was produced in two versions, one Cornish and one English). There is, in particular, a Cornish Film Festival which encourages the production of short films in Cornish, by awarding a grant and a mentor for the production of one film a year, on a competitive basis.

As far as news print is concerned, there is only a weekly Cornish language column in the *Western Morning News*. Publishing, on the other hand, is doing well and includes full-length novels, as well as Cornish language materials. Periodicals, comic books and publications for children are also being published.

To this must be added the institution of the web, which has had a major impact by attracting interest from those areas where Cornish people emigrated, when work in the mines dried up, namely in the mining areas of Australia, South Africa and North America. In Australia, in particular, descendants of those emigrants have established links with the homeland, and become interested in the language. This was made possible thanks to the setting up of correspondence courses in 1982. This can only be good for Cornish tourism, and Cornwall in general, which is thus brought out of its isolation. At the 'taster' level the introduction of Cornish material in contexts such as choirs is a positive move, and the *Gorseth Kernow* continues to be a focus of attraction. The fact there has been an increasing demand for weddings and other public ceremonies to take place in Cornish is also encouraging. All this represents a remarkable feat for a supposedly 'dead' language.

## Concluding comments

The battle for Welsh no longer has to take place at an institutional level, but there is still a need for general acceptance by all that Welsh identity (and language) is compatible with British identity (and English). This battle still has to take place for the language to win a genuine reprieve: 20 per cent speakers is still a long way from the theoretical 30 per cent transmission needed for survival. A first near-miraculous step has been taken in this direction according to the last census. More need to follow. This progress illustrates, however, the importance of linguistic policies in this area. Wales has been exemplary in this domain, showing what can be achieved. Not surprisingly, the other Celtic languages look towards it for guidance and inspiration. The Gaelic Language (Scotland) Act 2005, in particular, is said to have benefited from the experience of those involved in the drafting of the Welsh Language Act 1993 and the Official Languages Act 2003.

Cornish is at the other end of the spectrum, having all but disappeared. Bringing the language back to life is a remarkable feat, attributable to the constant efforts of intellectuals and academics, on the one hand, and believers in the cause of Cornish as an essential part of Cornish identity on the other. This has led militants and activists to formulate both wishes and demands in terms which may seem over-emotional and inappropriate in the context of an objective analysis of the situation, but such excesses are essential for the success of what must have appeared to most people, including linguists, a lost cause.

It now seems that thanks to Herculean efforts, the language has become an officially accepted part of Cornish and British reality. The problem now is to turn the language into a desirable asset for the whole population, including newcomers from England, if it is not to remain a minority interest. The approach adopted by the *Strategy for the Cornish Language* report is to show how sustainable prosperity (in one of the poorest areas of Britain) may be achieved 'through sustaining and enhancing Cornwall's distinct natural environment, heritage, culture and image'. In this the language has a large part to play.

The problem of locals being swamped by incomers speaking the majority language is, in fact, common to nearly all RLs. The problem is how to convince the latter to fit in and adopt the culture of the area in which they have elected to live. It is also important that the newcomers be made welcome, so as not to end up with a socially exclusive society. Clearly, bombing second homes, as has happened in Wales, although understandable at a certain level, is neither acceptable nor will it achieve the desired effect.

Speaking a RL, particularly where it has been revived as in the case of Cornish, is like belonging to a social club. There is a solid core of members, to which new members must be added if the cause is to prosper. The next step should be making Cornish attractive to the whole population. It is encouraging, in this respect, that the *Strategy* document refers to using the language to help 'address social exclusion, where for example it means gaining a new skill and building self-esteem or in developing an increased sense of ownership among young people'. The term 'social exclusion' could certainly be broadened to include newcomers, both old and new.

# 7
# The Regional Languages of Scotland: Scottish Gaelic and Scots[1]

Scottish Gaelic, or, more simply 'Gaelic', belongs to the Q-branch of Celtic which also includes Irish (or Irish Gaelic) and Manx Gaelic. The fact that the term Gaelic may be used in both cases goes back to a period when the language spoken in Ireland and Scotland differed but little, particularly in writing. The two languages started to grow apart, however, after the tenth century, although they could still be considered as dialects of the same language in the thirteenth century, after which they gradually came to be considered different languages. It is therefore convenient when referring to present-day speech to refer respectively to Irish and Gaelic.

Scots, on the other hand, is a Germanic language, which developed separately from English from Anglian roots with a Norse influence, and an input from French. It was also influenced by Celtic roots. It became by the late Middle Ages the language of the Scottish Court and administration, displacing Gaelic in the process, which took refuge in the Highlands and Western Isles. Then Scots itself developed into a non-standard language, because of the increasing role played by English.

Scotland therefore has two RLs competing for space and visibility. One, Gaelic, has fewer speakers but a more distinct profile. Scots, on the other hand, has far more speakers, and is trying to improve its status. Both are endangered for different reasons and fighting for survival.

## Scottish Gaelic

Whereas Welsh saw its numbers increase in the last census to slightly over 20 per cent of the population, Gaelic is still in decline and only spoken by around 58 000 people which represents only just over 1 per cent of the population of Scotland taken as a whole (but density varies according to location, with the highest density in the Western Isles, where it reaches just over 67 per cent). This represents an 11 per cent decline over ten years. It appears, therefore, in danger of extinction. But Gaelic language enthusiasts and activists, and now those in the establishment officially involved in saving the language, feel that the census paints an unnecessarily gloomy picture, since major efforts are being made to reverse the situation, both at an individual and an institutional level.

## Historical development

Ever since the twelfth century, the forces against Gaelic have been such that it is amazing that the language should have survived to this day, for whereas Welsh was either ignored, seen as a bit of a nuisance in terms of social progress, or, at the very worst, seen with contempt, Gaelic was considered early on as inimical to the ruling classes. Indeed, from the time the term 'Highlands' started to be used during the late medieval period the language associated with the area came to symbolise the problem the Highlanders represented for the powers in place. To quote T. M. Devine (2000: 232):

> After the Reformation, the Highlands were not properly evangelised for the new faith and were regarded as irreligious, popish and pagan for generations thereafter. For the Scottish elites and the Presbyterian Church before 1700, the Highlands were alien and hostile, in need of greater state control and both moral and religious 'improvement'. The consensus was that the society had to be assimilated to the social and cultural norms that prevailed in the rest of Scotland because it was both inferior and dangerous.

Such a negative approach was also voiced in the modern era. Thus Price (1984: 53) quotes from James VI of Scotland's book of advice to his son, the *Basilikon Doron*, published in 1599, i.e. four years before he became James I of England: 'As for the Hie-lands, I shortly comprehend them all in two sorts of people: the one, that dwelleth in our maine land, that are barbarous for the most part, and yet mixed with some shewe of civilitie: the other, that dwelleth in the Isles, and are alluterly barbares, without any shew of civilitie.' Such an opinion led to the following policy: 'Follow the course I have intended, in planting Colonies among them of answerable In-Lands (i.e. Lowlander) subjects, that within short time may reforme and civilize the best inclined among them; rooting out or transporting the barbarous and stubborn sort, and planting civilitie in their roomes.' Thus was born the concept of 'Plantations' which came to typify the colonisation of Ireland. It was clearly tried out first in the Highlands.

The association of the language with Irish did not help, although the relationship existing between the Scots and the Irish is far from clear. The most accepted theory is that the 'Scottis' came from Ireland.[2] This is hardly surprising since, on a clear day, County Antrim in Northern Ireland may be seen from the Scottish coast. The first permanent colony, in Argyll, is dated from AD 501, although movements between the two coasts predate it, and continued afterwards. It consisted of an expansion of the northern Irish kingdom of Dál Riata into the Western Highlands and Islands. Absorption of the Pictish kingdom in the north, the Cumbric-speaking kingdom of Strathclyde and part of Anglian Northumbria, established by the eleventh century a largely Gaelic-speaking Scottish kingdom, which corresponded roughly to present-day Scotland. But G. Price (1984) has pointed out that relations between Scots, Britons and Angles remain unclear, particularly in terms of population movements. Various conflicting theories have been put forward, either stressing that a substantial part of the population was, indeed, Irish in origin, or else that the indigenous population simply acquired the Old Irish tongue. Or that the Q-branch came to Britain before going to Ireland.

The acceptance or denial of an Irish past is still an emotive subject. Thus in the eighteenth century Sir John Clerk went so far as to deny the country's Gaelic-speaking past, stating that the early Scots spoke Saxon (Devine 2000: 29). Without going this far, others have questioned the importance of the Irish/Scottish link. Thus an article appeared relatively recently in the *Times Higher Educational Supplement* (8 June 2001) entitled 'Scot roots are not Irish'. The author of the article states in the opening paragraph: 'The Scots are Scottish after all. A study has thrown doubt over the long-held belief that the Scots were originally an Irish tribe that invaded the British mainland 1,500 years ago.' The article then quotes a researcher in early medieval archaeology at Glasgow University, Ewan Campbell, as stating that he had found no reliable evidence that it was invaders who had founded the early kingdom of Dál Riata (or 'Dálriada') in the sixth century. Dr Campbell believes that it is more likely that the Scots were an indigenous, Gaelic-speaking people with strong cultural connections with the inhabitants of northeastern Antrim.

What is certain, however, is that the earliest known Scottish Gaelic text, which dates from the twelfth century and relates to the foundation of a monastery with its grants of lands and privileges, is written in a form common to Irish and Gaelic, although it already displays divergences. The language spread to southern Scotland, where Cumbric, a P-Celtic language similar to Welsh, was spoken. Early bilingualism at this point is said to have affected Scottish Gaelic syntax. By the eleventh century Gaelic was spoken in virtually the whole of mainland Scotland, and was still mutually intelligible with the form spoken in Ireland. And yet, immediately after achieving such success, Gaelic went into retreat: the last king to speak Gaelic as his native tongue, Malcolm Canmore, who reigned between 1059 and 1093, was also the one who introduced English as the language of his Court. This was because he had previously spent fifteen years in exile in England, had gained the throne thanks to the English and had married an English princess (she was in fact a Hungarian-born, French-speaking English princess). The Anglo-Normans, who were invited in by the king (as were the Flemish and Bretons) also introduced French as the language used by the nobility and the Court. It is reckoned (Price 1984) that by the time of Alexander III, the last king of the House of Canmore to come to power (1249–86), there was little Gaelic presence left in any of the domains associated with power. Diglossia therefore settled in far earlier in Scotland than in Wales, in relation to Gaelic.

Not surprisingly, there is not such a great a literary tradition, at least in terms of volume, as there is for Welsh, but there is an important tradition nonetheless, mainly based on poetry which remains strong to this day and is universally recognised. Unfortunately, the Gaelic tradition was not helped by printing and translation having come much later to Scotland than to Wales, for although the first book printed was a translation of the *Book of Common Order* (John Knox's Liturgy) in 1567, the New Testament was not translated until 1767, i.e. 200 years after the Welsh version, and the Old Testament in 1801. Lack of printing in Gaelic was due at first to most of the Highlanders not converting to Protestantism, which meant they were largely seen as the enemy from within, particularly after the defeat of the 1745 Rebellion, under the Young Pretender. When printing in Gaelic did take place, it was as a means to conversion. In this case, religion started by hindering and then saving the Gaelic language (see further details below).

Another massive blow to the Gaelic culture came during the late eighteenth and the nineteenth centuries, from the clearances, which dispersed the Gaelic-speaking population and destroyed their social structures. It was reasonably easy to evict the tenants, because their rights of tenure were not protected legally, but were dependent on a 'landlord-protector' principle. The failure to honour this duty caused incredible trauma and brought about the destruction of the social structures which had been in place. Those who survived and did not emigrate to America or elsewhere, ended up in the coastal areas. This transformed the linguistic geography of the country, by reducing the Gaelic-speaking strongholds to the coastal areas and the Western Isles.

The decline of the Gaelic-speaking society must also be set against the growing importance of 'Britishness' and a general sense of unity across Great Britain. Britishness was born officially of the Union of England and Wales with Scotland in 1707. This was seen, at the time, as a union of equals, born of the necessity to fight a common enemy, the papists. The new Britain was united, in particular, against the possibility of a Catholic king acceding to the British throne, and against various Catholic powers in Europe. This sense of unity was further developed at the time of the French Revolution, which horrified Britain, and the Napoleonic wars. Finally a real sense of a common British identity developed during the expansion of the British Empire. From then on, it was possible to combine two nationalities, a 'local' one and a British one. The energies of the remaining Highlanders were channelled into the army, where they became and remain famous, and into the machine that was the Empire. The cause of Gaelic was not completely forgotten but romanticised and integrated within the context of the new Imperial identity. As a result, Gaelic became seen by many of its speakers as useless in the new context.

It is only recently, with the collapse of the Empire and (relative) peace in Europe, that the whole problem of how to define Britishness has come to the fore. This problem was much discussed at the time of devolution, and remains a central theme for politicians such as Gordon Brown, who wish to revitalise the concept. At the same time, it is not surprising that given the present circumstances, some of which are not unique to Britain, regional (or sub-state) identities are trying to reaffirm themselves, which sometime implies promoting their most powerful marker, their RLs. This is not so much the case in Scotland, however, where national identity has traditionally been expressed not so much through language as having separate Scottish legal, ecclesiastical (formerly of great importance) and educational systems, and now its own parliament. And yet Gaelic clearly carries a particular sense of identity, hence its tentative revival, against all odds.

For efforts to destroy Gaelic have been systematic, and carried out over a long period of time. There were first of all the Statutes of Iona of 1609, making it compulsory for every man of 'good worth' (i.e. owning at least 'three score cows') to educate their eldest child in English. The Privy Council gave full support to this statute in 1616, stating that the English tongue was to be implanted and the Irish tongue, 'the principal cause of the continuance of barbarity and incivility . . . to be abolished' (Price 1984: 52–3). Further measures were taken by the Scottish parliament which decided in 1646 that an English school should be established in every Highland parish. Repealed in 1662, this provision was re-enacted in 1696 with the Act for the Settling of School. This was in line with the development of a national system of parish schools in the Lowlands established by law and under public control, which was very advanced for its time. Already extensive at the end of the seventeenth century, it was virtually complete by the end of the 1790s. In other words, policies which were beneficial in many respects to the population, leading as they did to general literacy, had a negative impact on Gaelic, which was ignored in this context.

The Church of Scotland was equally unsympathetic to Gaelic, associating it with popery. But it had to accept that preaching would have to be in Gaelic (or the 'Irish language'), the huge majority of the population being monoglot. The SSPCK (the Society in Scotland for Propagating Christian Knowledge) founded in 1709 was much less tolerant. It was conceived specifically to set up charity schools in the Highlands, to evangelise and specifically to destroy the Gaelic language, source of all evil. This approach lasted for about half a century, after which a more tolerant approach was adopted. This was signalled by the publication of the New Testament and then the Old Testament in Gaelic, in 1767 and 1801 respectively. It was also decided in 1767 that children should be taught to read in both Gaelic and English, and in 1824 it was decided to teach Gaelic-speaking children to read in Gaelic before they learned to do so in English.

As a result the position of Gaelic ended up better in the SSPCK schools than in the local parish schools. Its position was further improved after the foundation in 1811 of the Edinburgh Society for the Support of Gaelic Schools. Similar societies were founded in Glasgow in 1812 and Inverness in 1818. They adopted the principle of the 'circulating schools' which were similar to the Welsh 'itinerant' schools. The evangelical movement also had an important impact since the 1790s saw the founding of the Society for Propagating the Gospel at Home, which sent itinerant preachers to convey the Christian message in Gaelic. The Gaelic School Societies and the Highland Missionary Society followed in the same footsteps. As a result of all these efforts, by the end of the nineteenth century, a reasonably high level of literacy was widespread in the Gaelic-speaking area, and over 900 books had been published in Gaelic (Price 1984: 54).

Unfortunately the 1872 Education Act for Scotland, which instituted compulsory education between the ages of 5 and 13 made no such provision for the teaching of Gaelic. In 1875, schools inspectors were authorised but not required to test Gaelic-speaking children in Gaelic. This rarely happened in practice. In 1885 the Scottish Education Department allowed the use of Gaelic in infant and junior classes, but no higher up. This destroyed much of what had been achieved up until then, and was not remedied until the late 1950s (see below).

It is interesting to note that, although the Scottish Education Department, established post-1872, was accused by activists of *An Comunn Gàidhealach* (the Highland Association founded in 1891) of conducting a campaign against the implementation of the 1884 Napier Commission's decision that Gaelic should be part of the curriculum in Highland schools, this sin of omission was committed not only by English-speaking inspectors, but also Gaelic ones. This was because they viewed the campaign to revive the language as sentimentalist and contrary to the interests of the people involved. In practice, the Scottish Education Department did little to help Gaelic. The 'Gaelic clause' of the 1918 Act briefly mentioned the problem, requesting that 'adequate' provision be made for the teaching of Gaelic in Gaelic-speaking areas, but this had little impact in practice.

On the other hand 'Highlandism', which developed in the late eighteenth and nineteenth centuries played an important role in Gaelic's survival. Devine traces the roots of Highlandism back to the 1746 disaster when the Jacobites permanently lost the battle to put a Catholic king on the throne. The rebels having seen their power destroyed, it became possible to turn them from national traitors to national heroes, with Robert Burns (1759–96) at the forefront of this rehabilitation. Integrating the Highlanders into the army proved a remarkable success which further enhanced their reputation. And Sir Walter Scott (1771–1832) completed this rehabilitation by providing an idealised image of heroic Highlanders who, although they followed a mistaken cause, remained true and loyal to their ideals.

The Highland Society, created in London in 1778, also played a major part in preserving the ancient Highland traditions. In 1782 it managed to have the law forbidding the wearing of Highland dress repealed. One of the problems this entailed, from an identity point of view, was that the tartan, and all that went with it, started to become associated with Scotland as a whole, and not just the Gaels. Thus, in 1822, when various festivities were organised by Sir Walter Scott in honour of George IV's visit to Edinburgh, the king ended up dressed in full (fake) Highland regalia. Lord Macaulay, in particular, found it shocking that the king should show respect for the Scottish nation 'by disguising himself in what, before the Union, was considered by nine Scotchmen out of ten as the dress of a thief' (Devine 2000: 235). It is a fact, however, that the British royal family have been wearing tartan ever since.

This new sympathetic approach to the Highlands was also enhanced by the impact of the publication of Gaelic poems translated by James Macpherson. He also published in 1765 a collection of poems he attributed to Ossian, a legendary Gaelic bard. They were, in fact, no more than his own refashioning of poems known in Ireland and the Highlands, but they had immense international success. This was another case of fabricating the past, so common at the time. (It is still common now, particularly in the context of 'historical' films; see, for example, the much criticised *Braveheart*.) As a result of all these efforts Gaelic has survived, but only just. Whereas the 1891 census established a figure of 253 415 speakers this had dropped to 65 978 in 1991. The figures had dropped again by 10 per cent in the 2001 census to 58 652 speakers. To these must be added 7413 with some skill in the language, bringing the total number of those with some competence in Gaelic to 66 065.[3]

### Present-day efforts to fight back

This gloomy picture may be counteracted by the rather more complex picture which emerges from the report based on the 2001 census. According to the report, Gaelic is thriving as well as declining. For if the number of Gaelic speakers fell by 7300 during the 1990s, the number of Gaelic readers increased by 3200 and the number of people able to write in Gaelic rose by 3100. The census suggests that Gaelic is declining in its traditional heartlands, particularly in the Western Isles, but growing in many other parts of Scotland – and among young people. Around 430 more young people, aged 5–9, could speak Gaelic in 2001 than in 1991. It is moving from being (largely) an oral language to being a language spoken, read and written.

This is mainly due to the considerable improvements made in recent years in the provision of Gaelic-language education and media. It is to be hoped that positive results will start appearing in the next census in 2011. The main problem at present is Gaelic collapsing in the context of the family, the neighbourhood and the Church. Like Welsh, it has now spread to urban areas in the Lowlands (see below), but, like Welsh in a similar context, its roots remain fragile, and whether intergenerational transmission will take place as a result of Gaelic medium education is far from certain. It is what is hoped for and what the militants are striving for.

Gaelic medium education and media were not just born out of the blue, but were the result of nearly a century of efforts. Gaelic could be studied as part of a university degree in Celtic from 1882, and the first society created for the promotion of Gaelic was *An Comunn Gàidhealach* (The Highland Association) in 1891 (see above). It set up a festival of competitions for Gaelic music, poetry and drama, *National Mòd*, similar to the *Eisteddfods*. A professional director was appointed in 1966, and became involved with political issues. 1963 saw the foundation of the government-assisted *Comhairle nan Leabhraichean* (Gaelic Books Council). This led to the publication of an all-Gaelic magazine, a bilingual fortnightly magazine in the late 1960s, a book club in the 1970s (both no longer in existence) and recently a monthly newspaper, *An Gàidheal Ùr*, which is an *An Comunn Gàidhealach* project, and a publishing house, Acair, for the publication of educational material, chiefly in Gaelic (MacKinnon 2000: 52).

The mid-1980s saw the creation of *Comunn na Gàidhlig* (the Association for Gaelic) which is funded by a governmental development agency, which became responsible for education and the media, while *An Comunn Gàidhealach* specialised in cultural matters. In 1987, the Scottish Arts Council started funding a *Pròiseact nan Ealan* (a national Gaelic Arts Project)

Gaelic medium schools came later to Scotland than Wales, but their origins are in developments which started much earlier (MacKinnon 2000: 53). From 1958 Gaelic was used as an initial teaching medium in the early primary stages in Gaelic-speaking areas, and could be studied as a second language at secondary level. By the 1970s it was introduced as a second language in many of the Highland schools and an early project on bilingual education was developed in the Western Isles Islands Area in 1975. The first playgroup movement started in 1982, and in 1988 the Highland Region established two Gaelic medium nursery schools. Nurseries, which are council controlled and cater for the 4–5 age group, are more formal than the voluntary playgroups and more recent. By 2005–6, the enrolment in Gaelic medium nurseries had reached 641 in 60 units.

The first two Gaelic medium primary 'units' (i.e. a class within an otherwise Anglophone school) were created in 1985 in Glasgow and Inverness (they are now formally described as 'departments' within the Highland Council). By 2005–6 there were 2068 children being educated through the medium of Gaelic in 61 'units' and one all-Gaelic school in Glasgow. Another is due to open in Inverness in April 2007.

In 2005–6 there were 315 pupils receiving Gaelic medium education in secondary schools. There were 981 studying Gaelic as a subject for fluent speakers and 2718 as a subject for learners.[4] These figures may seem impressive, and indeed they are if one thinks that thirty years ago there were none. But much more needs to be done to save Gaelic, which is why the Ministerial Advisory Group on Gaelic, appointed by the Scottish Executive, concluded in a report published in 2002, *A Fresh Start for Gaelic*, that to arrest the decline, intake into the Gaelic medium schools would have to be at least 2 per cent of all primary students present, whereas at present the intake is only about 0.35 per cent. This echoes MacKinnon's conclusions, who also pointed out that in the Western Isles, where nearly 70 per cent of the population (67.23 per cent to be precise) is Gaelic-speaking, only 25 per cent of children benefit from Gaelic medium education.

Until recently, the government accorded grants for such education according to the Grants for Gaelic Language Education (Scotland) Regulations 1986, which gave £3 of executive money to local authorities for every pound they spent on Gaelic medium education. But while such grants are invaluable, they cannot sustain the system alone since at no point in the past were the local authorities compelled to provide such education. But pressure from the Gaelic community led to the inclusion of a clause in the Standards in Scotland's Schools Act 2000 introducing some element of compulsion since it requires local authorities to include in their yearly statement an account of what has been achieved in response to local demand for such a type of education. And the situation has changed again with the Gaelic Language (Scotland) Act 2005 (see below). But one of the main problems remains the fact that demand is necessarily small. As a result, it only led in the past to the establishment of 'units' (or 'departments') in otherwise English-speaking schools, rather than fully-fledged Gaelic-speaking schools.

Another aspect of the problem is that, as in Wales, population movement has brought Gaelic speakers to areas they had not inhabited since the twelfth century or thereabouts, young people moving from the Gaelic heartlands to the cities in search of work, particularly Glasgow. Thus by 1991, 55.5 per cent of Scotland's Gaelic speakers lived within Lowland Scotland. Thus the non-speaking Gaelic south is becoming 'Gaelicised' in the same way as South Wales has become 'Welshified'. As a result, and because of the 'parents' Charter' which was supposed to give parents choice over their children's education, education in Gaelic has had to be provided not only in the Highlands but also in the Lowlands, and this has had the effect of sparking off enthusiasm for learning Gaelic in other age groups. Indeed 40 per cent of all Gaelic learners are now in the Lowlands, and 25 per cent of Gaelic medium schools are also in the Lowlands (there are, for example, three preschool units catering for 50 children in the city of Glasgow). The problem is that, as in Wales, such 'new shoots' are fragile, given the strongly English and/or Scots environment in which the children are brought up.

De-Gaelicisation of the Gaelic heartlands, on the other hand, is partly due to many women having left – and continuing to leave – the traditionally Gaelic-speaking areas in search of work in the cities. This has entailed those men remaining there having to go further afield to find a bride, who will often be English or Scots speaking only. Research also shows that even the young women who remain *in situ* are less supportive of Gaelic than the men (MacKinnon 2000: 48–9). All of which makes the fight to retain Gaelic all the more difficult. As a result, according to the 2001 census, there were only 7.39 per cent Gaelic speakers left in the Highlands.

Other major problems affecting the transmission of Gaelic are the shortage of qualified teachers able to teach through the medium of Gaelic and the scarcity of educational resources, although efforts are being made in this area (McLeod 2003a). Sabhal Mòr Ostaig, the Gaelic college of higher education on the island of Skye, set up a research unit in 1992, to study the problem.

It is also hoped that *Bòrd na Gàidhlig* (the Gaelic Language Board) will help since it has got governmental backing. It was originally a company wholly owned by the Executive, but it became a statutory public body in accordance with the Gaelic Language (Scotland) Act 2005 (this change of status explains why it has slightly altered its name several times since its inception in 2002–3, this latest version dating from 2006).

What some (but not all) in the Gaelic community want is all-Gaelic schools rather than units in Anglophone schools, and full secondary education in Gaelic. Although the government pays for 75 per cent of the initial running costs for Gaelic medium education, the balance is paid by the local authorities, which get part of their money from local taxes and business rates, and may be subject to pressures against 'wasting' money on 'useless' languages. Moreover, what the local authorities have to give their money to is still not clearly defined from a statutory point of view, since the 2000 Education Act does not make clear whether 'making provision for Gaelic' refers to simply teaching Gaelic or providing Gaelic medium education. Nor do the local authorities have to establish any developmental objectives.

On a more positive note, the Western Isles council became bilingual in 1975, and set up bilingual road signs, gave out bilingual notices etc. The aim was to give Gaelic some visibility in an area where it is still spoken. Four local authorities followed suit at the time. Another important part in the fight for survival is the role of the media, particularly radio and television.

There is a BBC radio station (Radio nan Gàidheal) which broadcasts nationally, on its own bandwidth, although some parts of the country are unable to receive these programmes. This represents approximately 65 hours output per week, or over 3000 hours annually. 2003 marked 80 years of Gaelic radio broadcasting. Important efforts have also been made to increase the presence of Gaelic on film and television. The Scottish Office started providing an annual television fund for Gaelic in 1992–3 (it had already started giving grants for the funding of Gaelic education since 1986). A television fund was established which allows for around 300 hours of programmes in Gaelic on BBC and ITV combined (MacKinnon 1998), including peak-time provision every night on digital. There was also a *Comataidh Craolacidh Gàidhlig* (a Gaelic Broadcasting Committee) responsible for administering government funding for Gaelic programmes, but it had no power to commission or schedule such programmes (MacNeil 2003). This problem has now been redressed (see below), and a purely Gaelic digital channel is planned for early 2007. Enough to make French RL militants dream sweet dreams! Moreover, viewing figures are most encouraging, although it would appear that the audience tends to view programmes because they are in Gaelic, and not for their content, which is not sufficiently audience-orientated, except where children's programmes have been concerned.

There have been, in particular, gaps in provision for young people and learners, where television is concerned, since the Gaelic Broadcasting Committee had no power over commissioning or scheduling, as mentioned above. This was left to others such as BBC Scotland and the commercial channels (see below). It also seems, according to MacNeil that viewing opportunities are still restricted, with over a third of the total Gaelic output, between 2002–3, in late evening or post-midnight slots. MacNeil has also pointed out that most provision for children is shown while children are at school, and that there is very little over the summer months. What is being requested at present is a fully Gaelic channel, to prevent further marginalisation of the language.

It was this kind of complaint which led to much campaigning on the part of militants, which, in turn, led to the Communications Act

2003 which created a new body, the *Serbhisnam Meadhanan Gàidhlig* (Gaelic Media Service), with expanded powers compared to those of the Gaelic Broadcasting Committee. The new body may engage in making programmes in Gaelic and in training people to do so. The result is not perfect but represents marked progress (Dunbar 2003b).

Another step forward was when *Bòrd na Gàidhlig* became a statutory board as from 13 February 2006 when the Gaelic Language (Scotland) Act 2005 came into force. It takes over from *Comunn na Gàidhlig* its educational responsibilities but with more powers, with the latter continuing its work in terms of after-school care, clubs, camps etc. This *Bòrd* is also responsible for creating, within a year, a National Plan. This entails setting out the philosophy which should be the foundation upon which the development of Gaelic is to be based. It also entails detailing specific plans to promote Gaelic, both at the national level and at the level of all public authorities, of which the local authorities are only a minority. The plans are to be agreed with the relevant bodies, and indeed will be drawn up by the bodies themselves, assisted, where appropriate and feasible, by *Bòrd na Gàidhlig*. The latter will also engage with those bodies not covered by the Act, which may wish, nonetheless, to prepare a non-statutory Gaelic language plan.

The Gaelic Language (Scotland) Act 2005 seems to also make Gaelic an 'official language of Scotland commanding equal respect to the English language'. 'Seems' because the wording of the Act is odd. Under 'Constitution and functions of *Bòrd na Gàidhlig*, there is a clause which states that its functions are to be exercised with a view 'to securing the status of the Gaelic language as an official language of Scotland commanding equal respect to the English language through (a) increasing the number of persons who are able to use and understand the Gaelic language, (b) encouraging the use and understanding of the Gaelic language, and (c) facilitating access, in Scotland and elsewhere, to the Gaelic language and Gaelic culture.' This seems to refer to the future, and yet Gaelic was listed for Part III protection in the context of the European Charter for Regional or Minority Languages, is fully recognised by the Scottish Executive and its use is permitted in parliament as long as suitable notice is given. In other words it seems to be 'official', but not equal, at least in practice. This has led the more cynical to point out how governments can reduce the effectiveness of their policies through inaction and the granting of inadequate funds (see Kirk and Ó Baoill's summary of McLeod 2003b: 3–4).

It would be churlish, however, not to recognise the immense progress achieved so far from an institutional point of view. It is also worth noting that, from a purely linguistic point of view, Gaelic is lucky in not presenting great dialectal variation. Those which existed are becoming less marked, partly because of the impact of broadcasting which tends to break down barriers. Orthography has changed little through the centuries. The first review of Gaelic Orthographic Conventions was in 1981 for use in school examinations from 1985, and a further review was carried out at the end of 2005, but the issues to be resolved were not seen as being particularly problematic, with the possible exception of what to do about the rapidly disappearing dative case. This *de facto* standardisation means that the language is ready to take off. Whether it does or not will depend on the willpower, desires and opinions not only of its speakers, but, more importantly, its potential speakers.

## Scots

The position of Scots is nearly diametrically opposed to that of Gaelic, both linguistically and in terms of its numbers of speakers, but since its identity as a language remains vague, Scots tends to be the poor relation in Scotland, although efforts are being made to improve its status.

Linguistically, it is fragmented into a number of dialects or varieties, and lacks standardisation in spelling, which has long been a problem to writers in Scots. (To give an example, the *Scottish National Dictionary* gives lists of variants, which may be of historical or regional origin, or may be simply accidental or idiosyncratic.) As far as the number of its speakers are concerned, a 1996 government estimation put their number at around 1.5 million speakers out of a population of just under 5 million. This is already an impressive number for a RL, but according to some people, the real number is much higher, with more or less everybody speaking Scots. It is, according to one Scots specialist, 'the tung ye hear when ye gang thro the streets o Scotland's touns and cities, in Aiberdeen or Ayr, Banff or Buckhaven, in the glens o Argyll an the streets o Glesca' (McHardy 1996: 7). Others disagree with this, pointing out that there is a cline between 'thin Scot' and 'dense Scot' (see below), with only the latter counting as real Scots.

The fact that no official figure can be given is due to the absence of any questions on Scots in past censuses. This was due mainly to the problem of how to define Scots (see below). Hence there are widely diverging assessments of the strength of the language. For some it is doing well, with numerous 'bottom-up' and 'top-down' developments taking place,[5] whereas for others for whom Scots is defined mainly in terms of the forms derived from Old Scots, or literary Scots, the language is quickly disappearing, having become 'a bastard lingo compounded of rudimentary Scots on the one hand and mispronounced English on the other' (quoted in Corbett 1997: 20). The historical development of the language explains such widely diverging points of view.

## Historical development

From the reign of Malcolm III (1054–96) Gaelic lost ground to what was first of all called *Inglis* and then *Scots*.[6] Scots derives from Anglian speech as spoken in Northumbria and the south east of Scotland, which was later influenced by English and Flemish settlers in the burghs of eastern Scotland. It displaced Gaelic on the eastern side as far north as the Moray Firth, and also in most of the south west. It also displaced a form of early Welsh spoken by the Strathclyde Britons, which may have acted as a sub-stratum specific to the area. When it spread further north, to Orkney and Shetland, it displaced the Norse language, Norn, which had become extinct in those areas by the eighteenth century. In doing so, Scots again acquired a distinctive flavour which survives to this day in those areas. Hence an information leaflet published in 2002 by the University of the Highlands & Islands Project had an introduction in not only Gaelic and English, but also Scots, Shetlandic and Orcadian. To this has since been added Doric.

The problem of Scots identity does not reside, however, in its dialectal variation (most languages show such variation), but because it was seen, in medieval times and as late as the sixteenth century, by those who wrote it as a form of English or *Inglis* (see Price 1984). On the other hand, this written form clearly did not comply with the form of standard English being developed by the Chancery and others (see Chapter 2) and which had eliminated most dialectal forms of English from the formal and official written language. This was due to Scotland and England forming separate states, even after the accession of James VI of Scotland to the English throne in 1603, since Scotland retained most of its distinctive institutions until the Act of Union of 1707. As a result Scots was used in all contexts: official documents, being the language of the Court, private correspondence, contracts, sermons, scholarship and literature, although the first written records in Scots do not appear to predate the late fourteenth century.

The development of Scots towards becoming a national official language followed much the same path as English. Thus in 1398 the Scottish parliament started using Scots rather than Latin in its legislation. As was the case for English, writers embellished their language with numerous borrowings from prestigious languages, such as Latin and

French. French in particular had an important influence on Scots. As a result, although many French words appear to have been borrowed both by English and Scots, there are a number which are restricted to Scots alone.

After the advent of printing, however, southern standards on spelling, grammar and vocabulary made themselves felt on Scots. As was the case for English, writers were anxious to have as broad a readership as possible, which led, after the establishment of printing, to Anglicisation of the language. This phenomenon became particularly marked in the seventeenth century. Smith quotes in this respect the Catholic writer Ninian Winget, who attacked John Knox, for using 'Southeron': 'If you, through excessive attention to novelties, have forgotton our old plain Scots which your mother taught you, in times to come, I must write to you concerning my thinking in Latin, because I am not acquainted with your Southern speech.'[7]

The biggest blow came from the fact that the Scottish Reformation (1560) led Scotland to look more towards Protestant England as an ally, rather than Catholic France as had been the case for the previous two and a half centuries, under the *auld alliance*, and English, not Scots, then became the language of religion. No Bible in Scots was produced at the time to replace the Latin of pre-Reformation times. An English Bible was therefore read in Scottish churches: first the 1560 Geneva Bible, and later the King James Authorised Version of 1611. Calvin's *Forme of Prayers* (1562) and *Catechism* (1564) also became known to the Lowlands population. Moreover, in 1579, a Scottish law established that every householder over a certain financial level had to be able to prove possession of a Bible and a Book of Psalms in the 'vulgar language', i.e. English. The Church therefore had already started destroying Scots, long before the Act of Union of 1707.

As a result, Scots moved closer to English, at least in its written form, and eventually it came to be seen as a 'dialect' of English, i.e. a kind of sub-variety, or, even worse, as 'bad English'. As a result, the Golden Age of Scots literature, which was in the fifteenth and sixteenth centuries, came to an end, first with the union of crowns in 1603 and then the union of parliaments in 1707. There was a flurry of literary production in the eighteenth century, Robert Burns being its most famous representative, but even he used English for more elevated discourse. A Scots prose tradition developed during the nineteenth century in the popular press and in fiction, and a renaissance after World War One, led by Hugh MacDiarmid, which 'set out to create a medium of literary expression by drawing on all the resources of Scots, present and past' (Price 1984: 189–90). This form of 'elevated' Scots, called 'Lallans' (from Lowlands) has been criticised as 'synthetic'[8] or 'plastic' and for being alien to its spoken version. Others, such as J. Derrick McClure, maintain that Hugh MacDiarmid had restored Scots' dignity as a literary language, and had changed, single-handedly, the course of its history. It is now promoted by the Scots Language Society.

The criticism levelled at Lallans certainly seems unfair since literary language tends, by definition, to be quite different from the spoken language from which it may emerge. It is at this point that Scots started to suffer from pundits, and others, wishing to identify the written language with the spoken, which would preclude it from ever acceding to modernity. But, as Smith has pointed out, modern-day novelists do not appear to use Lallans much, and prefer to use a form of Scots which reflects working-class urban speech. He gives Irving Welsh's 1986 novel *Trainspotting* as an example. But even then Scots tends to represent only the characters' speech, creating again a diglossic approach, which Smith considers to be reminiscent of Burns' distinction.

This diglossic situation developed from the time English became a sign of social prestige, which led to the domain of Scots shrinking and becoming restricted to oral speech used in the context of the home. This evolution was neatly summed up by David Murison (quoted in Price 1984: 191), editor of the *Scottish National Dictionary*: 'Scots became more and more restricted in use and scope, having lost spiritual status at the Reformation, social status at the union of the Crowns, and political status with the Parliamentary Union.'

The language lived on, among the less educated on the one hand, and also among intellectuals, whose defence of Scots usually has a strong nationalistic flavour. This has led to numerous studies of the language in its various forms. Already in the nineteenth century, a four-volume *Etymological Dictionary of the Scottish Languages* had appeared, and a study of *The Dialect of the Southern Counties of Scotland* was a landmark in the history of dialectology (later copied in Germany and France). Then, in the twentieth century, the *Scottish National Dictionary*, which deals with the language from 1700 onwards, appeared between 1931 and 1976, and includes ten volumes. Scots boasts, in fact, more than 50 000 words different in Scots from English. A systematic study of present-day Scots was undertaken by Professor Angus McIntosh as part of the Linguistic Survey of Scotland project based at Edinburgh University.

Commenting on the survey, Price states that it came 'perhaps, just in time'. He goes on to state that having been excluded from all official contexts, and being open to the influence of English to a degree much greater than Gaelic for obvious reasons, 'what one hears over the greater part of the south or east of Scotland where Scots used to be spoken is merely a regional form of southern English, with a Scottish accent and a Scots element (greater or smaller according to the locality and according to the individual) in its vocabulary.' He also quotes the editor of the *Scottish National Dictionary* as having forecast that by the twenty-first century, 'it is doubtful whether it will be anything that is recognizably Scottish, at least in the ordinary historical meaning of the term' (Price 1984: 192). With this one may, however, disagree.

The reason for disagreeing is that such attitudes are strictly prescriptive. They imply, indirectly, that outside influences spoil languages, which no longer survive in a 'pure' form. They reject all forms of change which are not purely natural and inherent in the language itself, but brought about by external forces (which most are). It is hardly surprising that English, a collateral language of Scots, should have influenced its development. This does not mean that it is no longer 'Scots'. Indeed viewing Scottish programmes on television has led many a southern English speaker to wish for subtitles.[9]

To be fair to Price, he explains in his introduction that the distinction between language and dialect cannot be based merely on linguistic criteria, citing the mutually intelligible Danish, Norwegian and Swedish case, which are now accepted as the different languages of different nation-states. He points out that the concept of Scots is 'extremely nebulous' and that it is not easy to distinguish between what is Scots and what is not. He even mentions that he changed his mind four times in the course of writing his book. Matters are still unclear in this respect, despite devolution and the official recognition of Scots as a language, both at national and international levels.

### The fightback

In 1993, Scots was listed by EBLUL as a separate language, and in 1994 in the Killilea Report. In 2001 Scots came under Part II protection under the provisions of the European Charter for Regional or Minority Languages. This amounts to official recognition of Scots as a separate language rather than a dialect of English.

Despite this, Scots was not mentioned in the 2001 census, although whether to include a question on the language was debated by the Scottish parliament. This was because the findings from research carried out by the Registrar General for Scotland showed that depending on how the question was formulated, the answer could be very different, and the results therefore untrustworthy. The Scottish Executive's proposal not to include such a question was approved by the Scottish parliament. This decision might be reversed, however, since trial censuses are to be run to assess how best to word a question about Scots, ready for the next general census of 2011.

But the problem of whether Scots is a distinct language or not from English continues to be debated. J. J. Smith has pointed out that English itself was once a dialect of West Germanic and only gradually emerged as a separate entity, as did Dutch, German, etc. (J. J. Smith 2000: 159). The problem is determining when the dialect emerges as a language in its own right. This has to be to a large extent a political decision. And indeed the proponents of Lallans are political activists working for an independent Scotland, in which Lallans would be used in all contexts. Thus J. Corbett reproduces a letter in *Language and Scottish Literature* (Corbett 1997: 14–15) written by the National Convener of the Scottish National Party, Alex Salmond, which is in Lallans. This, in turn, could turn unionists off the whole idea.

Various suggestions have been made as to how to define Scots. For J. J. Smith, the relationship between Scots and English in linguistic terms is much the same as that between the Scandinavian languages, or Dutch and certain varieties of German. They are all part of a continuum, which goes from the mutually intelligible to the unintelligible. McClure (1979, 1995) suggested a model based on two axes, one with a continuum between literary and colloquial Scots, and the other between 'dense Scots' and 'thin Scots'.[10] The newest term in this field is 'Civil Service Scots' (see below).

Whether a Scot will consider him or herself as a Scots speaker will depend on where they stand both politically and socially. For, as Smith points out, there are three groups of speakers in Scotland. There are those who speak *standard English*, either because they are English immigrants or members of the Scottish aristocracy. There are those who speak *Scots*, which has become the general preserve of the working classes, rural and urban. And there are those using *Scottish standard English*, which has been defined as standard English with a Scottish accent and some Scotticisms. It is an extremely prestigious form of speech, which lies on the English–Scots continuum between the two: English at one end, symbolising power and social and economic opportunities, while Scots, at the other end, symbolises home, the familiar, but also lower social classes.

In order to fight back, Scots has to prove itself not to be a purely working-class language, and there has been some work done in this direction. It now displays an impeccable pedigree, with the *Concise Scots Dictionary* (1985) distinguishing an Old English or Anglian period, going from the seventh century when the Angles established themselves in Scotland to around 1100, an Older Scots period which went from 1100 to 1700 and a Modern Scots period from 1700 onwards. The Older Scots period is divided into Pre-literary Scots, Early Scots and Middle Scots.

It also has to establish itself in the educational system. It has done so to a certain extent, in that plans have been set afoot to enable teachers to use Scots in the schools. This involves two problems: how to teach it and what to teach. Most teachers have had little training in the language, and the latter may vary quite substantially from area to area. The solution adopted so far has been a 'polynomic' one, i.e. the children are taught the local variety, while introduced to others. New materials have also been produced to help with the problem of inadequate teacher training provision. A package known as *The Kist/A' Chiste* (Scots and Gaelic for 'the chest') has been published for schools, and includes texts for the different Scots dialectal areas, and for Gaelic. There are those opposed to this, on the grounds that what should be taught should be the standardised Lallans form, in order to build up a national language. The present policy, on the other hand, is based on respect 'for the language children bring to school'.

Unfortunately, the introduction in the Advanced Higher English and Communication syllabus of a section on Scots which allowed a study of Scots depending on areas and in different domains, has only had a very low uptake on the part of students (Blain and Gifford 2003). The other problem, apart from lack of materials and teacher training, is clearly a lack of motivation on the part of the learners.

Media coverage of Scots is very limited. The problem is that there is fierce competition between papers, and none is likely to embark on experimenting with Scots when there is no demand. At present English is still the language of print, although Scotticisms do appear, when dealing with local affairs. There are also some daily papers and local papers which either carry columns in Scots or refer to the variety spoken in the locality. Magazines also publish both fiction and poetry in Scots.

Scots has a greater presence in broadcasting, however. Radio Scotland, the only all-day national broadcaster, has a duty to provide a wide range of programmes, and as a result, some programme directors have encouraged presenters to use Scots words and expressions in a wide range of programmes ranging from football to gardening.[11] There is no Scots channel as such, because of a desire not to ghettoise programmes (previous ethnic programmes proved to be unsatisfactory in not attracting the audiences they aimed for). The aim is to include Scots within mainstream programmes, and to develop an evolutionary process in this direction. For many this is quite unsatisfactory, however (see Stuart McHardy 2003 for example).

In television drama, city speech, such as that of the Glasgow character 'Rab C Nesbitt' put a form of Scots on the map (although whether or not it is 'Scots' is a subject of debate), but research shows that even in programmes which set out to explore Scottish life, the language element is often ignored or inadequately represented (Robinson 2003). Again this is felt by many to be quite unsatisfactory. What is asked for is a channel devoted to programmes representing Scotland's rich language diversity.

On the other hand, drama in Scots has developed consistently in recent years. It deals not only in original works in Scots but also in translations from authors as far apart as Molière and the Quebecker, Michel Tremblay. Since the latter includes different varieties of Joual and Québecois French in his plays, these translate particularly well into Scots,[12] since the difference of denseness between varieties of Scots corresponds neatly with the differences in Montreal speech. (The oldest generation speaks rural Scots, the middle generation speaks urban Scots, and the young generation speaks standard Scottish English; see Corbett 1997: 19.) Comedy programmes in Scots are also said to have brought the language to those who most readily rejected it.

For Scots to survive in a non-diglossic situation, it has to be used in all public domains. There is room for both hope and despair in this context. On the negative side much has been written on the lack of progress since devolution: 'It would not be unreasonable to argue that the main characteristics of the Executive's language policy are inconsistency and incoherence' (Hance 2005: 71). The accusation of inconsistency is due to the very different approaches adopted to the funding and support given to Gaelic and Scots. The accusation of incoherence is due to policies being set up merely because of external pressure, at the point when it can no longer be ignored. The main complaint is that although the Executive may make great mission statements in relation to language policies, which appear to give Scots and Gaelic equal weight, this is hardly ever carried out in practice for Scots by the Executive's agencies which refuse to take the language seriously.

A different approach could be adopted. Thus J. Corbett and F. Douglas, in a study on 'Scots in the Public Sphere', outline the considerable progress made so far. For this study, they used the Stewart (1968) questionnaire as a basis, and 'ticked the boxes'. To the question 'Is the language used as an official language by the governing authorities?', there is a partial yes, since devolution. The breakthrough was the *Report on the Education, Culture and Sport Committee into Scots, Gaelic and Minority*

*Languages in Scotland* (the McGuigan Report) of 2003. This was followed by a Scots version of the leaflet *Makkin your voice heard in the Scottish Pairliament* and a pamphlet by the Pairty Group on the Scots Language based on the Universal Declaration of Human Rights. *A Scots Parliament*, by James Robertson, written in Scots, is also on sale at the parliament bookshop. These publications are written in 'Civil Service Scots', which is meant to be simple and accessible. But such initiatives do not appear to have been often replicated by local authorities, one exception being Perth, where the Scots Language Resource Centre, founded in 1993, is based.

On the other hand, in 2003, the British Council asked J. Corbett to furnish a Scots version of the Council's mission statement, which figures alongside the English and Gaelic versions, under the 'diplomatic relations in the language' question. As far as its use in religion is concerned, the 1983 translation of the New Testament into Scots makes it finally possible for a Scots translation to be read in churches. A colloquial *Glasgow Bible* was published in 1997, and a new version of the complete Bible in pared-down Scots, based on Ogden's *Basic English Vocabulary*, was imminent at the time of writing. This pared-down Scots is similar to the functional Civil Service Scots. Answers to questions such as 'Is the language used in the capital? In the media?' are difficult to answer since it depends whether 'thin' Scots is considered acceptable or not. It is easy, on the other hand, to answer the question as to whether Scots is used for literary purposes or not, since there is 'abundant evidence' of activity in this domain.

Corbett and Douglas (2003) conclude that although the use of Scots is still patchy, in contrast to 1968 when Stewart drew up his list of target domains, when Scots was used in very few, enormous progress has been made. The development of Civil Service Scots is particularly important in this regard, since it takes Scots from the domain of the literary to the domain of the useful in everyday life.

## Concluding comments

A heartening aspect of linguistic policies in Scotland is the relative lack of animosity between the two RLs, Gaelic and Scots, partly because of the need to avoid self-destructive hostility, although bitterness at obvious inequalities is bound to surface. The situation is interestingly different from the one in Brittany, where there is a clear line of demarcation between the two languages. In Scotland, both Gaelic and Scots have little by little infiltrated, at different times, large parts of the whole country.

Another difference is that Scots is the language of patriots, of kings who fought and managed to maintain Scottish independence for centuries. The Scots, like the Gaels, but unlike the Gallo speakers, have numerous heroes whose exploits they may sing. This makes Scots a nationalistic language in its own right despite its linguistic links with English. And since both languages are national, there are people who indeed speak both, and militate for both, which is quite remarkable.

Gaelic's fight for survival is difficult because of the very small proportion of Scottish speakers of Gaelic. But the government does seem to be trying hard to save it, although it is frequently argued that it is still not doing enough. The next census, or more likely the one after that, i.e. in 2021, will be all-important in determining how successful these efforts are, particularly in renewing the practice of language transmission within the family.

The fight for Scots survival is progressing, although institutionally at a much slower rate. But time is not quite so crucial, despite the demise of Scots having been announced over 200 years ago: there are still plenty of speakers, although many do not admit to speaking anything else but English. The problem here is whether 'thin' Scots is the beginning of the end, or is a platform to accede to 'dense' Scots, and also whether Civil Service Scots develops a life of its own. The problem is essentially a social one. As J. J. Smith said (2000: 168): 'Scots will be valued only when the human users of Scots will be valued', which sums up the problem. Devolution should make this possible if there is genuine commitment, not only on the part of language activists, but of society as a whole. This is far from certain, but what does seem clear in Scotland is a move towards more linguistic openness.

# 8
# The Regional Languages of Northern Ireland: Irish and Ulster Scots[1]

There are two RLs in Northern Ireland which now benefit from official recognition: Irish Gaelic, or, more simply, Irish, and Ulster Scots. This constitutes a recent state of affairs, for whereas Irish has always been on the scene, the appearance of Ulster Scots is very recent and intimately linked both with the process of ensuring peace in Northern Ireland and the signing of the European Charter for Regional or Minority Languages. Previously it was, to a very large extent, either an unknown language or one presumed to be extinct.

Language, in Northern Ireland, is therefore very much a political issue, in which religious affiliation plays a major part in terms of a sense of national identity. Irish is nowadays associated mainly with Catholic Nationalism, although not exclusively so. Ulster Scots is associated, nearly exclusively, with the Protestant Unionist British tradition. In other words, Protestants tend to feel themselves to be British, whereas Catholics tend to feel that they are Irish. It is quite possible, in this situation, to be a 'Protestant' atheist or a 'Catholic' atheist. In other words, the divide is not simply religious, in the sense that people do not argue about religious dogma. The terms 'Catholic' and 'Protestant', in Northern Ireland, have become mere labels to distinguish two different cultures and allegiances.[2]

It was not always so, or at least not to the same extent: Douglas Hyde (1860–1949), the founder of the Gaelic League in 1893, whose dream it was to keep Irish alive in those areas where it was still spoken, and later to restore it as the spoken language of the country, was Protestant. And earlier on, it was reported at a Presbyterian synod that various ministers were in the habit of preaching in Irish in the counties of Londonderry,

Antrim, Armagh and Tyrone (Price 1984: 41). Even today some Irish speakers in Northern Ireland are Protestant. But the tensions which are present there today and the symbolic value in terms of identity now attached to Irish and Ulster Scots within the context of the religious divide, make the language situation in Northern Ireland very different from elsewhere in the United Kingdom.

Both languages have ties beyond their political borders. Irish in Northern Ireland cannot be seen separately from its counterpart in the Irish Republic, where it is the official language of the state (even if it does not in practice function as such). Nor can Ulster Scots be dissociated from Scots, which spread to Northern Ireland mainly from the seventeenth century onwards, where it developed its own characteristics. But whereas Irish being an official language of the Republic helps Irish in Northern Ireland, the same cannot be said to the same extent of Ulster Scots, since Scotland can give only academic help. The paradox now is that Scots, which is spoken by many in Scotland, gets very little support from the Scottish government, whereas Ulster Scots, which appears to be spoken by very few (if any as a complete language) has been granted considerable means to expand from what many consider to be a non-existent, or at least a very tenuous, base. Such is the power of politics. It is also because of politics that the revival of both languages has to be seen side by side, the one seeking better treatment, in the case of Irish, the other seeking equality of treatment, in the case of Ulster Scots.

## Irish in Northern Ireland

### Historical background to Irish in Ireland as a whole

The development of Irish in Northern Ireland cannot be dissociated from that of Irish in the rest of Ireland, since partition did not come into effect until 1922 (the Anglo-Irish Treaty was signed in December 1921), when three of Ulster's traditional counties became part of the Irish Free State, and the Republic of Ireland in 1938, while the other six remained part of the United Kingdom.

Irish can be divided into a number of historical periods in which the development of the language corresponds with various external influences, which affected its development. Thus Proto-Irish corresponds to the pre-Christian and pre-literate era. The transition to Old Irish corresponds to the introduction of Christianity in the fifth century which brought about contact with Latin and led to the introduction in the sixth and seventh centuries of a monastic system in Ireland. The new monasteries quickly became seats of learning, both sacred and secular.

There is a large body of material, which dates back to this period, in both Latin, mainly for religious matters, and in Irish, for sagas, genealogies, praise poetry, satire, works on grammar and proverbial texts (see Harrison 1992). Linguistically, many Latin words entered the Irish language during this period, which stretches from the seventh to the tenth centuries. At this point the Norse invasions ushered in another linguistic period, marked by a few lexical borrowings in terms of commerce and seafaring, but without the language being deeply affected. This is termed the Middle Irish period, and lasted from the tenth century to the end of the twelfth.

Early Modern Irish goes from the thirteenth until the seventeenth centuries. It was influenced by the arrival of the Anglo-Normans, who brought both French and English with them, post-1169. The monasteries again played a role, because with the Normans came European monastic orders and monks who spoke French or English. (Indeed there are many tales of conflict and even murder between the native Irish clergy and the foreigners.) The mix of Irish and French/English in the monasteries became a new factor in terms of language change. Borrowings from French were mainly in terms of the military (including military architecture), and the law. The latter survived in French until the fifteenth century. English, on the other hand, the language of the followers of the Anglo-Normans, affected all aspects of language, and not just the lexical. This period lasted from the thirteenth century until the beginning of the seventeenth century, when the Flight of the Earls,[3] in 1607, brought about the collapse of the Irish socio-cultural framework.

It was early on during this period that secular learning was banished from the monasteries. From then on, separate secular schools for learning were established, which lasted for 400–500 years. During this period a written standard language was established and taught in these schools, which precluded the use of dialectal forms. Poets, during this period, received patronage from the noble classes, in exchange for which they used their knowledge and skills to confirm the status of their patrons. Their main production was highly stylish and formulaic praise poetry (Harrison 1992).

The following period, Modern Irish, goes from the seventeenth century to the late nineteenth century, and corresponds to an increase in dialectal divergence in the spoken language (the written language remained relatively standardised). For example, the influence of the Norman French stress pattern had an impact on Munster Irish, which it did not have on Ulster Irish. Dialectal divergences affected not only phonology, but all aspects of the language. Moreover, as Irish-speaking districts gradually shrank to more isolated areas, contact between the various *Gaeltachts*[4] diminished and divergence became ever more marked. Four major dialects are usually recognised: Leinster (which had disappeared by the end of the nineteenth century), Munster, Connacht and Ulster. This is also the period when Scots, brought in by the planters from the Lowlands (see below), started to have an impact on the language.

There are some differences of opinion as to how disastrous the seventeenth century was in terms of the language. Some consider it to have been catastrophic, since it marked the beginning of its decline. But others (such as Ó hIfearnáin 1992) have pointed out that Irish remained very vigorous until Culloden in 1746, when all hope of a Jacobite success was lost (see below).

The period from the late nineteenth century to the present day is usually labelled Late Modern Irish, and was marked by the rise of Irish Nationalism, which was to lead to the establishment of an Irish Free State and the separate entity of Northern Ireland in 1921. It was marked by a strong revivalist movement which favoured both the Irish language (the movement led by Douglas Hyde[5]) and intellectual life in general which led to a great flowering of Irish literature written in English but with an unmistakably Irish character, best known in the writings of W. B. Yeats (1865–1939).[6] There was, in fact, disagreement between the various intellectuals involved in the Nationalist movement as to the role the Irish language should have in Irish Nationalism. Thus, whereas Hyde saw Irish as 'the best claim we have upon the world's recognition of us as a separate nationality', Yeats set out to create a special brand of English, which was to have 'an indefinable Irish quality of rhythm and style' (N. Davies 2000: 814).

Such a linguistic account of the development of Irish makes it look smooth and linear and does not take into account the fact that various areas of Ireland lost their linguistic independence at different periods in time. Thus, by the tenth century, a Scandinavian population had settled in Dublin, which became part of a Norse-Gaelic cultural zone, which also included the Isle of Man, Galloway and the Hebrides. This did not have a profound influence on Irish, whereas the arrival of the Normans at the end of the twelfth century constituted a far more serious challenge. It is at this point that new forms of land tenure and a different political system were set in place. Both English and French were used by the Anglo-Normans, whose influence was strongest in the area of the Pale around Dublin. The latter eventually became the point from which English spread to the whole of Ireland.

That was not initially a foregone conclusion, for outside the Pale the incomers tended to learn Irish, marry into Irish families and adopt Irish customs. The grip of England on language use in Ireland was weak even within the Pale,[7] to the extent that the Kilkenny Statutes were passed in 1366 to stop English settlers, under pain of losing their land, from going over to Irish. But these statutes are said to have been fairly ineffective and failed to check an Irish resurgence, which held its own until well into the sixteenth century.[8] The social and economic structures of Ireland were, however, undermined by military force. The latter involved military raids, with the vanquished lords being granted their lands back as feudal fiefs, in exchange for their declaring allegiance to the English monarch, obedience to English law, ceasing to wear Irish garments, and by learning English (Moody and Martin 1994: 179).

Changing from Irish to English law was particularly important in the battle of English against Irish. The earliest legal code in Ireland and in Irish, *Feineachas* (*féin* meaning 'self'), was an oral one, but the arrival of Christianity had led to written forms of these laws appearing. Although the form of Irish used then gradually became archaic, there was the usual reluctance to change the wording, which made lawyers indispensable. This continued even after the arrival of the Anglo-Normans, who came with their own code, but the latter was originally employed only in the Pale and other centres under their control. It was not until the seventeenth century that English Common Law spread to other parts of the country. The institution of Manor Courts, the Court of Assizes and Quarter Sessions brought English law, and English, to different parts of the country. Then, in 1737, the Administration of Justice (Language) Act (Ireland) was enacted which forbade the use of any other language than English in court. This law is still on the statute books in Northern Ireland (but not in the Republic of course). Another such law which applies only to Northern Ireland since it was passed in 1949, the Public Health and Local Government (Miscellaneous Provisions) Act (Northern Ireland) 1949, forbade councils from using street-names other than English ones (Napier 2003).

Another element in the decline of Irish was due to English settlers being brought over in the seventeenth century to take over the lands of the dispossessed Irish aristocracy. The establishment of this new Protestant upper class by Cromwell[9] (1599–1658) had the effect of removing Irish not only from all legal contexts, but also as the normal language of administration and the higher levels of commercial activity.

Where the English failed was in enforcing the Reformation, despite ordering the clergy to address their congregations in English as early as 1540. English, not Irish, was to be the language of religion. But for this to become possible, the population had to be converted, hence the first printed material to be published in Irish[10] being a Catechism in 1571. This was followed by the Old Testament in 1602, the Book of Common Prayer in 1608, a new translation of the Old Testament in 1685 (by Archbishop Bedell), and other Irish language publications (but these died out from early on in the eighteenth century). The Presbyterian Church, particularly in Northern Ireland, also sent Irish-speaking missionaries into rural areas, and produced Irish language education materials, including a grammar of Irish (Ó Dochartaigh 2000).

Protestant books and materials in Irish were seen, however, as an attempt at proselytisation. As a result, they received a hostile reception, and were rejected by the Catholic clergy. Thus Grace Neville's study of the language shift from Irish to English as exemplified in the Archives of the Irish Folklore Commission, *Coimisium Béaloideasa Éireann*, states that the Protestant Bible in Irish was known as the 'souper's Bible', a 'soup House' being one in which 'soup was doled out to hungry people provided they accepted, read or listened to the Protestant Bible in Irish being read'. She also mentions a reference found in these archives to a 'sort of Irish (language) school where the souper's Bible was taught, in Irish of course', and where the teacher was reputed to be paid for every convert made (Neville 1992: 27–8). This rejection of Irish in the religious context soon became associated with the idea that it was not a good enough language to pray in, one priest even being quoted as saying that its use made a 'mockery of it' ('it' being the Christian faith). In other words, in the case of Irish, translation of religious works into Irish turned out to be counterproductive for the language. In this the Irish situation differs fundamentally from the case of Welsh and Scottish Gaelic. This anti-Irish approach on the part of the Catholic clergy also went against an older Irish tradition, since from the earliest days of Christianity, a substantial amount of religious writing had been produced in Irish.

The end result was that English ended up being the language of both secular and religious power, with Irish becoming a disenfranchised spoken language, and indeed one associated with the French concept of *patois*. This did not happen right away, since many of the Gaelic nobility who had fled to the continent early in 1607 maintained an international Gaelic community. They established, in particular, many colleges throughout Europe to maintain and develop Irish culture, with a view to its future re-establishment in Ireland. (This was supposed to happen with the restoration of the Stuarts to the English throne, at which point the great Irish chieftains would have regained their lands.) The language was, at that point, so strong that when, in an Irish college in Lille which included both lay students and seminarists, the name of a new rector who did not speak Irish was put forward in 1764, there was a massive outcry, and another Irish-speaking rector had to be found (Ó hIfearnáin 1992: 37). But after the Jacobite Rising in Scotland, partly financed by Irish bankers and merchants, failed in 1745–6, all hope was lost. This was followed by a decline in Gaelic scholarship in Irish colleges on the continent, as merchants and bankers lost interest and integrated in to the country where they had chosen to live.[11] After this, Irish disappeared from nearly all formal registers and only survived in the poorest rural parts, although it has been pointed out that the peasantry possessed a rich literary oral culture of high quality.

The Act of Union of 1801 with Great Britain was followed by further efforts to Anglicise Ireland, in particular the foundation, in 1832, of the 'National Schools', which functioned entirely in English and did much to spread that language, thanks in part to the tacit agreement of parents (see below). A few years later, a series of famines (the most serious being in 1845) killed or drove abroad a large proportion of the Irish poor, who were also Irish speakers. The impact was clear: according to the 1851 census,[12] 23.3 per cent of the population spoke Irish. Thirty years later, in 1881, the figure had dropped to 18.2 per cent, and in 1911, the date of the last census in a united Ireland, the figure was down to 13.3 per cent. Irish had become a minority language. Moreover, most of the Irish speakers left were bilingual.

This was mainly due to the reluctance of parents to transmit their language to their children. Thus Grace Neville's archives make numerous references to parents using every means at their disposal to encourage their children to speak English, seen as the best language for economic survival, and to discourage their use of Irish. She states:

> Linguicide, from whatever source it flows, is accepted time and time again with the same fatalism as bad weather, potato blight or any of the myriad crosses people encountered. Expressions of indignation, anger and frustration at such treatment might be expected. I have encountered none. Indeed, how 'the Irish was beaten out of us' is often recalled with humour, as if, consciously or not, the informant's aim was first and foremost to entertain and amuse the collector.[13]

These archives refer to 'the dirty Irish', 'that old Irish' and so on.

By the time Ireland gained independence, in 1920, the language was seriously endangered. This was despite the wave of romantic nationalism which had led writers towards the end of the nineteenth century to take an interest in Irish folklore and literature. Indeed Hyde's declared aim, which was to de-Anglicise Ireland and re-establish Irish as the normal language of the state, led to many adults learning the language, and Irish was introduced in many of the National Schools. But after independence, support for individual efforts in this direction were handed over to the state, which realised that by then, for Irish to be re-established, it would have to be taught to over 90 per cent of the population. The implications in terms of resource allocation were horri-fying. As a result, 'the government effectively lowered its sights and took shelter in a number of low-level reforms, accompanied by the rhetoric of external symbol' (Ó Dochartaigh 2000: 31).

Ó Dochartaigh points out that the only serious attempt made in the early days was through the schools system, since the decline of Irish in the nineteenth century was attributed to the establishment of the National Schools. This did not take account of the socio-economic needs of Irish speakers, hence the lack of success of a policy based purely on education. There were also practical problems involved. One was in terms of the font to be adopted – the Irish font desired by the 'true Gaels' or the Roman font favoured by the modernisers. Adopting the Irish font would have meant having two typewriters in every office, which would clearly have been too expensive. The whole issue took until the 1960s to be fully resolved in favour of the Roman font.

Another problem was establishing a standard norm to be used in official contexts. A Reform Committee was set up by the government in Dublin to select the most appropriate forms, which were to be chosen from the three main dialects, Connacht, Munster and Ulster. The aim was to end up with a simplified system, but without any of the chosen forms being in any way reconstructed. The brief was to combine aspects of all three dialects, to form a whole. But the end product was not received by all with equal enthusiasm as the way towards a codified and therefore usable national language. Some felt that the language planners had not been fair to all the dialects, and that Ulster Irish in particular had had a raw deal. Others found the rules too strict, and resented not being allowed enough freedom to use dialectal forms. Others favoured more or less borrowings from English. This led to the idea that the rules could be relaxed in all non-formal domains, i.e. they only had to be strictly adhered to in legal and official documents.[14]

Spelling reform constituted another pressing problem which had to be solved if the language was to be taught and used in official contexts. This was because spelling had become very archaic, with numerous let-ters representing sounds no longer pronounced in natural speech. But standard spelling rules were not agreed until 1958, and, despite having taken so long to elaborate, they still do not satisfy everybody.

A more immediate problem for the new Irish government and those which followed was the paucity of well-trained teachers and teaching materials. There is still, for example, a need for a new English–Irish dictionary, the best available at present having been first published in 1959. Various word-lists for technical terms in philosophy, science, education, psychology, IT, etc. are available, but have not yet been incorporated in bilingual dictionary format.

From a policy-making point of view, it was not until 1978 that the Irish government established *Bord na Gaeilge* as a statutory language body with annual funding. Until then the only bodies involved were about a dozen voluntary groups, of which the most important were affiliated to the Gaelic League (*Conradh na Gaeilge*), each with an interest in some particular aspect of Irish culture. After independence, instead of trying to pressurise the British government for support, as in the past, they turned to the new Irish state. The problem was their 'fissiparous tendencies'. Thus Ó Dochartaigh (2000: 31) reports the standard joke in any new Irish language organisation, according to which the most commonly used sentence was 'And when do we have to split?' This led to the creation of the more efficient National Congress for the Irish Language (*Comhdháil Náisiúnta na Gaeilge*), founded in 1943. Both bodies still exist, but without their respective functions being clearly delimited, which again weakens the language lobby (Ó Dochartaigh 2000: 30–3).

Thus when the 1937 Irish Constitution stated that Irish was the first official language, this was no more than the expression of a desire, the reality of everyday life being in English. In later years, however, the government was to give a great deal of practical support to the language in numerous contexts, not all of which have had general national support. Thus, the considerable help given to the *Gaeltacht* region has given rise to jealousy and opposition, particularly from those Irish people who did not feel the need to learn Irish to have an Irish identity. They see the revival of Irish as a retrograde step towards parochialism and exclusionism, in contrast with the more exciting forward-looking future offered by the EU.

The 1991 census seems, nonetheless, encouraging in terms of language revival in the Republic since it established that 32.5 per cent of the population claimed they were were Irish speakers (1 095 830). It may be assumed, however, that a maximum number of people claim this knowledge since Irish is seen by them as a badge of cultural, ethnic and national identity. It has also been pointed out that such statistics disguise the fact that the number of native speakers of Irish is continuing to decline in real terms, and that these high figures are due to the acquisition of Irish as a second language at school, without intergenerational transmission automatically following. As a result, despite major efforts, Irish is still very much a minority language in its own country. This constitutes a warning to other RLs, namely that state policy, however positive, is not enough on its own to reinstate a language.[15] There has to be a strong desire on the part of the population.

Such a desire may come from unexpected quarters, such as the situation in Northern Ireland, where, until very recently, Irish had to fight hard for recognition. The fact that speakers of Irish were also fighting for equality, and that their identity became associated with the Irish language, no doubt helped to give it a dynamism viewed with envy south of the border (Ó hIfearnián 1998: 202). Indeed, as polarisation between the two communities in Northern Ireland has increased, there has been a parallel development in interest in Irish among the Nationalist/Catholic people, as witnessed by the growth in Irish medium schools, and the use of Irish road and street-names in Nationalist areas (around the culture centre in Belfast, the *Cultúrann*, many other signs are in Irish, such as doctors' surgeries, pubs and shops).

But the situation in what is now Northern Ireland had its own characteristics even before 1921, because it was the region most affected by the 'Plantations', i.e. settlers brought in to take over lands previously owned by Irish Catholics. The principle was that land equalled power and wealth, and that their removal from the Catholic insurgents would weaken resistance to English rule. If Ireland would not become Protestant, then Protestants would have to go to Ireland, and repopulate it.[16] This policy, which started in the sixteenth century, was not limited to Ulster, but it is there that it took its most extreme form. It took off mainly after the Flight of the Earls in 1607 since their abandonment of their lands was considered a treasonable act, which led to their confiscation to the benefit of Protestant colonists or planters, who came mainly from Lowland Scotland. Cromwell's conquest of Ireland (1649–50) and William III's defeat of the Catholics at the Battle of the Boyne in 1690 further increased this movement of population, which also had, as a side-effect, the introduction of Scots into Ulster (see below).

The newcomers had, from the very beginning, their own traditions, institutions, religion and language. Even their farming was different, with a preference for the cultivation of arable land over Irish pastoral farming. This created a new society separate from the indigenous people. Despite this, or perhaps because of it, Irish survived for quite a long time, particularly in mountainous districts, but the end of the nineteenth century saw its near total demise. The 1851 census gave 7 per cent Irish speakers in Armagh, by far the highest figure for Northern Ireland where the overall average was but 2.6 per cent, falling to 2 per cent by 1861. More importantly, by 1891 there were only fourteen monoglots left, eight by 1901, and four, all under the age of 10, in 1911. There were still, however, 28 279 bilinguals (Price 1984: 43–5).

### The fight for the survival of Irish in Northern Ireland

Unlike in the Republic where, ever since independence, policies have been in place to reinstate Irish as a living language, in Northern Ireland the British state has only recently started to support the language (see below). The 1991 census for Northern Ireland, which corresponds to the beginning of this period of gradual recognition, was the first to contain a linguistic question since Partition. The returns indicated that 142 003 people claimed a knowledge of the language (which is not, of course, the same as being bilingual, hence the disparity between this figure and the 28 279 bilinguals mentioned previously). This represented 9.46 per cent of the whole population and a little under one-third if the Protestant population is excluded (Ó hIfearnáin 1998: 212). These figures could be broken down into three categories: (i) those who could speak Irish, and could also read and/or write the language (86 636 persons or 5.77 per cent of the population), (ii) those who could speak Irish but could not read and/or write it (45 338 or 3.02 per cent of the population) and (iii) those who could only read and/or write the language (10 029 or 0.6 per cent of the population).[17]

Given the recent development of an enthusiastic movement for the revival of Irish in Northern Ireland, it would be interesting to be able to compare these figures with those of the 2001 census. Unfortunately, the questions asked were not exactly the same, since the 2001 census introduced the new category of 'understanding' the language. As a result of this additional category, the figure reached this time was of 167 490 persons (or 10.33 per cent of the population) who had some knowledge of the language, but of these 36 479 declared only an understanding the language. If this figure is deducted from the total this gives the lower figure of 131 011. But this is all hypothetical since it presumes that the persons who only ticked the 'understand' box, had not ticked anything in the previous census (see Ó Duibhin 2003 and MacKinnon 2003).

It is interesting to note that, as for the other Celtic languages in Britain, with the exception of Cornish, the distribution of speakers has changed geographically, with urbanisation having taken place. In the past, in what is now Northern Ireland, native speakers of Irish lived in communities which were geographically isolated and scattered in small pockets throughout the six counties. These *Gaeltachts* have long since ceased to exist, but with the development of bilingual networks in urban new areas, new *Gaeltachts* appear to be growing due to the influence of Irish medium schools which have the effect of concentrating Irish-speaking families around them. Not surprisingly, the British government signed up Irish for Part III protection of the European Charter for Regional or Minority Languages.

Education is the most important tool to save a language when intergenerational transmission has either ceased or become dangerously low. Efforts in this direction come, in the first instance, from language enthusiasts who set up voluntary bodies and associations, including schools, to further their aims. Irish is no exception: the first Irish medium school in Northern Ireland dates from 1971, but progress was slow at first, because of the negative attitudes of the state and official bodies. But after the 1989 review of the working of the Intergovernmental Conference of the Anglo-Irish Agreement, many more were founded. This was because the British government undertook at that point to support efforts to enhance awareness and appreciation of the Irish language in the context of encouraging greater mutual understanding across the community. It is within this context that the government accepted the use of the Irish version of personal names and official correspondence in Irish (although the reply was to be in English).

As a result, and despite lacking any state support and with only limited backing from the Catholic Church, the number of Irish medium nursery groups and Irish-speaking medium units in primary schools started to increase. In 2004–5[18] there were 32 Irish medium primary schools or 'units' (i.e. classes which function in Irish within an otherwise Anglophone school) which provided education for 2328 pupils. Preschool provision was provided in 44 'settings' which catered for 855 children.

This led to demand for post-primary Irish medium education and the first all-Irish secondary school opened in 1991. Elsewhere Irish medium post-primary education tends to take place in Irish units within English-speaking schools within the Catholic sector. For 2004–5 there were 530 pupils receiving post-primary education in Irish in three schools, one in Belfast, one in Derry and one in Armagh.

This improvement in numbers and in provision is largely due to changes following the 1998 Good Friday (or Belfast) Agreement, which guarantees funding by the Department of Education, where there is a demand. (Strict rules have been drawn up in this respect, which establish how many children at each level and in different areas are needed for an

Irish medium unit to be created. See Steele 2003 for details.) It also ensured there was greater cooperation between the various bodies[19] promoting Irish medium education. This stops at the tertiary level, however, although both Queen's University and the University of Ulster offer courses in the language.

Traditionally, Irish has also been taught as a subject in Catholic schools, but this does not automatically imply competence in the language. Moreover, pressure on curriculum time, brought about by the introduction of new subjects, has led to a decline in provision. Whereas in the past, schools tended to make Irish an obligatory subject, Irish is now, in many cases, an option among other modern languages, such as French and Spanish, which many pupils and parents perceive as more relevant to the needs of modern life. It would therefore seem that at the same time as the number of pupils attending Irish medium schools increases, there is also a decrease in the number of pupils learning Irish in the mainstream Catholic schools.

The fact remains, however, that the dynamism of the Irish language movement in Northern Ireland is sometimes viewed with envy in the Republic of Ireland, where there is not the same degree of enthusiasm, since there is not the same need to affirm a separate identity from that dictated by the state. It is such a need which led Gaelic enthusiasts in Belfast in the 1960s to develop a small urban *Gaeltacht*. This, in turn, grew into a bilingual community, actively engaged in using the language, but it is still too early to say whether this will lead to intergenerational transmission (Ó hIfearnáin 1998).

The current success does not mean there are no problems. The supply and training of teachers is the most difficult and one which is common to all RLs. Shortage of materials, and the problem of continuity across the different levels of education, are also common in all cases.

Apart from education, the media is the other great language-empowering institution. Once a language appears on radio, and even more so on television, it is seen as being legitimate. Moreover, for many nowadays the media has become the main centre of gravity around which many organise their lives (it would have been, traditionally, the family, the community or religion). It is therefore not surprising that broadcasting should be considered the most powerful of all institutions in manipulating the mind. And yet there are limitations as to what may be achieved in terms of programmes in the RLs, although the advent of digital television may have an immensely liberating effect.

If one takes the national channels, the problem for a body such as the BBC is that its programmes are supposed to reflect the diversity of the audience, which is paying for them. This means that Irish should be present on both radio and television, which it is, but only to a minimal extent. The problem is that the 89.64 per cent of the population who have no knowledge of Irish (according to the last census) do not want to see Irish programmes displace those they wish to see. This means that the BBC in Northern Ireland is necessarily, at present, overwhelmingly in English, with Irish rarely appearing at peak times. This is sometimes referred to as the 'displacement factor', and is a problem for all programming in the RLs. Indeed it is for this reason that many Welsh Anglophones favoured the creation of an all-Welsh channel, so that their own programmes were not displaced.

A problem, if such a channel were created for Irish in Northern Ireland, is how to fill it, given the very varied abilities of the potential audience, many of whom are no more than learners. The small number of potential viewers and listeners also precludes to a large extent the commercial sector from taking an interest in creating dedicated radio stations or television channels. But the need to include at least some programmes in Irish resulted in 2003–4 in four 30-minute TV programmes on life in Armagh. A new ten-part magazine was also planned (and was broadcast) for young people, and an Irish learning project was planned. That year, seven members of staff were dedicated to Irish language broadcasting. This clearly is very little but it is difficult to see how the BBC could do more at present, given the constraints already mentioned.

A possible solution is enabling reception in Northern Ireland of programmes broadcast by the Republic, on the Irish channel, TG4, which includes a large number of programmes in Irish. Such a solution was already promoted in the Good Friday Agreement: 'In the context of active consideration being given by the UK to signing the Council of Europe Charter for Regional or Minority Languages, the British Government will in particular in relation to the Irish language, where appropriate and where people so desire explore urgently with the relevant British authorities, the scope for achieving more widespread availability of Teilifis na Gaeilge [now TG4] in Northern Ireland.' The Agreement also states that the UK will also: 'seek more effective ways to encourage and provide financial support for Irish language film and television production in Northern Ireland' (McAlistair 2003b: 29–30).

Since 1998, the Northern Irish Department of Culture, Arts and Leisure includes a Linguistic Diversity branch. Its representative, Patricia McAlistair, has pointed out that the Agreement effectively recognises that TG4 is likely to remain for the foreseeable future the principal supplier of television programming to meet the needs of the Irish-speaking community in Northern Ireland, and that it is important to ensure that coverage by TG4 is expanded to reach all. Unfortunately the programmes cannot be seen at present in more than half of Northern Ireland, and reception is often very poor even where they can be. This does not result from disagreement between the British and Irish governments, but is linked with the inability to clear rights for much of their programming, such as sport, films and soaps (Eirug 2003) since TG4 is mainly self-funding. At the time of writing this problem had still not been solved.

RTE1 (Raidió-Teilifís Éirann), the equivalent of BBC1, is the national channel of the Irish Republic. It broadcasts mainly in English, but there are daily news bulletins in Irish, and occasional programmes in Irish. Plenty of people, from both communities in Northern Ireland, have aerials to receive it, since it is good for sport (especially rugby, the all-Ireland game) and films, as an addition to BBC and UTV.

Television is not the only important mediatic form. It has often been pointed out how very important radio has been in giving life to the RLs, often buried until then in books, between quotation marks, with grammar and vocabulary usually cleaned up to make them fit in with the linguistic standard version. In contrast with this, Raidió na Gaeltachta, which is based in the Republic, broadcasts in the three main dialects on an all-Ireland basis. It is not aimed explicitly to develop Irish but does so indirectly. It has, moreover, connections with BBC Radio Ulster and BBC Raidió nan Gàidheal, which presents a weekly bilingual programme in Irish and Scottish Gaelic.

Depending on the Republic for radio and particularly television programmes cannot be, however, a long-term solution since these programmes do not reflect the concerns of the Northern Irish population. Moreover, use of the southern dialect may cause problems for listeners and viewers whose linguistic competence is limited. But the government has committed itself to doing more, both in the Good Friday Agreement and when it gave Irish Part III protection. The latter guarantees encouraging or facilitating the production of audio and audiovisual works in Irish, giving financial assistance, and supporting the training of journalists and other staff for media using regional or minority languages. As a result, reports have been commissioned to examine what could and should be done.

The report *How to Broadcast the Irish Language in Northern Ireland*, which has been chosen among several as a starting point, made two recommendations: one was to train Irish speakers from Northern Ireland to work in television, the other was to set up a production fund in the region of £3 million per annum. As a result, a first training scheme ran in 2002, which was judged to have been very successful since many of its fourteen participants obtained employment in the industry or gained commissions with TG4.

This is clearly an area in which many changes are taking place. The general aim at present seems to be for increased programming in Irish from BBC Northern Ireland, greater availability of TG4 and the prospect of a film and television fund. But so far, the actual quota of programming is not as high as many would wish, for the reasons given above (Hegarty 2003).

Publishing, on the other hand, seems to be already in a very healthy state. There are numerous book launches and publishing houses, including in Northern Ireland. Irish also has a presence in newspapers. Thus the *Irish News*, which is the daily paper with the highest circulation in Northern Ireland, now has two full pages every day in Irish. There is also an Irish language newspaper, *Lá* (meaning 'day').

Finally the importance of the arts centre, *Cultúrann* in the Falls Road, must be mentioned given its role in promoting the Irish language and culture to the whole community. It forms, with the Irish medium school which is close to it, the heart of the new urban *Gaeltacht* in Belfast.

## Ulster Scots

### Historical background

Ulster Scots is a variety of Scots, which was imported into Northern Ireland mainly from the seventeenth century onwards. It was established in three main areas[20] where it developed its own characteristics. But it gradually became associated with working-class and rural speech, hence the contempt in which it is held by many today[21] who consider it to be no more than 'bad English'. It was not recognised by EBLUL in 1993 nor in the Killilea report in 1994.

The success of the Ulster Scots movement has been in drawing attention to its existence, to the literary achievements of Scots, the 'parent' language, and to Ulster writers who adapted Scots to their own particular needs (Herbison 2005). Thus Gilbert states that 'the case for Ulster-Scots lies in the antiquity of its origins, the continuity of literary tradition, etymology and, of course, the current usage in Northern Ireland' (Gilbert 2003: 87).

According to this point of view, large numbers of people – mainly Protestants descended from the planters – spoke Ulster Scots in the eighteenth and nineteenth centuries. But those who see the language as no more than an Unionist ploy to claim to have their own language in the name of equality with the Nationalists, are more cynical and claim that Ulster Scots has no speakers whatsoever. They maintain that what is spoken is English with a scattering of words and expressions derived from Scots. These, say its defenders, are the sad remains of a language in need of recognition and rebuilding.

Whether Ulster Scots exists in linguistic terms either as a language or even as a dialect of Scots (and some claim that Scots is nothing more than English with Scotticisms) is, to a large extent, irrelevant in terms of linguistic policies. A language exists, at least potentially, once it has been recognised politically, and Ulster Scots has now received such recognition by (i) the Good Friday Agreement 1998, (ii) the North/South Cooperation (Implementation Bodies) Northern Ireland Order 1999, (iii) the European Charter for Regional or Minority Languages 2001 and (iv) the Communications Act 2003 (later a disappointment). Whether it develops into a genuinely used language is another matter.

One advantage of its recognition is that school children using forms of speech not recognised as correct, but existing in Ulster Scots, can now be informed that these are part of a past heritage, rather than simply being told they are wrong. This is worthwhile both pedagogically and psychologically. Various institutional changes have taken place in order to make this possible (see below).

### The fight for the revival of Ulster Scots and corresponding new arrangements for Irish

When the Belfast or Good Friday Agreement was signed in 1998, it was clear that Irish would demand political recognition. At this point, however, some Unionists demanded recognition for Ulster Scots. The latter was duly recognised since the Good Friday Agreement aimed at giving guarantees to both the Nationalists, largely associated with Irish, and to the Unionists, some of whom claimed to speak Ulster Scots. Since nothing much was known about this language, and few were aware of its existence, the Ulster Scots Agency (*Tha Boord o Ulstèr-Scotch*) was set up to study the problem. It received £1.3 million in 2000–1; 75 per cent of its budget comes from Westminster and 25 per cent from Dublin.

This led to new arrangements being made for Irish, previously the sole responsibility of the Irish Republic. Irish is now handled by *Forás na Gaeilge*[22] (the Irish Language Agency) which is responsible for the language both north and south of the border, which constitutes a remarkable political departure. Its funding is the mirror image of that for Ulster Scots, since 75 per cent of its budget comes from Dublin and only 25 per cent from Westminster, which reflects differences of allegiance between the two languages. Irish also receives proportionately greater funds, since in 2001–2 its budget was 15 million euros (i.e. around £10 million as against the £1.3 million for Ulster Scots). Both agencies together form the North/South Language Body.

To go back to Ulster Scots, there has been evidence of government implementation of its Charter obligations towards Ulster Scots, since the Ulster Scots Agency has been able to plan a number of educational initiatives. It began by commissioning an Ulster Scots Primary School Project, which began in March 2002, which aims at producing Ulster Scots learning materials, since the Charter requires that all children should have access to an Ulster Scots education, if their parents so wish. The aim is not to teach a language (still in the process of being described), nor to teach through the medium of Ulster Scots (which at present amounts mainly to Ulster Scots interference in English). It is more a matter of recognising a form of speech, history and culture, which are part of Ulster's heritage. One of the main aims is to give children 'pride in their traditional tongue' (Avery 2003: 68) and to remove the complexes acquired from having their speech criticised as 'bad English'.

Those responsible for producing these materials have asked for the assistance from Scots language experts and publishers of books and other materials designed for Scots curriculum development. The aim in doing so is to emphasise the possibility of bilingualism and to recognise features of Scottish origin. Another important influence were the teachers of Ulster Scots from County Antrim and the Ards peninsula, who had pioneered the teaching of the language to children in an area where it was claimed its use was still significant. It is in this connection that the organisers of the project were warned not to introduce written Ulster Scots at the primary school stage, because of the risk of causing confusion in terms of the pupils' use of English spelling.

An orthography has been established for the purposes of developing learning materials, which has been criticised by some Scots specialists (Falconer 2005) who complain of the damaging effects of breaking up a linguistic continuum by the imposition of an untraditional orthography. They cite the case of Manx as an example. Its orthography, by being different from Scottish Gaelic and Irish, isolates it from the rest of Gaeldom. On the other hand, since the orthography of Manx is based on English conventions it could be argued that this makes it easier for English speakers to learn. Orthography is an area fraught with problems, with at least two opposing points of view: those who wish to go back to a past form, and the modernisers who wish to bring it up to date. This is what the revivalists of 'Ullans', by choosing a new orthography, appear to have done.

There are necessarily differences in aims and approaches for the safe-guarding and promotion of Irish and Ulster Scots, Irish being a highly developed language while Ulster Scots is still emergent. This is reflected within the context of the European Charter for Regional or Minority Languages, since Ulster Scots only benefits from Part II protection, whereas Irish benefits from Part III. This is why the Ulster Scots Agency (or *Tha Boord o Ulstèr-Scotch*) has been given the task of promoting greater use and awareness of Ulster Scots and its culture, whereas its Irish counterpart, *Forás na Gaeilge*, concentrates purely on language.

But both agencies, without having been given a specific media function, have indicated their interest in this area (McAlistair 2003b). Not surprisingly, Ulster Scots is still in its infancy in terms of broadcasting, but a start has been made by creating a Northern Ireland Ulster Scots Unit, which, in 2003, included three members. The first time any Ulster Scots was heard on BBC Radio Ulster was on 6 March 2002, when the first series of *A Kist o Wurds* started running. It ranged through a variety of topics and personalities, and the aim, according to the producer, was to use 'as much Ulster Scots as possible' (Spurr 2003: 41), thus implying the current absence of a well-developed language. He stated that many of the contributors use 'Ulsterised' English, and that Ulster Scots is still at the aspirational level. He pointed out that 'when more speakers and contributors can converse at ease, this will no doubt happen', which again illustrates the fact that what is involved is revival and not survival or revitalisation.

The problem is how to find contributors and how to find topics to deal with. The two-hour-long Ulster Scots Theme Night, first broadcast in 2003, was successful in that it combined music, speech and folklore, but this can only be an occasional kind of programme. During 2003–4 the aim was to provide twelve hours, a marked improvement, but as Chris Spurr, the producer, pointed out, most work on Ulster Scots speech so far has been carried out by 'enthusiastic amateurs' and 'it is difficult to see how any policy towards the development of Ulster Scots could be furthered without the input from professional linguistic and teaching expertise across all three levels of education, and from within Ulster' (2003: 44). This is why reference is made in broadcasting circles to the 'different developmental stages reached by the two languages'.

Having reached different developmental stages does not mean that there cannot be 'parity of esteem', and of funding, although the latter may be used for different objectives. Thus the proposed level of funding by the Irish language Broadcast Production Fund is supposed to be mirrored in the funding for the Ulster Scots Academy. It was announced on 23 July 2003 by the Secretary of State that a fund in the region of £12 million would be awarded to develop Irish language film and television over three years (Mac Póilin 2003). On the principle of parity of treatment this sum needs to be matched by a similar sum to the Ulster Scots Academy. There are, however, problems associated with such funds, namely that although people in the business world have been consulted on the issue by the DCLA (Department of Culture, Leisure and Arts), there has been no genuine public discussion on such a use of public funds. Some have also objected to the idea of an Ulster Scots Academy where they would have preferred a more embracing 'Language Academy'.

The Ulster Scots Academy has been very active, however, in helping Ulster Scots develop into a language. It was set up in 1994 by its parent organisation, the Ulster Scots Language Society, founded in 1992, which includes some 300 enthusiastic amateurs whose job it is to collect material in Ulster Scots. The aims of the Academy are more academic and include the promotion of the study of Ulster Scots, recognition of its affinities with Scots, the pursuit of documentation, research and publication. Its members are actively involved in making a tape-recorded survey of Ulster Scots speakers, and in establishing an electronic text base of the written tradition. Two dictionaries were completed in 1995 and 1996, a grammar in 1997, and a translation service is available. There were, at one point, civil service posts advertised in both English and Ulster Scots. This no longer seems to be the case, however, possibly as a result of direct rule from Westminster. This may, therefore, change if devolved government is restored.[23] Finally, and this seems symbolically important, a translation of the Bible is being carried out as a collective work by native speakers.

## Concluding comments

Irish has made great progress in Northern Ireland in terms of education, publishing and the media. This was made possible by its long literary tradition, and by the fact that it never quite died out. Numerous efforts in the Republic, while not always very successful, at least had the advantage of giving the language not only legitimacy, but also iconic value. This does not mean that the language is saved in Northern Ireland, but there is now at least a general institutional commitment to its survival. Whether it succeeds or not will depend on the effort of individuals, although there is still one task to be carried out by the British state, namely the revoking of the Administration of Justice (Language) Act (Ireland) of 1737 in Northern Ireland, without which it will never be possible to use Irish (or Ulster Scots) in the courts.

Ulster Scots is at the other end of the scale, its legitimacy doubted both on linguistic grounds and because of its close association with Unionism and Loyalism. If it is to become a credible language, much more serious academic research is required. At present, as a language, it is still in its infancy. On the other hand, it clearly has the potential to become one through elaboration and codification. Some argue that this makes it a purely artificial language, while others feel that since it is linguistically a variety of Scots (it was defined as such in the North–South (Implementation Bodies) (Northern Ireland) Order 1999) Scotland should be involved in its policy-making. But the main problem associated with Ulster Scots is that its whole existence depends on the political divide, and a demand for parity with Irish, granted mainly for peacekeeping reasons.

Clearly the authorities in Northern Ireland are faced with a completely new situation in which this demand for parity is not generally approved. Many people resent money going to a little-used language (Irish) or one which may not even exist (Ulster Scots), when there is a shortage of funds for other worthy projects. It has to be hoped, however, that by channelling energies into language and culture, be they Irish or Ulster Scots, difficulties may be diffused, making the expenditure worthwhile from everybody's point of view. The pitfall to be avoided at all costs is that the development of these RLs should lead to further community entrenchment. The only way to avoid this is to make both communities aware that they have a shared interest in each.

# Concluding Comments

There are, on the whole, far more similarities than differences in the history of the RLs in France and Britain in terms of how and why French and English became national languages, resulting in the destruction of the RLs. This was mainly achieved by the imposition of French and English in the domains of law, administration and education. But these tended to be pursued for idealistic reasons in France and pragmatic ones in Britain.

Another difference was that policy was imposed uniformly on a national scale in France, whereas in Britain different policies applied at different times to Cornwall, Wales, Scotland and Ireland. This was because Britain was never the homogeneous unit that France has always aspired to be and only shared a common interest when the self-interest of its constituent parts found a common purpose through the British Empire. Yet another factor, which also played a part, was the steady demographic increase in the English population in relation to the population as a whole.[1]

Religion also played a different part in the two countries. In Britain, the Reformation had a major linguistic impact, since religion was to be practised in the vernacular. The survival of the RLs, from then on, depended to a large extent on whether or not the Bible was translated into each RL and when, since this gave them considerable prestige (Irish being the exception). In France this did not apply, since Latin remained the language of the Church with only the Catechism and sermons in the vernaculars.

The ending of the British and French empires at around the same period, engendered a sense of national despondency in both countries. This was due to the loss of economic opportunities previously afforded, and triggered a renewal of interest in regional identity, seen nowadays as a form of compensation for the perceived homogenising effect of the move towards globalisation. The gradual recognition of the right to use one's own language as a human right at the level of the Council of Europe and the EU, and other international organisations, has also helped the RLs find a voice.

By the 1970s, when this movement really started to gather pace, the RLs in France and Britain were either only just surviving or on the verge of extinction if not already extinct. Although much has been achieved since then, in both countries, particularly in terms of education, it is in Britain that most progress has been made. This was confirmed by the ratification by Britain of the European Charter for Regional or Minority Languages, but the degree of protection accorded to each RL was largely influenced by political factors (e.g. Ulster Scots in Northern Ireland).

In Britain, all the RLs examined have received some kind of official recognition: Welsh, Gaelic and Irish having fared best of all. But this is not enough in the view of their advocates, since the current law does not give individual rights to use the RLs in all contexts. They have been described as 'administrative enabling' or 'planning based' laws, where the onus is on local government administration to claim rights under the law but not individual speakers. This does, however, represent enormous progress. Scots, Ulster Scots and Cornish have also seen their existence recognised. Although they only come under Part II protection, this too marks progress (and indeed a triumph for Cornish and Ulster Scots), but Scots speakers feel they have been dealt with unfairly by not being granted Part III protection given their large number of speakers.

No such progress has been achieved in France, where all efforts in this direction are submerged in a constitutional quagmire. The main hope in France is for the passing of 'enabling administrative laws' by the new regional assemblies, since these would circumvent the Conseil d'Etat and the Conseil constitutionnel, which are the main stumbling blocks to any progress.

Both countries have achieved much, however, in terms of education, although more so in Britain than in France in respect of making the RLs obligatory, as in Wales. The media is a much more problematic area because of the problem of 'audience displacement'. The obvious solution in Britain is to create dedicated radio stations and TV channels for the RLs (or 'national' languages). This is easier to conceive of since digitalisation, but fundamental problems remain: producing enough programmes, finding people qualified to do so, and solving the problem of who is going to pay when the audience is relatively small. So far only Welsh has a dedicated TV channel (although a Gaelic one is planned), but other channels provide some programmes in the RLs. Radio is generally less of a problem. In France, provision in this important area is even more inadequate, although slow progress is being made.

It remains to be seen whether, in the long run, these efforts will be successful in achieving more than the simple preservation of these languages. The outstanding problems are enormous in spite of the progress achieved. One of the most serious is 'regional scepticism', which means that the RLs are seen by those who could conceivably be expected to take an interest in them as part of their heritage, as parochial, backward-looking and limiting. They are seen as fostering exclusion within small areas, just when larger units such as the EU are developing and bringing great benefits in numerous quarters (the Irish economy being a typical example). This is reminiscent of the attitude towards the RLs during the creation of the French and British empires. Clearly those in favour of the RLs need constantly to promote their inclusiveness, the enriching effect of a second culture and their potential permanence at a communal level in a constantly changing world.

Another problem is to ensure intergenerational transmission as the outcome of educational policies. Without this the languages will ossify and ultimately die as natural means of communication. Transmission seems unlikely to happen at a satisfactory rate, since research shows that RLs learned in the primary school sector are often abandoned in later years. And yet, in the short term, everything depends on education in the RLs, which faces numerous problems, common to both countries, including a shortage of suitably trained teachers and lack of teaching materials. One of the problems is how to educate native and non-native speakers together. Usually those who have the RL in the context of the home are sacrificed. The same problem affects the media, with its very mixed audience.

Yet another problem is the matter of orthography. This is, at least, a solvable problem, with several possible solutions, ranging from a standardised form to the polygraphic. An associated problem is the existence of dialectal differences that people are unwilling to sacrifice. Once again the solutions range from a standardised to a polynomic version. But delays in reaching a solution can be very damaging, since this affects not only teaching but also all official documents.

These difficulties are associated with the need to develop the languages, which have often lost some of their registers, and need to be adapted to the modern world. The ways in which this can be achieved are open to debate, particularly in terms of the degree of interference which should be allowed from the majority language. This problem is even more marked for revived languages, which are often accused of being artificial and therefore not valid. This seems unfair since the official standardised languages are, themselves, highly artificial by definition. There still remains, however, the question as to who should be authorised to influence the form in which the RL is revived.

Success either for the revitalisation or the revival of the RLs is due, in the first instance, to a 'touch of madness' on the part of their defenders. Examples include leaders such as Gwynfor Evans, willing to fast to death for the establishment of a Welsh language TV channel, or Cornish militants risking prison for defacing English Heritage signs and replacing them by signs in Cornish. But apart from such catalysts, it tends to be the work of mainly educated people. For the languages to be truly revitalised, however, the impetus must also come from other sectors of society. What is at stake is the need to establish bilingualism (and multilingualism in some areas), since the likelihood of monoglot RL speakers seems highly unlikely,[2] and the advantages of bilingualism have to be 'sold' to society as a whole. This may well be the most difficult hurdle, particularly where the poor and uneducated are concerned, since spending money on 'useless' languages will not be seen as a priority. And even where there is a consensus, there still needs to be a sense of realism about the availability of resources and the speed at which language policies may be implemented.

Large countries seem less able, ideologically, to adapt to the principle of developing their RLs, particularly if they are centralised like France. In Britain there is no longer the same degree of ideological objection. Devolution, in particular, has led to a marked improvement for most – but not all, since Scots seems very hard done by. Decentralisation in France is also having a beneficial effect in some regions. But on the whole, France is far behind Britain in terms of what is accorded to the RLs, which, unlike in Britain, still have no official status whatsoever.

So far the policies which have worked in both countries have been mainly local and aimed at increasing the prestige of the RLs. Opportunities have been created to bring together mature speakers and young learners, and to create activities linked with language (for example religious services, holiday camps, festivals – music being particularly important in many cases). Efforts have been made to increase their visibility in public domains, such as business (letter headings, corporate logos, etc.), law, administration, bilingual signage, and so on. The economic impact in terms of tourism has also been analysed (tourists have the great advantage in that they are not permanent and do not dilute community identity). Electronic technology, particularly the web, has also acted as a springboard for further developments.

The next stage is to transcend the diglossic stage, which includes the introduction of compulsory education in the state system; the possibility of using the RL in a work context – including in local government offices – and the availability of mass media in the RLs. Whether this will ever become a reality will depend partly on the commitment of all social classes, and the presence of a 'touch of madness'. It will also depend on developments in international politics. The rise of the British and French empires was inimical to the RLs but the rise of the EU has had the opposite effect and an emerging international recognition of language as a human right leaves room for hope.

What needs to be aimed for is acceptance of the fact that having a common language, in this case French or English, does not need to mean having only one language. Multilingualism needs to be seen in terms of cultural pluralism rather than in narrowly political terms. This is very much the approach of most RL activists, in both Britain and France (where it is also the policy of DGLFLF). But Britain is far more advanced along this path than France, because of the latter's Jacobin tradition. There are moves, however, even in France, in the direction of more tolerance and awareness of the presence and worth of languages other than the official one.

# Notes

## Introduction

1. This label is given when fewer that 30 per cent of the population are ensuring intergenerational language transmission. See *Language Death* (Crystal 2000) and *Language Shift: Theoretical and Empirical Foundations of Assistance to Threatened Languages* (Fishman 1991), which detail the various stages a language needs to go through to become completely rehabilitated.

## Chapter 1    The Rise of French as an Official National Language

1. The *Helvetii*, threatened by the Confederation of the *Suebi*, attempted to cross the lands of the *Aedui* on the Lower Saône in search of a new home on the Atlantic seaboard. The alarmed *Aedui* then called on Caesar to help repel them, having had a long-standing treaty of friendship with Rome.
2. His own language was probably Franconian, but Romance would have been the language spoken by his soldiers. Hugues Capet was the first king (987–96) to speak Gallo-Romance.
3. There are, however, some Old High German texts which predate 842.
4. This terminology is based on there being two ways of saying 'yes', *oïl* in the north and *oc* in the south. The term was used by Dante at the beginning of the fourteenth century, but it seems to have been used even earlier, to represent a *fait accompli*.
5. Rivarol (1753–1891) was a French writer, and a violent polemicist, who has remained famous mainly for his *Discours sur l'universalité de la langue française* (1784), in which he tried to prove that French was the best language in the world.
6. Although this ordinance is mainly remembered for its historical component, it was meant to regulate registration of gifts, the function of notaries, to provide registration for civil status etc.
7. It was told by the grammarian Ramus in 1572, but there are no traces of it in the official archives of the period (comment from M. Alessio (DGLFLF)).
8. There were rules during the Middle Ages as to what people could wear depending on their social status. Some seem quite comical today, such as the law, but briefly enforced, which stated that all prostitutes were to wear their clothes inside out.
9. The very first was, in fact Palsgrave's *Eclaircissement de la langue française* (1530), but its aim was to contrast French and English.
10. The *département* was the administrative unit set up in 1790 by the revolutionary Assemblée constituante.
11. The exact wording of the report may be found in De Certeau, Julia and Revel (1975: 302). H. Walter (1988) considers, however, these figures to be only approximate since it is not known how the abbé Grégoire reached these

conclusions, nor whether they included women and children. She considers that if in 1790 the population of France was around 25 million, there were no more than 12 persons out of 100 who could speak French properly, and less than one in four could understand it (1988: 101–2). See also R. Wardaugh in *Languages in Competition* (1987: 102).

12. The Girondins acceded to power in 1792 but were blamed for military defeats in 1793, at which point they lost power.

13. Originally the 'Jacobins' were members of a French political club established in Paris. The name derives from the fact that they met in the old monastery of the Jacobins, who were Dominican friars. Their aim was to maintain and propagate the principles of democracy and absolute equality. They stood for a unified, centralised government in a unified, centralised state. The principle of France *une et indivisible* goes back to them.

14. 'Cette entreprise, qui ne fut pleinement exécutée chez aucun peuple, est digne du peuple français, qui centralise toutes les branches de l'organisation sociale et qui doit être jaloux de consacrer au plutôt, dans une République une et indivisible, l'usage unique et invariable de la langue de la liberté' (De Certeau, Julia and Revel 1975: 302).

15. The Convention succeeded the *Assemblée nationale* and governed the country from 1792 to 1795.

16. An administrative unit similar to the English 'parish'.

17. 'Depuis l'ordonnance de Villers-Cotterêts de 1539 – qui dispose que la justice est rendue en français – et la création de l'Académie française en 1635 – qui a donné à notre langue un gardien – la langue française, ciment de l'unité nationale et élément fondamental de notre patrimoine, a fait l'objet de politiques publiques.' Ministère de la culture et de la francophonie, NOR:MCCX9400007L.

18. 'la langue française est pour eux leur premier capital, le signe de leur dignité, le passeur de l'intégration, le diapason d'une culture universelle, le partage d'un patrimoine commun, *une part du rêve française.*' J. Toubon, Minister for Culture and Francophone Affairs, quoted in *Le Monde*, 4 August 1994, p. 16.

19. See 'Le français, "première condition" de la réussite scolaire', by G. Varro in *Education et Société Plurilingues*, no. 8 (June 2000).

20. Loi No. 94–665, 4 August 1994 (JO, 5 August 1994) and Décret No. 95–240 (JO 5 March 1995).

21. '*Les martyrs de l'orthographe.* Tous les enfants qui peinent aujourd'hui pour apprendre l'orthographe du français peuvent maudire le lundi 8 mai 1673, jour funeste où les académiciens ont pris la décision d'adopter une orthographe unique, obligatoire pour eux-mêmes et qu'ils s'efforceraient ensuite de faire accepter par le public. Dans l'angoisse des zéros en dictée, cette orthographe, à la fois abhorrée et vénérée, continue au XXe siècle à avoir ses martyrs et ses adorateurs.'

22. E.g. there was a famous debate which opposed *ouïstes* and *non-ouïstes*, the problem being whether to say *corbeau* or *courbeau*, *forbu* or *fourbu*; in fact the decisions were all taken word by word, no attempt being made to put forward a general rule.

23. This well-known expression – or even battle cry – is difficult to translate. It basically compares the French language to a light lighting up the world.

24. See H. Walter (1988: 116) but J.-M. Eloy informs me that the French orthographic specialist, Nina Catach, maintained that she had never found any trace of such an obligation, which she considered to be apocryphal. See Nina Catach, in *French Today: Language in its Social Context*, ed. C. Sanders (1993: 140).
25. 'Celui qui a besoin de recourir à un autre pour écrire ou même lire une letter, pour faire le calcul de sa dépense ou de son impôt, pour connoître l'étendue de son champ ou le partager, pour savoir ce que la loi lui permet ou lui défend; [. . .] celui-là est nécessairement dans une dépendance individuelle, dans une dépendance qui rend nul ou dangereux pour lui l'exercice des droits du citoyen.'
26. See case 154 / 89 / CEE.
27. 'Si la politique en faveur de la langue française est une constante de l'action gouvernementale, elle n'en doit pas moins faire l'objet d'une aussi constante vigilance, d'une volonté sans faille. Elle doit sans cesse évoluer, se rénover, se moderniser pour garder son efficacité,' in *L'essentiel sur l'emploi de la langue française*, DGLFLF, 2002.
28. This is the article which states that France is one and indivisible.

## Chapter 2   The Rise of English as an Official Language

1. In *The Ecclesiastical History of the English Nation*, which was finished in 731, Bede's aim was to tell how Christianity was brought to Britain but in doing so he also wrote the first history of Britain.
2. The Eisteddfod is the traditional Welsh gathering for the encouragement of the bardic arts of music, poetry and literature.
3. *The Anglo-Saxon Chronicle* is a compilation of texts from different sources which, together, give a year by year account – sometimes brief, sometimes lengthy, and for some years nothing at all. It covers the period going from AD 1 to the eleventh and twelfth century, and differs from most European chronicles in that it was kept in Old English, and not in Latin. It was started under the influence of Alfred the Great.
4. But Crystal warns us not to completely trust labels such as 'Saxons' or 'Angles' since they reflect nowadays different social realities which are essentially territorial and culturally homogeneous, whereas in the days of Bede such labels may have merely 'reflected the orderliness of his [ = Bede's] own mind'. Crystal also points out that Bede did not use such labels consistently, referring to the same people sometimes as *Angli* and sometimes as *Saxons*. He even suggests that *Anglo-Saxon* came to refer to the Saxons in England (Crystal 2004: Chapter 1).
5. A *calque* is the transfer of a neologism based on a dead metatphor (or 'catchresis' such as 'the leg' of the table). An example would be 'sky scraper' and '*gratte-ciel*'.
6. The spelling used is in fact Anglo-Norman, but F. Morgan Nichols, who prepared the 1865 edition of *Britton* states that: 'The language of William the Bastard and his Norman followers may probably have been a provincial dialect, but the French spoken at the court of Edward I did not materially differ from that spoken by St Louis, and the language of *Britton* resembles very

much that of Joinville' (Introduction, pp. xlvi–xlvii in *Britton*, ed F. Morgan Nichols, Oxford: Clarendon Press, 1865).

7. A 'count' was a formal statement of claim, declaring the cause of the action.

8. This was the phonological change which affected the long vowels, transforming them into diphthongs. Only the short ones remained unchanged, as in *cat/pig/box* which are written as they are pronounced. Whereas words containing long vowels such as *mice* or *make* are pronounced quite differently. As Bragg puts it, 'Before the Great Vowel Shift . . ."I name this boat Pete" would have been pronounced "Ee nahm mee bought Peht" ' (2003: 101).

9. These were and still are private schools reserved at first for the aristocracy, then for the moneyed elite.

10. Its editor was James Murray whose ambition was to indicate for every single English word when and how it first appeared, and how it may have changed through time both phonetically and semantically. Quotations taken from all kinds of contexts were to illustrate each phase of each word's development. To do so he obtained the help of 2000 volunteer readers responsible for collecting the quotes. It represented a mammoth task and it constitutes a work of reference still valid today.

11. In France, the prestige accent was the accent of Touraine, the area where so many kings and aristocrats had their châteaux, from the Renaissance on.

## Part II   The Regional Languages Spoken in Metropolitan France

1. I am indebted for useful suggestions and comments for the whole of Part II to Michel Alessio, who is responsible for all the French Regional Languages at the *Délégation générale à la langue française et aux langues de France*, and to Jean-Michel Eloy, Professor of Linguistics (Sociolinguistics and Glottopolitics) at the University of Picardie, in Amiens.

2. Defined in the *OED* as 'rough speech' and as a 'provincial form of language spoken in a restricted area and having no literary status', also 'sub-dialect'.

## Chapter 3   Regional Languages Official Elsewhere

1. The first from 1833 to 1839 and the second from 1872 to 1876.

2. The term 'race' has had different connotations at different times. It was often used in France in the early part of the twentieth century to refer negatively to a group of people (Lyautey, for example, uses the term *cette* race to refer to the French parliamentarians, whom he particularly disliked). The term did not, then, automatically imply notions such as those of colour. Similarly, in Britain it was quite normal to refer to the British 'race'.

3. It is worth remembering that it was not only the Basques who were interested in their origins. Everybody was, and many theories, many of them ludicrous, were put forth. More recently, research has highlighted the Basque special 'blood' factor (the Basques supposedly have the highest concentration of type O and the highest incidence of Rh negative blood). But this is hardly enough to define a 'race'. Research has also been carried out by opponents of Basque nationhood trying to prove that the Basques came from somewhere

else. This is because being 'indigenous' appeared to give them rights. Hence, alongside genuine research born of natural scientific curiosity, research was also carried out with a hidden agenda. According to Kurlansky (2000: 26), from the sixteenth century on, historians receiving government salaries from Madrid wrote histories trying to disprove their being indigenous populations of the region. Yet this is most probably the case since all other theories have been disproved, at least until now.

4. 'Pour la détruire, il faudrait détruire le soleil, la fraîcheur des nuits, la qualité des eaux, l'homme tout entier.'

5. *Pratiques et representations du catalan, Région Languedoc-Roussillon*, Institut Médiapluriel Méditerranée, Montpellier, 1998. Quoted, as are the other figures, in Sibille (2000: 42).

6. Duvoskeldt in J.-M. Eloy (ed.), *Des langues collaterals: Problèmes linguistiques, sociolinguistiques et glottopolitiques de la proximité linguistique*, Vol. 1, pp. 161–70.

7. JO, 09/06/1983, p. 5254.

8. See INSEE, Chiffres pour l'Alsace: Revue numéro 12, December 2002.

9. The following results were summarised in a paper given at the annual Association for French Language Studies Conference in Quebec in 2000.

10. JO, 25/09/1991, p. 12498.

11. JO, 11/06/2003, p. 9818.

# Chapter 4   Regional Languages Not Official Elsewhere

1. It is estimated that some 70 originally Gaulish words remain in French. Survivors include words common in agriculture such as *boue* (mud), *chemin* (lane), *mouton* (sheep), and an alternative to the Roman *mille* (= 1485 metres), *la lieue* ( = 2222 metres), which survived as a unit of measurement until the arrival of the *kilomètre* in 1795 (the term is still used in expressions such as *à vingt lieues à la ronde* – 'for miles around', *être à cent lieues de penser que* – 'to be far from imagining that'). Another interesting survivor is *bouge* meaning a leather bag, which became *bougette*, a small leather bag, which gave us the English word 'budget' (Walter 1994: 232–4). Gaulish words also survive in place-names; it is noticeable that these are few in Provence, largely because it was the first area to be Romanised and also because the Gauls expanded into the area only at a late date and in smaller numbers. They are also less frequent in Aquitaine.

2. In Auzanneau (ed.), *Plurilinguismes, Situations régionales françaises et frontalières*.

3. Corsica also came under British rule between 1794 and 1798 before going back to being French – the period having been short and Paoli having taken refuge at one point in London, the attitude towards Britain is still quite positive among the islanders.

4. The presence of 20 000 repatriates was a source of bitterness for the locals who felt the newcomers were being offered unfair advantages, while they remained in a miserable state.

5. Diglossic is used here to refer to a High and Low use of two different languages, and not just two varieties of the same language.

6. In the *Giorgi vs Masaspino* case mentioned in Chapter 1.

7. The Italians landed in Corsica in 1942 which led to the setting up of particularly strong resistance movements, loyal to France. Corsica was the first *département* to be liberated in 1943.

8. There are numerous historical reasons for this. One goes back to the kind of organisation put in place by the Genoese who gave considerable powers to a certain number of Corsican families, who then became very powerful.

9. For further details on terminological problems in naming Occitan, see relevant chapters in Boyer and Gardy (2001), Hammel (1996) and Clairis et al. (1999).

10. The *De Vulgari eloquentia* classified languages according to their way of saying yes – *oïl*, *oc* and *si*, from the Latin *hoc* in the south and *hoc ille* in the north).

11. The present author who lived in the area in the 1950s remembers that parents tended to speak to their children in French, even if it was their second language, to give them a better chance in life (*pour qu'ils puissent monter à Paris*, i.e. so that they could leave their underprivileged area and find jobs elsewhere, mainly in Paris). But *patois* was still used by adult speakers amongst themselves, with solidarity and shared identity overtones, and when addressing social inferiors such as labourers, or cows and other animals.

12. This orthography, often termed *Mistralien*, was in fact the system developed by J. Roumanille (1818–91). It is the result of a compromise between French spelling, the traditional etymological and grammatical spelling of the Marseilles poets, and local pronunciation.

13. *Circulaire du recteur le 1er avril 1977, jugement sur le recours introduit par 'Défense et promotion des langues de France'*, 27 September 1979.

14. As they were after 1789 in Occitan and Breton-speaking areas, for example, in order to stifle them.

15. *Francien* is the name given in recent times to the dialect which emerged from the Ile-de-France.

16. It has been suggested that the distinction between *oc* and *oïl* languages may have started with the Merovingians and completed under the Carolingians (751–987). Varieties then appeared within these two groups, but without affecting their underlying unity. It is only later that fault lines became deeper and led to the 'dialects' which characterised these languages during the later period.

17. JO, 09/06/1983, p. 5254.

18. See the Killilea Report to the European Parliament, 1994, A3 – 0042/94.

19. JO, 17/09/1993, p. 12996.

20. Sibille (2000: 42) calls it the *zone francique*, a term used by Pierre Bec in his *Manuel de philology romane*. But he states himself that this term is ambiguous since it also refers to the Germanic form of speech spoken in the Moselle–Rhine–Luxemburg areas. Hence no label has been given here.

21. Poitevin-Saintongeais is an exception among the *langues d'oïl* since it started off belonging to the Occitan group before coming under *oïl* influence. Hence its present *oïl* structure combined with *oc* traits.

# Chapter 5   Revitalising the Regional Languages of France

1. JO, 09/06/1983, p. 5254.

2. Guadeloupe, Martinique, Guyane, Réunion, St Pierre et Miquelon.

3. Loi no. 2005–380 published in the JO on 24 April 2005.
4. Published in the JO of 14 May 2005 and in the *Bulletin officiel de l'Education nationale*, no. 21, on 26 May 2005.
5. The *collège* corresponds to the first four years of secondary school and the *lycée* corresponds to the last three.
6. ABCM stands for Association pour le bilinguisme en classe dès la maternelle.
7. See the *Circulaire* 83–547.
8. The *Bressola* thought of making such a request in 1999, but this came to nothing at the time because the main teaching unions objected to their acquiring a public status.
9. Loi no. 2000–719 of 1 August 2000, published in the JO on 2 August 2000.
10. Loi no. 2004–669 of 9 July 2004, published in the JO on 10 July 2004.
11. Decree no. 2004–1312 26 November 2004, published in the JO on 30 November 2004.
12. Figures derived from the *Rapport du Parlement sur l'emploi de la langue française*, 2005.
13. The DRACs come under the Ministry of Culture and Communication, for all other cultural matters.
14. These terms are sometimes updated in the press, 'Jacobin' becoming *souverainiste*, i.e. those who put the unity of the nation above all else. But according to regionalists, it is possible for a state to allow the regions their own identity in terms of institutions and culture without endangering overall cohesion. For example, Daniel Cohn-Bendit advocates the application of the principle of subsidiarity to the relationship between the state and its regions. The 'communautarians', on the other hand, want a Europe of regions that ignores the concept of nation-state. Despite the Jacobins sometimes waving the fear of communautarianism in order to cause fright, the concept has no real following in France.
15. The *départements d'outre mer* and the *territoires d'outre mer*.
16. CE 15/04/1996, no. 165114.
17. CE 10/07/1996, no. 171104.
18. CE, 24/06/2002, nos. 01NC00524 and 01NC00525.

# Part III   The Regional Languages of Britain

1. The second half of the twentieth century has been marked, in particular, by a profusion of excellent studies on the subject, some of which, such as Trudgill's, have introduced new aims and methodologies, and a shift of interest from dialectology to sociolinguistics, which have had worldwide implications.
2. Reported in *The Guardian*, 8/2/06.
3. The UK government did, however, sign the European Charter for Regional or Minority Languages on behalf of the Isle of Man in relation to Manx. The language was signed up for Part II protection although Part III is being considered since Manx already fulfils some of the Part III requirement. Manx is a language which has come back from the dead, since the last native speaker is said to have died in 1974, but there are, according to the last census, 1689 people who can speak, read or write it out of a population of 76 315. This is mainly because it was introduced into the school system in 1992, and there is also

one Manx Medium School in existence. This spectacular recovery has made it a particular model for Cornish, which has been trying to do the same.

4. This was because the Celtic Druids, although they knew about writing, were unwilling to give up their greatly respected oral tradition.
5. Another area of conjecture is whether these two branches came into existence before the Celts arrived in the British Isles, or happened later.
6. The Isle of Man probably started off by being Brythonic speaking but ended up being Goidelic (or 'Gaelic') because of population migration from Ireland.
7. There are also figures for the earlier periods which may be deduced from comments made by the ministers of individual parishes in their returns for the various *Statistical Accounts* needed for the Church to be able to assess their flocks' needs, including their linguistic needs. These will not be considered here since the focus of this book is towards present-day problems.
8. Such as writing but not reading, for example.

## Chapter 6   The Regional Languages of England and Wales

1. I am indebted to Ian Jones of CAMOC's international committee on museums of cities, for his comments on Welsh, and Jenefer Lowe, Cornish Language Development Manager, for her help with Cornish.
2. See the complaints made at the time of the 'Welsh Tickbox Census Campaign'.
3. Spelt either 'Mann' when used on its own or 'Man' in 'the Isle of Man'.
4. Cumbric collapsed in about the eleventh century, because of competition from both English and the Goidelic speakers who had migrated from Ireland to Argyll.
5. Janet Davies, in *The Welsh Language* (1999), points out that versions of the word, with this second meaning, survive in the marchlands of the Empire, hence the Walloons of Belgium, the Welsch of the Italian Tyrol and the Vlachs of Romania (see p. 7).
6. Although this may have been wrongly attributed to him, see Price (1984: 95).
7. It could be claimed that they composed their works in Cumbric, rather than Welsh, except that it is reckoned there was no great difference between the two at the time.
8. Not only for religious reasons, but also for political reasons, i.e. the Protestantism of Wales would counterbalance the Catholicism of Ireland, among others.
9. Huw Edwards in the excellent BBC 4 programme 'The Story of Welsh', 2003.
10. This is not true, of course, for Occitan which had a standardised literary form which was used all through the medieval period.
11. Some claimed that Welsh was a sister language of Hebrew and predated the Tower of Babel, others that the Welsh were descendants of the Trojans (J. Davies 1999: 29–30).
12. Edward Williams ('Iolo Morganwg') did not hesitate to fabricate literature to further his aims, one of which was to establish that the Welsh bardic order descended from the Druids. Forgeries of this nature were quite common in the eighteenth century, in the context of revivalist movements.

13. These educational reports were always published bound with blue covers, hence this particular one being referred to as the Blue Books.
14. This fundamental divergence of views as to the desirability of saving Welsh, or, on the contrary, its pointlessness, is not specific to Welsh. It continues, both in Britain and France, to bedevil efforts to save the various RLs from extinction.
15. Much has been written about teachers imposing *le signe* in Wales as in France, i.e. usually making a pupil caught speaking a RL wear an ignominious sign to this effect. In Wales it was a tablet on which there was a W and an N, standing for 'Welsh Not'. But some think that this was not practised as often as present mythology would have it.
16. Hence the nationalist motto *Cofio Trewerin*, i.e. Remember Trewerin.
17. Welsh in Schools, SDB 3/2000 and SB 16/2004, The National Assembly for Wales Statistical Directorate.
18. Government statistics quoted by Dunbar (2003a).
19. Both quotes are from news.bbc.co.uk/1/hi/wales/2758291.stm and are dated 13/2/2003.
20. To the extent that during the referendum on the Assembly, Anglesey was too close to call. This would have been unthinkable in the 1960s, as may be seen from the maps in Aitchison and Carter (1994).
21. Quoted in *The Economy Takes Centre Stage: Monitoring the National Assembly, December 2000 to August 2001.*
22. It is said that when the Welsh actor, Richard Burton, met Anthony Hopkins, he asked him if he spoke Welsh. Hopkins said no, and Burton said: 'Then you are not a Welshman.'
23. A submission by the Cornwall County Council to the Local Government Commission, in 1994, reads as follows: 'Cornwall's "independence" was recognised in later medieval times by the twin consitutional accommodations of the Duchy of Cornwall and the Stannaries.' See www.cornish. heritage.care4free.net/page23.htm.
24. The most famous were: the *Ordinalia*, a cycle of mystery plays written between 1350 and 1450; the *Pascon agan Arluth* (The Passion of our Lord), a religious poem, also in Middle Cornish; *Beunans Merisasek* (the Life of St Meriadoc) which dates probably from around 1504; and *Gwereans an Bys* (The Creation of the World), dated 1611. Bishop Bonner's *Homilies* were translated into Cornish c. 1556–8.
25. Old Cornish corresponds to the period stretching from the ninth to the thirteenth centuries, Middle Cornish to that of the thirteenth to sixteenth centuries, and Late Cornish corresponds to the period of the seventeenth and eighteenth centuries.
26. *Strategy for the Cornish Language*, County Hall, Truro, 2004.
27. The report may be found on www.gosw.gov.uk/gosw/publications/ Cornish.htm.
28. Available from Cornwall County Council, www.cornwall.gov.uk.
29. Campaigning for Cornish names has gone on for quite a time. There was, in particular, a campaign run by militants to deface English Heritage signs in Cornwall, particularly at the site of Tintagel. Seeing the latter named 'English' seemed so insulting that it led to actions which in turn led to prison sentences. English Heritage has now adopted the form 'English Heritage in

Cornwall', which could seem worse, but it has also put up some signs in Cornish to diffuse the situation.

## Chapter 7   The Regional Languages of Scotland

1. I owe much in terms of information to Peadar Morgan, Language Planning Manager for the *Bòrd na Gàidhlig* who was kind enough to read this chapter and make numerous suggestions and corrections, this being an area where change is the order of the day. Any errors which remain are, of course, the author's responsibility.
2. It is assumed that the original inhabitants spoke a form of Brythonic, and possibly an unknown Pictish language, and maybe other indigenous languages.
3. The 2001 census distinguished four categories of linguistic proficiency, but the report gave seven permutations of these categories: (i) Speak, read and write Gaelic, (ii) Speak but neither read nor write Gaelic, (iii) Speak and read but cannot write Gaelic, (iv) Read but neither speak nor write Gaelic, (v) Write but neither speak nor read Gaelic, (vi) Read and write but do not speak Gaelic, (vii) Other combinations of skills.
4. All figures for 2005–6 are compiled by the Gaelic Department, University of Strathclyde, Jordanhill Campus, January 2006.
5. J. J. Smith's terminology (2000: 167). 'Bottom-up' refers to changes coming from the lower social classes, i.e. the least educated, whereas 'top-down' refers to changes coming from the most educated sector of the population.
6. The first recorded example of the use of *Scottis* with today's meaning of *Scots* dates from 1494. Previously the term referred to Gaelic (Price 1984: 187).
7. 'Gif ze, throw curiositie of nouationis, hes forzet our auld plane Scottis quhilk zour mother lerit zou [,] in tymes coming, I sall wryte to zou my mynd in Latin, for I am nocht acquyntit with zour Southeron.' Quoted by J. J. Smith (2000: 165).
8. Its promoter too used the term 'synthetic', but with a positive sense, since it represented an effort to achieve a supra-dialectal language.
9. The same applies to Geordie, and no doubt other markedly different dialects of English.
10. Corbett criticises this approach for not including either the chronological or the urban–rural dimensions, but accepts that it is a useful initial form of classification (Corbett 1997: 18). But McClure (1995) recognises this dimension, without integrating it into his model.
11. It would appear that a Head of Radio Scotland is/was, herself, a native Gaelic speaker and radio broadcaster, which illustrates the ambiguities and complexity of the linguistic situation in Scotland.
12. Which is not totally encouraging for Scots, since Joual has been abandoned as the national language of Quebec in favour of standard French.

## Chapter 8   The Regional Languages of Northern Ireland

1. I am indebted for much useful information and many apposite comments to John Salters, who was Director of the Centre for Modern Language Teaching (Post-Graduate Education), Queen's University Belfast. Any errors are mine.

2. The reason Unionists are at present (in 2006) reluctant to share power with Nationalists in the governance of Northern Ireland is that Unionists wish to see Northern Ireland remain part of the UK, whereas the Nationalists (in general) want a united Ireland. Unionists do not relish the idea that part of the Northern Ireland devolved government wants to abolish that government and become part of the Republic of Ireland. Nationalists within the devolved government in Stormont, where power was shared until its collapse, are therefore seen as the enemy within, a kind of Trojan horse.

3. The battle of Kinsale in 1603 marked the downfall of the last Gaelic lordships and the end of the old Irish world. Although pardoned by James I, most of the leaders, who were also the landowners, fled, leaving their people defenceless. This is generally known as the 'Flight of the Earls'.

4. A *Gaeltacht* is an area which includes a majority of Irish speakers.

5. Douglas Hyde became President of the Irish Republic between 1938 and 1945. He was also the first Professor of Irish at the newly created National University of Ireland, founded, along with Queen's Univesity Belfast, in 1908.

6. Others include J. Synge, S. O'Casey, S. Beckett and S. Heaney, without this list being in any way exhaustive. Some of their work provoked such an uproar in Ireland that some of these writers moved permanently to England or Paris.

7. The Pale included Louth, Meath, Dublin and Kildare. This area was separated from the rest of the country by a double ditch six feet high to repel Gaelic Irish invaders. See Moody and Martin (1994: 169).

8. No more attempts were made after 1366 to check the use of Irish, but a law was passed in 1537 relating to hairstyle and dress, which forbade Gaelic usages in this matter.

9. Cromwell landed a puritan army at Dublin in 1649. The settlement which followed included dividing the Catholic landowners into two groups, those guilty of involvement and those not. The first lost all their estates, while the second retained a proportion of the land they had held but not the same land.

10. There was of course a great deal of material in manuscript form. The earliest texts date from the twelfth century, but much of the material they contain was copied from writings that were centuries older.

11. The Hennessys of Cognac are a good example of a family having donated to the Irish colleges but who settled in France permanently (see T. Ó hIfearnáin 1992: 39).

12. Which is not totally reliable because of being in a footnote, and being self-evaluative. It is, however, useful as an indication of the situation.

13. Neville quotes an informant recounting how a 'tally stick' was given to children to take home, and each time the parents heard the child mutter a word of Irish, they would make a notch in the stick, which would be handed back to the teacher the next day. Punishment would ensue, depending on the number of notches. Neville uses this example to encapsulate the collusion between parents and teachers in this matter (1992: 26–7).

14. For interesting proposals for a more flexible approach to the standard based on current usage in the *Gaeltacht* and a simplified grammar of the language to be taught in schools, see Nicholas Williams (2002), *Caighdeán Nua don*

*Ghaeilge (A New Standard for Irish)*, Aimsir Óg (publishers), *Páipéar Ócáideach 1 (Occasional Paper 1)*.

15. Some sociologists have expressed scepticism as to the efficacy of education in social reconstruction, particularly in Northern Ireland, in the context of the 'integrated schools'. Some people feel this same scepticism may apply to education in the RLs.

16. This was because Protestant England wanted to be safe from attacks from Catholic Europe, which could have come via Catholic Ireland.

17. It is important, when assessing all such figures, to take into account that they will undoubtedly also include persons who may have put themselves down as knowing Irish, either because of an optimistic assessment of their own capabilities, or to make a political point.

18. Figures drawn from the *Comhaile na Gaelscolaíochta* Annual Report, the latter being the representative organisation for Irish-medium education in Northern Ireland (labelled 'north of Ireland' in the report).

19. Northern Ireland differs from Scotland and the rest of the United Kingdom in that education is not the sole responsibility of the local authorities, but of the Department of Education. It is administered through Education and Library Boards.

20. See maps reproduced in McCrum et al. (1986: 154) and in Gilbert (2003). The areas concerned are centred essentially around St Johnson, Dundonald, and the Bushmills and Ballymena areas.

21. The fact that Ulster Scots tends to be turned into ridicule by Nationalists, some non-sectarian Protestants and even some Unionists, is illustrated by a story which circulated a couple of years ago according to which, when street-names in a Loyalist area were replaced by names in Ulster Scots, they were supposedly pulled down by the locals who thought they were in Irish. This story may be apocryphal, but the point it is trying to make is obvious: for some people Ulster Scots does not exist as such.

22. *Forás* means growth, development, progress.

23. Bairbre de Brún (Sinn Féin), when she was Minister for Health in the Stormont Executive, ordered that all advertisements for appointments, contracts etc. in the field of health and medicine should be in Irish as well as in English, but this order was not extended to Ulster Scots.

## Concluding Comments

1. See Norman Davies in *The Isles: a History* (2000). He points out that a study of the demographic change in the UK in terms of percentage of each nation shows that whereas in 1801 the English represented 58.1 per cent of the total population, this figure had reached 78.8 per cent in 1999–2000. During this period only Wales saw its population increase slightly (from 4.1 per cent to 4.6 per cent), whereas Scotland's went from 11.2 per cent to only 8.1 per cent.

2. But William Lamb, working on building up a corpus of spontaneous Gaelic, has suggested: 'there is the ... intriguing possibility that advances in computer technology – specifically automatic machine translation – will make it possible to be a minority language monoglot, but still be able to spontaneously communicate with nearly every other human being on the planet' (2005: 135).

# Bibliography

Adamson, I. (2005) 'The Ullans Academy', in J. M. Kirk and D. Ó Baoill (eds), *Legislation, Literature and Sociolinguistics: Northern Ireland, the Republic of Ireland and Scotland*, Belfast Studies in Language, Culture and Politics, Vol. 13, Belfast: Queen's University.

Aitchison, J. and Carter, H. (1994) *A Geography of the Welsh Language 1961–1991*, Cardiff: University of Wales Press.

Andreani, J.-L. and Ajchenbaum, Y.-M. (eds) (2005) *La Corse, histoire d'une insularité*, Paris: Le Monde/Librio.

Angarrack, J. (1999) *Breaking the Chains: Propaganda, Censorship, Deception and the Manipulation of Public Opinion in Cornwall*, Camborne: Stannary Publications.

Auzanneau, M. (1995) 'Français, patois et mélange . . . ou variétés de discours en Poitou?', *Langage et société*, No. 71, Revue trimestrielle publiée à la Maison des Sciences de l'Homme, Paris.

Avery, H. (2003) 'Ulster Scots in Education in Northern Ireland', in D. Ó Riagáin (ed.), *Language and Law in Northern Ireland*, Belfast Studies in Language, Culture and Politics, Vol. 9, Belfast: Queen's University.

Awbery, G. (1998) 'Welsh', in A. Ó Corráin and S. Mac Mathúna (eds), *Minority Languages in Scandinavia, Britain and Ireland*, Uppsala: Uppsala University.

Balibar, R. (1993) *Histoire de la littérature française*, Paris: Presses Universitaires de France.

Barbour, S. and Carmichael, C. (eds) (2000) *Language and Nationalism in Europe*, Oxford: Oxford University Press.

Bécat, J. and Sibille, J. (2003) 'Le Catalan', in B. Cerquiglini (ed.), *Les langues de France*, Paris: Presses Universitaires de France.

Blain, N. and Gifford, A. (2003) 'Scottish Political Identity Construction in the Media: Learning and Teaching Questions Around the Theme of Inclusiveness', in J. M. Kirk and D. Ó Baoill (eds), *Towards our Goals in Broadcasting, the Press, the Performing Arts and the Economy: Minority Languages in Northern Ireland, the Republic of Ireland and Scotland*, Belfast Studies in Language, Culture and Politics, Vol. 10, Belfast: Queen's University.

Blanchet, P. (1996) 'Problématique de la situation ethnolinguistique du Pays de Retz (L.- Atlantique): pratique et identité en zone de marche', in F. Manzano (ed.), *Langues et Parlers de l'Ouest*, Cahiers de Sociolinguistique no. 1, Rennes: Presses Universitaires de Rennes.

Bothorel-Witz, A. and Huck, D. (2003) 'Alsace et Moselle', (Alsace) in B. Cerquiglini (ed.), *Les langues de france*, Paris: Presses Universitaires de France.

Boyer, H. and Gardy, P. (2001) *Dix siècles d'usage et d'images de l'Occitan: Des Troubadours à l'Internet*, Paris: L'Harmattan.

Bragg, M. (2003) *The Adventure of English: the Biography of a Language*, London: Hodder & Stoughton.

Broadbridge, J. (1998) 'Attitude to Alsatian as an Expression of Alsatianness', in D. Marley, M.-A. Hintze and G. Parker (eds), *Linguistic Identities and Policies in France and the French-speaking World*, London: CILT.

Broudig, F. (2003) 'Le breton', in B. Cerquiglini (ed.), *Les langues de France*, Paris: Presses Universitaires de France.

Carrington, D. (1971) *The Granite Island: a Portrait of Corsica*, London: Longman.

Carton, F. (1981) 'Les parlers ruraux de la region Nord-Picardie: situation sociolinguistique', in A. Tabouret-Keller (ed.), *International Journal of the Sociology of Language*, 29, The Hague and Paris: Mouton.

Carton, F. (2004) 'Orthographier le picard: aperçu historique du débat entre "phonétistes" et partisans de graphies "françaises" ', in J.-M. Eloy (ed.), *Des langues collatérales: Problèmes linguistiques, sociolinguistiques et glottopolitiques de la proximité linguistique*, Paris: L'Harmattan.

Catach, N. (1993) 'The Reform of the Writing System', in C. Sanders (ed.) *French Today: Language in its Social Context*, Cambridge: Cambridge University Press.

Caubet, D., Chaker, S. and Sibille, J. (eds) (2002) *Codification des langues de France*, Paris: L'Harmattan.

Cerquiglini, B. (1999) *Les langues de la France. Rapport au Ministre de l'Education nationale, de la Recherche et de la Technologies, et à la Ministre de la Culture et de la Communication*, Paris: Délégation générale à la langue française et aux langues de France.

Cerquiglini, B. (ed.) (2003) *Les langues de France*, Paris: Presses Universitaires de France.

Chiorboli, J. (2002) 'La codification des langues polynomiques: L'orthographe du corse', in D. Caubet, S. Chaker and J. Sibille (eds), *Codification des langues de France*, Paris: L'Harmattan.

Clairis, C., Costaouec, D. and Coyos, J.-B. (eds) (1999) *Langues et cultures régionales de France: Etat des lieux, enseignement, politiques*, Paris: L'Harmattan.

Clanché, F. (2002) *Langues régionales, langues étrangères: de l'héritage à la pratique*, No. 830, Paris: INSEE.

Colley, L. (1996) *Britons: Forging the Nation 1707–1837*, London: Vintage.

Corbett, J. (1997) *Language and Scottish Literature*, Edinburgh: Edinburgh University Press.

Corbett, J. and Douglas, F. (2003) 'Scots in the Public Sphere', in J. M Kirk and D. Ó Baoill (eds) *Towards our Goals in Broadcasting, the Press, the Performing Arts and the Economy: Minority Languages in Northern Ireland, the Republic of Ireland and Scotland*, Belfast Studies in Language, Culture and Politics, Vol. 10, Belfast: Queen's University.

Cormack, M. (2003) 'Programming for Gaelic Digital Television: Problems and Possibilities', in J. M. Kirk and D. Ó Baoill (eds), *Towards our Goals in Broadcasting, the Press, the Performing Arts and the Economy: Minority Languages in Northern Ireland, the Republic of Ireland and Scotland*, Belfast Studies in Language, Culture and Politics, Vol. 10, Belfast: Queen's University.

Coyos, J.-B. (2004) *Politique linguistique: Langue basque et langue occitane du Béarn et de Gascogne*, Bayonne: Elkar.

Crystal, D. (1995) *The Cambridge Encyclopedia of the English Language*, Cambridge: Cambridge University Press.

Crystal, D. (2000) *Language Death*, Cambridge: Cambridge University Press.

Crystal, D. (2004) *The Stories of English*, London: Penguin.

Cunningham M. (2003) 'BBC Radio Scotland and Scots', in J. M. Kirk and D. Ó Baoill (eds), *Towards our Goals in Broadcasting, the Press, the Performing Arts and the Economy: Minority Languages in Northern Ireland, the Republic of Ireland and Scotland*, Belfast Studies in Language, Culture and Politics, Vol. 10, Belfast: Queen's University.

Davies, J. (1999) *The Welsh Language*, Cardiff: University of Wales Press & Western Mail.

Davies, N. (2000) *The Isles: a History*, London: Macmillan.

Dawson, A. (2002) 'Le picard: langue polynomique, langue polygraphique?' in D. Caubet, S. Chaker and J. Sibille (eds), *Codification des langues de France*, Paris: L'Harmattan.

Dawson, A. (2004) 'Théorie des correspondances dialectales et autonomie phonologique du picard', in J.-M. Eloy (ed.), *Des langues collatérales: Problèmes linguistiques, sociolinguistiques et glottopolitiques de la proximité linguistique*, Paris: L'Harmattan.

De Certeau, M., Julia, D. and Revel, J. (1975) *Une politique de la langue: La Révolution française et les patois*, Paris: Gallimard.

*Des Langues plein les poches: Les Langues de France* (2005), Coll. du Moutard de Poche, no. 25, Lyons: Editions du Moutard.

Devine, T. M. (2000) *The Scottish Nation 1700–2000*, London: Penguin.

DGLFLF (Délégation générale à la langue française et aux langues de France) (2005) *Rapport au Parlement sur l'emploi de la langue française*, Paris: Ministère de la Culture et de la Communication.

Dunbar, R. (2003a) 'Legislating for Language: Facing the Challenges in Scotland and Wales', in D. Ó Riagáin (ed.), *Language and Law in Northern Ireland*, Belfast Studies in Language, Culture and Politics, Vol. 9, Belfast: Queen's University.

Dunbar, R. (2003b) 'Gaelic-medium Broadcasting: Reflections on the Legal Framework from a Sociolinguistic Perspective', in J. M. Kirk and D. Ó Baoill (eds), *Towards our Goals in Broadcasting, the Press, the Performing Arts and the Economy: Minority Languages in Northern Ireland, the Republic of Ireland and Scotland*, Belfast Studies in Language, Culture and Politics, Vol. 10, Belfast: Queen's University.

Duneton, C. (1973) *Parler Croquant*, Paris: Stock.

Duvoskeldt, E. (2004) 'Néerlandais standard ou West-Vlaamsch dialectal en Flandre française: étude diachronique des représentations', in J.-M. Eloy (ed.), *Des langues collatérales: Problèmes linguistiques, sociolinguistiques et glottopolitiques de la proximité linguistique*, Paris: L'Harmattan.

EBLUL (1993) *Mini-guide to the Lesser-used Languages of the EC*, Brussels: EBLUL.

Eirug, A. (2003) 'Towards the BBC's Minority Language Policy', in J. M. Kirk and D. Ó Baoill (eds), *Towards our Goals in Broadcasting, the Press, the Performing Arts and the Economy: Minority Languages in Northern Ireland, the Republic of Ireland and Scotland*, Belfast Studies in Language, Culture and Politics, Vol. 10, Belfast: Queen's University.

Elcock, W. D. (1960) *The Romance Languages*, London: Faber & Faber.

Eloy, J.-M. (ed.) (1998) *Evaluer la vitalité: Variétés d'oïl et autres langues*, Amiens: Université de Picardie-Jules Verne.

Eloy, J.-M. (2004) 'Des langues collatérales: problèmes et propositions', in J.-M. Eloy (ed.), *Des langues collatérales: Problèmes linguistiques, sociolinguistiques et glottopolitiques de la proximité linguistique*, Paris: L'Harmattan.

Etiemble, R. (1964) *Parlez-vous franglais?* Paris: Gallimard.

EUROLANG bulletins.

Euromosaïc Report, *The Production and Reproduction of the Minority Languages in the European Union* (1996), European Commission, Luxembourg: Official Publications of the European Communities.

Eysseric, V. (2005) *Le corpus juridique des langues de France*, Paris: Délégation générale à la langue française et aux langues de France.

Falconer, G. (2005) 'Breaking Nature's Social Union: the Autonomy of Scots in Ulster', in J. M. Kirk and D. P. Ó Baoill (eds), *Legislation, Literature and Sociolinguistics: Northern Ireland, the Republic of Ireland and Scotland*, Belfast Studies in Language, Culture and Politics, Vol. 13, Belfast: Queen's University.

Favereau, F. (1996) 'Poullaouen revisité: 1984–1994, impressions d'enquête de terrain sur la pratique du Breton dans le Poher', in F. Manzano (ed.), *Langues et Parlers de l'Ouest*, Cahiers de Sociolinguistique no.1, Rennes: Presses Universitaires de Rennes.

Favereau, F. (2002) 'Les orthographes du Breton', in D. Caubet, S. Chaker and J. Sibille (eds), *Codification des langues de France*, Paris: L'Harmattan.

Fishman, J. (1991) *Reversing Language Shift*, Clevedon: Multilingual.

Fowler, H. W. (1996) *Modern English Usage*, Oxford: Oxford University Press, 3rd edn.

Fusina, J. (1999) *Parlons Corse*, Paris: L'Harmattan.

Fusina, J. (2003) 'Le corse', in B. Cerquiglini (ed.), *Les langues de France*, Paris: Presses Universitaires de France.

Gauthier, M. (1995) 'Le Sud des Etats-Unis dans les relations de voyage britanniques (1783–1837)', unpublished PhD, Bordeaux.

Gilbert, A. (2003) 'Ulster-Scots Education in Northern Ireland: the History of the Language', in D. Ó Riagáin (ed.), *Language and Law in Northern Ireland*, Belfast Studies in Language, Culture and Politics, Vol. 9, Belfast: Queen's University.

Grossman, R. (1999) *Main basse sur ma langue*, Strasbourg: La Nuée Bleue.

Guiraud, P. (1978) *Patois et dialectes français*, Paris: Presses Universitaires de France.

Hammel, E. (1996) *Aide-mémoire, Langues et cultures régionales et région Languedoc-Roussillon 1985–1996*, Perpignan: Libres del Trabucaire.

Hammel, E. and Gardy, P. (1994) *L'occitan en Languedoc-Roussillon 1991*, Perpignan: Libres del Trabucaire.

Hance, M. (2005) 'The Development of Scots Language Policy in Scotland since Devolution', in J. M. Kirk and D. P. Ó Baoill (eds), *Legislation, Literature and Sociolinguistics: Northern Ireland, the Republic of Ireland, and Scotland*, Belfast Studies in Language, Culture and Politics, Vol. 13, Belfast: Queen's University.

Harrison, A. (1992) 'Introduction', in J. Brihault (ed.), *L'Irlande et ses langues: Colloque de Rennes 1992*, Rennes: Presses Universitaires de Rennes.

Hegarty, K. (2003) 'BBC Northern Ireland and Irish', in J. M. Kirk and D. Ó Baoill (eds), *Towards our Goals in Broadcasting, the Press, the Performing Arts and the Economy: Minority Languages in Northern Ireland, the Republic of Ireland and Scotland*, Belfast Studies in Language, Culture and Politics, Vol. 10, Belfast: Queen's University.

Héran, F., Filhon, A. and Deprez, C. (2002) 'La dynamique des langues en France au fil du XXe siècle', in *Population et Sociétés*, Bulletin mensuel d'information de l'Institut National d'Etudes Démographies, No. 376.

Herbison, I. (2005) 'The Revival of Scots in Ulster: Why Literary History Matters', in J. M. Kirk and D. Ó Baoill (eds), *Legislation, Literature and Sociolinguistics: Northern Ireland, the Republic of Ireland, and Scotland*, Belfast Studies in Language, Culture and Politics, Vol. 13, Belfast: Queen's University.

Huck, D. (2002) 'Les dialectes en Alsace: fonctions et statut de l'écrit dialectal et normes graphiques. Etat d'un non-débat', in D. Caubet, S. Chaker and J. Sibille (eds), *Codification des langues de France*, Paris: L'Harmattan.

INSEE (Institut National de la Statistique et des Etudes Economiques) 'Langues régionales, langues étrangères: de l'héritage à la pratique', No. 830, February 2002, Alsacien, revue numéro 12, December 2002, Breton, No. 92, January 2003, Aquitaine, No. 110, September 2002, Picardie, No. 125, February 2004.

Jones, G. (1977) 'Being and Belonging', BBC Wales Annual lecture, 14 November, Cardiff: Qualitex Printing Ltd.

Jones, M. (1999) 'Sociolinguistic Perspectives on Modern Breton', in M. Auzanneau (ed.), *Plurilinguismes: Situations régionales françaises et frontalières*, June 1999, No. 17, Paris V.

Judge, A. (1993a) 'French: a Planned Language?' in C. Sanders (ed.), *French Today: Language in its Social Context*, Cambridge: Cambridge University Press.

Judge, A. (1993b) 'Linguistic Legislation and Practice', in R. Sampson (ed.), *Authority and the French Language*, Münster: Nodus Publikationen.

Judge, A. (1994) 'La planification linguistique française: traditions et impact de la communauté européenne', in J. Rousseau (ed.), *Dossier le langues régionales*, Revue internationale d'éducation, No. 3, September, Paris: CIEP.

Judge, A. (2000) 'France: "One State, One Nation, One Language?" ' in S. Barbour and C. Carmichael (eds), *Language and Nationalism in Europe*, Oxford: Oxford University Press.

Judge, A., (2002) 'Contemporary Issues in French Linguistic Policies', in K. Salhi (ed.), *French In and Out of France: Language Policies, Intercultural Antagonisms and Dialogue*, Bern: Peter Lang

Judge, A. (2003) 'Les langues minoritaires, la Charte et le facteur corse', in M. Landick (ed.), *La langue française face aux institutions*, Paris: L'Harmattan.

Judge, A. (2004) 'Linguistiques politiques, langues collatérales et langues différenciées dans le cadre du Royaume-Uni', in J.-M. Eloy (ed.), *Des langues collatérales: Problèmes linguistiques, sociolinguistiques et glottopolitiques de la proximité linguistique*, Paris: L'Harmattan.

Judge A. and Lamothe, S. (1995) *Stylistic Development in Literary and Non-Literary French Prose*, Studies in French Literature, Vol. 19, Lewiston/Queenston/ Lampeter: Edwin Meller Press.

Judge, S. (2002) 'Language as a Human Right: a Legal Problem for France', in K. Salhi (ed.), *French In and Out of France: Language Policies, Intercultural Antagonisms and Dialogue*, Bern: Peter Lang.

Kurlansky, M. (2000) *The Basque History of the World*, London: Vintage.

Lamb, W. (2005) 'The Sociolinguistics of Contemporary Scottish Gaelic', in J. M. Kirk and D. Ó Baoill (eds), *Legislation, Literature and Sociolinguistics: Northern Ireland, the Republic of Ireland, and Scotland*, Belfast Studies in Language, Culture and Politics, Vol. 13, Belfast: Queen's University.

Law, A. (2003) 'Language and the Press in Scotland', in J. M. Kirk, and D. Ó Baoill (eds), *Towards our Goals in Broadcasting, the Press, the Performing Arts and the Economy: Minority Languages in Northern Ireland, the Republic of Ireland and Scotland*, Belfast Studies in Language, Culture and Politics, Vol. 10, Belfast: Queen's University.

Léon, A. and Roche, R. (2003) *Histoire de l'enseignement en France*, Paris: Presses Universitaires de France.

Lodge, A. (1993) *French: from Dialect to Standard*, London: Routledge.

MacKinnon, K. (1998) 'Gaelic in Scotland', in A. Ó Corráin and S. Mac Mathúna (eds), *Minority Languages in Scandinavia, Britain and Ireland*, Uppsala: Acta Universitatis Uppsaliensis, Studia Celtica Uppsaliensa 3.

MacKinnon, K. (2000) 'Scottish Gaelic', in G. Price (ed.), *Languages in Britain & Ireland*, Oxford: Blackwell.

MacKinnon, K. (2003) 'Celtic Languages in the 2001 Census: How Population Censuses Bury Celtic Speakers', in J. M. Kirk and D. Ó Baoill (eds), *Towards our Goals in Broadcasting, the Press, the Performing Arts and the Economy: Minority Languages in Northern Ireland, the Republic of Ireland and Scotland*, Belfast Studies in Language, Culture and Politics, Vol. 10, Belfast: Queen's University.

MacNeil, C. (2003) 'The State of Gaelic Broadcasting in Scotland: Critical Issues and Audience Concerns', in J. M. Kirk and D. Ó Baoill (eds), *Towards our Goals in Broadcasting, the Press, the Performing Arts and the Economy: Minority Languages in Northern Ireland, the Republic of Ireland, and Scotland*, Belfast Studies in Language, Culture and Politics, Vol. 10, Belfast: Queen's University.

Mac Póilin, A. (2003) 'Irish Language Television in Northern Ireland', in D. Ó Riagáin (ed.), *Language and Law in Northern Ireland*, Belfast Studies in Language, Culture and Politics, Vol. 9, Belfast: Queen's University.

Manzano F. (1996) 'Sur le statut sociolinguistique du Gallo: une identité en question', in F. Manzano (ed.), *Langues et Parlers de l'Ouest*, Cahiers de Sociolinguistique no.1, Rennes: Presses Universitaires de Rennes.

Mar-Molinero C. (2000) 'The Iberian Peninsulas: Conflicting Linguistic Nationalisms', in S. Barbour and C. Carmichael (eds), *Language and Nationalism in Europe*, Oxford: Oxford University Press.

Marley, D. (1995) *Parler Catalan à Perpignan*, Paris: L'Harmattan.

Martin, J.-B. (2002) 'Graphie du provençal: bref état des lieux', in D. Caubet, S. Chaker and J. Sibille (eds), *Codification des langues de France*, Paris: L'Harmattan.

McAlistair, P. (2003a) 'Implementing the European Charter in Northern Ireland: the Role of the Public Service', in D. Ó Riagáin (ed.), *Language and Law in Northern Ireland*, Belfast Studies in Language, Culture and Politics, Vol. 9, Belfast: Queen's University.

McAlistair, P. (2003b) 'The Department of Culture, Arts and Leisure's Language Diversity and Broadcasting Policy', in J. M. Kirk and D. Ó Baoill (eds), *Towards our Goals in Broadcasting, the Press, the Performing Arts and the Economy: Minority Languages in Northern Ireland, the Republic of Ireland and Scotland*, Belfast Studies in Language, Culture and Politics, Vol. 10, Belfast: Queen's University.

McCausland, N. (2003) 'Ulster Scots and the BBC – Current Situation', in D. Ó Riagáin (ed.), *Language and Law in Northern Ireland*, Belfast Studies in Language, Culture and Politics, Vol. 9, Belfast: Queen's University.

McClure, J. D. (1979) 'Scots: Its Range and Uses', in A. J. Aitken and T. McArtur (eds), *Languages of Scotland*, Edinburgh: Chambers.

McClure, J. D. (1995) *Scots and its Literature*, Amsterdam: Benjamins.

McClure, J. D. (2002) 'The Identity of Scots: a Contemporary Problem', in *Studia Indogermanica Lodziensia*, Lodz: University of Lodz.

McCrum, R., Cran, W. and R. MacNeil (eds) (1986) *The History of English*, London: Faber & Faber.

McHardy, S. (1996), Preface to G. Telfer, *Robert Bruce: a Scots Life*, Argyll: Argyll Publishing.

McHardy, S. (2000) Introduction to *Robert Bruce*, Argyll: Argyll Publishing.

McHardy, S. (2003) 'Broadcasting and Scots', in J. M. Kirk and D. Ó Baoill (eds), *Towards our Goals in Broadcasting, the Press, the Performing Arts and the Economy: Minority Languages in Northern Ireland, the Republic of Ireland and Scotland*, Belfast Studies in Language, Culture and Politics, Vol. 10, Belfast: Queen's University.

McLeod, W. (2003a) 'Gaelic-medium Education in Scotland', in M. Scott and R. Ni Bhaoill (eds), *Gaelic-Medium Education Provision: Northern Ireland, the Republic of Ireland, Scotland and the Isle of Man*, Belfast Studies in Language, Culture and Politics, Vol. 8, Belfast: Queen's University.

McLeod, W. (2003b) article in Gaelic summarised by the editors, in J. M. Kirk and D. Ó Baoill (eds), *Towards our Goals in Broadcasting, the Press, the Performing Arts and the Economy: Minority Languages in Northern Ireland, the Republic of Ireland and Scotland*, Belfast Studies in Language, Culture and Politics, Vol. 10, Belfast: Queen's University.

Moal, S. (2003) 'How Can One Be a Breton Speaker in the Twenty-first Century?' *Contemporary French Civilisation*, Summer/Fall, 27, 2.

Moignet, G. (ed.) (1969) *La Chanson de Roland*, Paris: Bordas.

Moody, T. W. and Martin, F. X. (eds) (1994) *The Course of Irish History*, Cork: Mercier Press.

Morgan Nichols, F. (ed.) (1865) *Britton*, Oxford: Clarendon Press.

Napier, S. de (2003) English résumé of 'An Dlí agus Cúrsaí Teanga i dTuaisceart Éireann', in D. Ó Riagáin (ed.), *Language and Law in Northern Ireland*, Belfast Studies in Language, Culture and Politics, Vol. 9, Belfast: Queen's University.

Neville, G. (1992) ' "He spoke to me in English; I answered him in Irish": Language Shift in the Folklore Archives', in J. Brihault (ed.), *L'Irlande et ses langues, Colloque de Rennes 1992*, Rennes: Presses Universitaires de Rennes.

Nolan, J. S. (2006) *French Language Policy and the Multilingual Challenge, from Maastricht to an Enlarged Europe from 1992 to 2004, with particular reference to the case of Gallo*, unpublished (as yet) PhD, University of Limerick.

*Òc-Ben!* (2003) Manual for teaching Occitan, elaborated under the direction of Jean Salles-Lousteau, Paris: CNDP, Bordeaux, CRDP d'Aquitaine.

Ó Dochartaigh, C. (2000) 'Irish in Ireland', in G. Price (ed.), *Languages in Britain & Ireland*, Oxford: Blackwell.

Ó Duibhin, C. (2003) 'A Comment on the Presentation of the Results of the Irish Language Question in the 2001 Census of Northern Ireland', in J. M. Kirk and D. Ó Baoill (eds), *Towards our Goals in Broadcasting, the Press, the Performing Arts and the Economy: Minority Languages in Northern Ireland, the Republic of Ireland and Scotland*, Belfast Studies in Language, Culture and Politics, Vol. 10, Belfast: Queen's University.

Ó hIfearnáin, T. (1992) 'Capuchon, Lame et langue: l'Irlandais et l'Europe Continentale au 17e siècle', in J. Brihault (ed.), *L'Irlande et ses langues, Colloque de Rennes 1992*, Rennes: Presses Universitaires de Rennes.

Ó hIfearnáin, T. (1998) 'Irish', in A. Ó Corráin and S. Mac Mathúna (eds), *Minority Languages in Scandinavia, Britain and Ireland*, Uppsala: Acta Universitatis Uppsaliensis, Studia Celtica Uppsaliensa 3.

Oyharçabal, B. (2002) 'L'unification orthographique et morphologique du basque standard', in D. Caubet, S. Chaker and J. Sibille (eds), *Codification des langues de France*, Paris: L'Harmattan.

Payton, P. (2000) 'Cornish', in G. Price (ed.), *Languages in Britain & Ireland*, Oxford: Blackwell.

Petit, J. (2001) *L'immersion, une révolution*, CEE: Jérôme Do Bentzinger.

Philipp, M. (2003) 'Alsace et Moselle', (Moselle) in B. Cerquiglini (ed.), *Les langues de France*, Paris: Presses Universitaires de France.

Plucknett, T. F. T. (1956) *A Concise History of the Common Law*, London: Butterworth.

Pontier, J.-M. (1997) *Droit de la langue française*, Paris: Dalloz.

Pontier, J.-M. (2003) 'Le français et la loi', in M. Landick (ed.), *La langue française face aux institutions*, Paris: L'Harmattan.

Pooley, T. (2004) 'Le picard vu par les jeunes lillois', in J.-M. Eloy (ed.), *Des langues collatérales: Problèmes linguistiques, sociolinguistiques et glottopolitiques de la proximité linguistique*, Paris: L'Harmattan.

Price, G. (1984) *The Languages of Britain*, London: Arnold.

Price, G. (ed.) (2000) *Languages in Britian & Ireland*, Oxford: Blackwell.

Purves, D. (2003) 'Scots Identity', in J. M. Kirk and D. Ó Baoill (eds), *Towards our Goals in Broadcasting, the Press, the Performing Arts and the Economy: Minority Languages in Northern Ireland, the Republic of Ireland and Scotland*, Belfast Studies in Language, Culture and Politics, Vol. 10, Belfast: Queen's University.

Rickard, P. (1974) *A History of the French language*, London: Hutchinson.

Robinson, C. (2003) 'Scots in Soaps', in J. M. Kirk and D. Ó Baoill (eds) *Towards our Goals in Broadcasting, the Press, the Performing Arts and the Economy: Minority Languages in Northern Ireland, the Republic of Ireland and Scotland*, Belfast Studies in Language, Culture and Politics, Vol. 10, Belfast: Queen's University.

Rogers, B. (2003) *The Bank Manager and the Holy Grail*, London: Aurum.

Rossillon, P. (1995) *Atlas de la langue française*, Paris: Bordas.

Sanders, C. (ed.) (1993) *French Today: Language in its Social Context*, Cambridge: Cambridge University Press.

Sibille, J. (2000) *Les langues régionales*, Paris: Flammarion.

Sibille, J. (2002), 'Ecrire l'occitan: essai de présentation et de synthèse', in D. Caubet, S. Chaker and J. Sibille, *Codification des langues de France*, Paris: L'Harmattan.

Sibille, J. (2003) 'Le francoprovençal', in B. Cerquiglini (ed.), *Les langues de France*, Paris: Presses Universitaires de France.

Simoni-Aurembou, M.-R. (2003) 'Les langues d'oïl', in B. Cerquiglini (ed.), *Les langues de France*, Paris: Presses Universitaires de France.

Smith, J. (2005) 'The Sociolinguistics of Contemporary Scots', in J. M. Kirk and D. Ó Baoill (eds), *Legislation, Literature and Sociolinguistics: Northern Ireland, the Republic of Ireland, and Scotland*, Belfast Studies in Language, Culture and Politics, Vol. 13, Belfast: Queen's University.

Smith, J. J. (2000) 'Scots', in G. Price (ed.), *Languages in Britain and Ireland*, Oxford: Blackwell.

Smyth, A. and Montgomery, M. (2005) 'The Ulster-Scots Academy', in J. M. Kirk and D. Ó Baoill (eds), *Legislation, Literature and Sociolinguistics: Northern Ireland, the Republic of Ireland, and Scotland*, Belfast Studies in Language, Culture and Politics, Vol. 13, Belfast: Queen's University.

Spurr, C. (2003) 'The BBC Northern Ireland Ulster Scots Unit', in J. M. Kirk and D. Ó Baoill (eds), *Towards our Goals in Broadcasting, the Press, the Performing Arts and the Economy: Minority Languages in Northern Ireland, the Republic of Ireland and Scotland*, Belfast Studies in Language, Culture and Politics, Vol. 10, Belfast: Queen's University.

Steele, P. (2003) 'Gaelic Medium Education in Northern Ireland', in M. Scott and Ní Bhaoill (eds), *Gaelic-Medium Education Provision: Northern Ireland, the Republic of Ireland, Scotland and the Isle of Man*, Belfast Studies in Language, Culture and Politics, Vol. 8, Belfast: Queen's University.

Van de Louw, G. (2003) 'Le flamand occidental', in B. Cerquiglini (ed.), *Les langues de France*, Paris: Presses Universitaires de France.

Walter, H. (1988) *Le Français dans tous les sens*, Paris: Robert Laffont.

Walter, H. (1994) *L'aventure des langues en Occident*, Paris: Robert Laffont.

Wardhaugh, R. (1987) *Languages in Competition*, Oxford: Blackwell.

# Index

**Numbers in bold refer to principal entry**